Food for Thought, Character and Soul

Visit www.booksurge.com to order additional copies.

Food for Thought, Character and Soul

Recipes and Blessings Included

Rabbi Philip M. Posner

Go thy way, eat thy bread with joy
and drink thy wine with a merry heart,
for God now accepts thy works.
— Eccles. 9:7

Contents

> Soul Talk
> With: Presidents Abraham Lincoln, Jimmy Carter,
> Nelson Mandela and the Prophet Amos
> Recipes in honor of the above: Rosalynn Carter's Cheese Rings,
> Babote, Stuffed Leg of Lamb, Red and White Raspberry Pie

> Arrested—Looking for Compassion
> With: Mother Antonia ,Viktor Frankl, Craig Kielburger and
> Albert Schweitzer
> Recipes in honor of the above: Hungarian Goulash with Potatoes,
> Phad Thai, Raspberry Lemon Cake with a Chocolate
> Frosting , Pumpernickel.

> The Forgiving Place
> With: Bill and Hillary Clinton, Archbishop Desmond Tutu and
> Joseph of the Bible
> Recipes in honor of the above: Poached Salmon with Creamy Beurre
> Blanc Sauce, Sephardic matzah leek pie, Tutu Chicken, Ginger
> Custard Peach Pie

Dedication

THIS BOOK IS dedicated to my children, Micah and Hillel Posner, and all the other wonderful people who by the character of their lives inspire us to try to make a difference, bringing more compassion, forgiveness, righteousness, kindness, moral courage, justice, and empathy to our personal lives, our community and the world.

I am grateful for all the wonderful cooks I have personally known: Helene, whose food like her *humentashen,* contains Jewish soul; Elizabeth who taught me "presentation," Patti whose own cook book, *Angels in the Kitchen,* taught me the importance of food and story; my chef adviser and friend, Rollo Storey, for whom I cooked or baked all the book's recipes. And finally my mother, *aleha ha shalom,* who was not only a wonderful cook but whose spirit, like the heady smell of her honey cake, filled my kitchen with the knowledge that she was *shebing nachos;* celebrating parental, joyful pride on the other side: "My son, Philip, has written a wonderful book."

Thanks & Acknowledgments

HOPEFULLY, MY READERS will appreciate how much I have thoroughly enjoyed writing, cooking and doing the research for this book. In great part the pleasure so derived came from all the wonderful individuals who helped me with sound advice, ideas and suggestions: Dr. William Lee Miller, author of *Lincoln's Virtues*; Linda Hern, The Nebraska Historical Society; Esther Schor, author of *Emma Lazarus*; Rev. Fred Shuttlesworth, co-founder SCLC; the NPS staff at Sagamore Hill – TR museum; Rabbi Gary Zola and staff at the American Jewish Archives; the staff at the UCLA and USC libraries; Col Jack Brennan, re. President Nixon; Marlene Bethlehem re. Nelson Mandela; Rajmahan Gandhi, re. his grandfather; Marjanne from Holland, re. Etty Hillesum; Jason and Mrs. Joanne Rogers re. Mr. Rogers; Dr. Franz Vesely and the family of Viktor Frankl; Archbishop Tutu's secretary; Drs. Chuck Wall and Sam Oliner.

Then there were those courageous persons who listened to or read some, or all of the chapters, offering their insights and wisdom, Sy Green, *alav ha shalom*; Gail Glasser; Judy Baer; Joy Dunston; Jane Fellman; Shirley Gottfried; Brenda Racoosin, Bob and Ginny Baird, Rabbis Sam Stahl, Allan Krause, Shoshanah Devorah, Chanah Talare, and Barry Kogan.

And of course, there were my fellow cooks and bakers who gave me ideas for recipes, my son Hillel Posner, Scarlet Newman, Dannete Brooks, Maria Baumgartner and especially Judy Baer for editing the recipes, and my chef adviser and friend Rollo Story.

I have always enjoyed writing, but have often lacked confidence in doing so. I am, therefore, indebted to all those who encouraged me to believe that I could write, even a book, Rowena Levin; Marcia Krosner; and Gale Park.

With them, I am also grateful to those who encouraged me to pursue my dream of writing a book that combines character and food, my wife, Patti, herself the author of a wonderful cook book, "Angels in The Kitchen"; my volunteer editor, Michael McLaughlin; my friend Jim Davis, for his help with the blessing chapter; our book illustrator, Dick Sommers; Jose Duran artist for the book marks, Myrna Shreve, recipe sampler illustrator; the many hard working and helpful individuals at my publisher, Book Surge, especially the editorial staff; and Mother Antonia, whose love and compassion, as with all the other role models inspired me to hopefully write something relevant.

As with every author there are those whose inspiration continues on in the gift of memory. I recall exactly the place and time when one of my seminary professors, Norman Mirskey, *alav ha shalom,* said "Phil why don't you write a book that deals with empathy and ethics." And, with him that day stood my beloved doctoral advisor, Rabbi Stanley Chyet, *alav ha shalom.* Their souls, together with my mother, herself a voracious lover of books, and my father are part of that eternal character that continues to bless this soul.

Most of all it has been an honor to have either spiritually felt the presence of, or actually been in communication with many of the inspiring role models for this book. Of course, I alone am responsible for any errors or mistakes that may have inadvertently found their way on to these pages.

Philip M. Posner, December 7th, 2007

Introduction and the
'Tree of Life' Character Bookmark

01, 102, 103...... If you had been in the cookbook section of a well known book store chain in San Antonio, Texas, last August, you might have noticed a man with a large mustache and a colorful *yarmulke* counting cook books...... 412, 413, 414......There was an incredible array of such books, some with amazing titles like *Trailer Park BBQ-In*. That man was me, and I was determined to get some sense of the competition, at least quantitatively. Would you believe, in that one store there were one thousand and seventy-nine different cook books? And that number did not even include diet cookbooks, vegetarian, vegan cook books, or those that involved cooking with wine or liquor. Nor did they include kosher cookbooks—which reminds me, I should say up front: the recipes in *Food for Thought, Character and Soul* are not necessarily kosher. Some fall in that category, others do not.

So, why another cookbook? Of course, every author likes to think his or her book is special. As far as I know, however, this "cookbook" is unique—the first to link food, ethics and character with famous personalities—a kind of ethical cookbook.

Throughout history, food, behavior and social bonding have been intrinsically connected. No doubt, the strong recollection of my mother's excellent and nutritionally balanced meals, together with the animated social conviviality and ethical discussion that I still associate with our dinner table, is part of what motivated me to write this book. And, I am certainly not the only clergyman to associate the good taste of food with character and enjoyment. In Jane Grigson's book, *Food with the Famous*, the author writes of the Reverend Sydney Smith, 1771–1845:

He learned to cook, loved good food, and felt that he could feed or starve a man into virtue or vice. That character, virtues and so on "are powerfully affected by beef, mutton, pie-crust, and rich soups." Digestion was the secret of life, the source of humour and friendliness [1]

Further, food and social behavior was, and in some societies still is, a matter of family social rank, such that those who were responsible for the food gathering or the hunt often ate first. In eighteenth century America, for example, food and behavior were tied together in social etiquette. When guests were present for dinner, "the quantities" of the dishes served "were often small—creamed spinach might only be topped with four eggs, even though upward of ten people were sitting round the table." So, you were dependent for your meal on what was directly in front of you "and on the good manners of the people on either side... In other words, a successful dinner depended not only on the cook's skill, but on the civilized behaviour of the company." [2]

But food is not only a matter of enjoying its good taste with family and friends. Food also calls to mind the spiritual, physical, and material dimensions of life. That is and why the Psalmist connects God, the Creator, with food and values: *Bless the Lord, O my soul... who causes herbs for the service of man and wine that makes glad the heart of man"* [3]

And because food is a requirement for our very spiritual and physical survival, breaking bread together is both a symbol for hospitality and a universal symbol for sustenance. "Praised are You O Lord for bread that sustains man's heart... so that we may make the earth yield bread." (In fact, these final words are the source for the Jewish grace before meals.)

On the other hand, the fact that there have always been millions of people who lack sufficient food to sustain their physical health means that people have fought over food and the land upon which food is grown.

It is no accident that in some Semitic languages, including Hebrew, the word for bread, *lechem*, is the root for the word war: *Milchamah*. Even when sustenance is not a source of physical conflict, man's ability to obtain food has been connected to power:

On a journey into Italy, Thomas Jefferson bribed a porter to take out rice from Piedmont; then fearing that he might not succeed, filled his own pockets with rice—the penalty, had either been caught, was death, so jealously guarded was the export of rice from the Po valley. [4]

Therefore, as a metaphor for ethical qualities hospitality, gratitude, spiritual sustenance, war, and power, food is a valuable reminder of our freedom to choose between the consequences of war or peace, suffering, or happiness.

It is the thesis of this book that principled role models are a practical source of inspiration for the ethical choices we make in our own lives. Some may feel ethically commanded or inspired through God's revelation. Others may be motivated by the humanistic ethical criteria of Immanuel Kant, or by specific universal ethical constructs such as compassion, righteousness, kindness and love. Whatever criteria we use as the basis of our ethical decisions, healthy individuals can universally appreciate and be inspired by a Martin Luther King, an Albert Schweitzer or the Prophet Amos.

However, as much as we may admire the character virtues of those whom we value as ethical role models, it is important to acknowledge that our ethical virtues are not absolute. Dr. King possessed an awesome ethical sense of social righteousness but evidently lacked a similar sense of righteous behavior when it came to spousal fidelity. President Lincoln had a great sense of justice, but he also suspended the right of habeas corpus during the Civil War. And, while I greatly admire President Carter (as the reader will see) for his great sense of righteousness, I and many others strongly felt that the choice of his title for his recent book on Israel and the Palestinians displayed a singular lack of fairness.

Nevertheless, the opportunity to interact with the role models found in this book and the ethical values they personify can help us live healthier, more fulfilled lives. Further, through the creative power of memory and our own acute sense of taste, such qualities unite us with what is universally good in a way that links us to the past, sanctifies the present, and provides us with feelings of hope for humanity's salvation—our future collective good.

Whether we celebrate the compassion of a Mother Teresa with a simple bowl of grapes, or give thanks for the inspiring kindness of Mr.

Rogers with his favorite Filipino Spinach Egg Rolls, we have the honor to celebrate with them at our very own table.

And so at the end of each chapter the reader will find recipes that are connected to these inspiring role models. The last chapter also contains ecumenical blessing or prayers of grace that encapsulate the good taste and ethical value associated with these individuals.

So, imagine chairs next to the ones where our friends or loved ones are seated, at our collective dining table. See in those chairs President Abraham Lincoln, whose tenacity for a righteous cause saved our nation; former President Jimmy Carter, whose dedicated labors on behalf of justice and peace have inspired the world; Archbishop Desmond Tutu, who never gave up on the role of reconciliation to heal his nation; and President Teddy Roosevelt, who legislated economic justice for all Americans, managing great power with wisdom and compassion.

And don't forget Elie Wiesel, a personification of the command to love the stranger. He is also seated at our collective table.

These personalities, and many others, occupy a seat in our admiration and memory, even if they are long deceased. In the virtue of their character, their spiritual presence continues to inspire our own individual goodness, righteousness, empathy and love.

Lastly, in an age when it is so easy to be numbed into indifference by the un-ethical around us, these character models, and so many more—including the ones you, our readers, privately name in your heart—encourage us to courageously persevere for a righteous and nobler future.

Whether we are joined at our meal by the religious or secular community, a family gathering, or are seated with friends, we have the opportunity to celebrate a banquet of memory with a nourishing plate—those ingredients that truly sustain individuals now and society forever.

Our greatest hope is imagining our readers seated around their dinner tables with children, family and friends, reading these stories, enjoying good food, and thanking God, each in his or her own way, for all that nurtures our body, character, soul, and humanity.

— *Rabbi Philip M. Posner, DD, DHL, with Chef Rollo Storey.*
Illustrations by Dick Sommers.

'Tree of Life' Character Bookmark

DO YOU KNOW someone deserving of a thank you for a quality that you especially love about that person?

You can complement the ethical aspect of *Food for Thought, Character and Soul* by sending the book as a gift with a *Tree of Life*, character bookmark, which says, "Dear ....

Rabbi Posner's book comes to you with admiration and respect for ethical qualities I/we especially love about you. Kindness, compassion, empathy, forgiveness, and moral courage is like a *Tree of Life*, growing tall in virtue, shading humanity with our goodness."

Of course, when we behave ethically we don't necessarily need a thank you. We know in our hearts what we did was right. However, in a world where we also know there is too much apathy and evil, a little thank you or a big one doesn't hurt.

Further, living with character reminds us or others that the world is sustained and strengthened by every ethical deed. (As I was typing the previous sentence my computer automatically intervened, in green letters it informed me, "Your computer needs to be restarted for updates to take effect." It was as if, even this inanimate thing was agreeing that we animate beings need to constantly update our ethical selves for the world to run more beautifully and efficiently.)

There are obviously such ethical attributes, including honesty, humility, patience, etc. However, each of the ethical attributes that form the basis of this book encompasses the idea of universal goodness. For example, while honesty, humility, or patience also exemplify goodness, one can be honest but also unjust or unkind. Empathy, kindness, justice, moral courage or righteousness, however, possess an inclusivity of goodness and character that nurture or coincide with all other ethical attributes.

A packet of character bookmarks, the art work of the Mexican artist, Jose Duran, can be ordered with the book, or as a separate item at **Rabbiposner.com**

Chapter I

Soul Talk

To bring the dead to life is no great magic. Few are wholly dead. Blow on a dead man's embers and a live flame will start. —Robert Graves

This is a work of creative nonfiction. Within this chapter, the author uses creative license to expand upon biographical and autobiographical information. The actual participation of living persons or historical figures as role models in any particular setting or scene is entirely fictional.

I WAS EXCITED, NERVOUS and hungry—hungry for the food and excited for the dish of righteousness coming to my house. Four very special guests would be dining with me. Two were of this world, and two had already passed over to the other side.

Setting the table lessened my nervousness, especially when it occurred to me that good food and character is another dimension of God's providence. Humanity is sustained with good food. And our spiritual selves are nourished by the virtue of character that spans all time and lives in every soul.

"Honey, the forks go on the right side of the plates and the spoons on the left? Right?" Then I wondered, "Do those from the other side use cutlery?"

My wife entered the dining room, "Forks and spoons? Do they even eat?"

"Honey, they must. I have prepared their favorite recipes, and besides you remember the Chassidic tale about a traveler who gets to see heaven and hell? He decides to visit hell first. But he doesn't see any fires and flames. Instead he sees an extraordinarily long banquet table, prepared for a feast, with large bowls of steaming food.

"The smell and aroma aroused his appetite. Seated all around the table and the appetizing food were men and women, but they were shrieking with hunger and fainting with thirst. They tried to feed themselves, but were unable to do so because of the ridiculously long forks and spoons they had been given, so long that they could not reach their faces and get the food to their mouths.

"The traveler then goes to see heaven. Surprisingly, there are no clouds and castles. But here too there's an extraordinarily long dinner table, prepared for a feast. There were the same large bowls of appetizing food, around the table, with the same number of people, seated with the same giant forks and spoons. Nothing has changed, and he is about to cry out in horror. Then he realized that there was no shrieking, instead everyone was laughing and smiling. The traveler is amazed, and then he smiles, too—he sees the people in heaven are using their giant forks and spoons to feed each other."[5]

"Great story," she replied, "and now we will have another question to ask our guests from the other side: 'Will you feed us, and we you?'"

"You know, honey, your question reminds me how much I especially value your soul—the spiritual side of you. Imagine how much more will we be nourished by the very presence of our guests who bring to the table the eternity of their souls experience."

She asked, "Is that why you call this encounter with us and those from the other side 'character soul talk?'"

"Exactly, through the character of our lives, past, present and future, our souls are extended expressions of a dialogue that merge with our memories and become one."

"By the way, you said you were serving their favorite recipes," my wife said. "What food will be on the table when you discuss righteousness with them?"

Before I could answer her, there was a sudden, loud knock at the door. I opened it and there stood Abraham Lincoln in a very tall stovetop hat. His appearance was different then when he ran for his first elective office in 1832. Then, he was described by an associate as "... very tall, gawky, and rough-looking."[6] Now his physical presence had the kind of ephemeral look one imagines for those from the other side. But his soul was so animated that I immediately felt his sincerity, his righteousness, his strength of devotion to the cause that had consumed him, especially his last five years on earth.

"Are you going to let me in?" he inquired.

It took me a moment to respond. Seeing "the Great Emancipator" I felt enveloped into his being, as if our souls became part of the other.

His presence confirmed my belief that our souls and our character are manifestations of an eternal dialogue that exists between humanity and God. Though no communication was yet expressed, I knew it would issue forth. Souls talk.

Standing there before my silence, Lincoln caught my thoughts and said,

"Rabbi, you look like you are bridging this moment with past and future ones."

"Mr. Lincoln, you are a keen observer. Please come in, and forgive me. I was relishing our encounter, how we will share what we were, are now and are yet to be."

"Relishing? Is that a joke regarding food, rabbi?" Lincoln asked with humor in his eyes. "I hope not because relishes remind me of indigestion long past."

"Not to worry, Mr. President. In fact, my wife just asked me what we would be eating," I continued, my eyes squinting with my own attempt at humor. "Your constitution as with your beautiful soul will continue to endure at my table with meats, salad, vegetables, cake and the topic of our righteousness. President Lincoln, I am so honored to have you as a guest."

"I am honored to add what I know of righteousness," said Lincoln as we headed for the living room.

"The prospect of it all reminds me of the time friends invited me to a meal," I said. "I went feeling lousy, but the food and the camaraderie were so wonderful that I left feeling nourished and enriched."

"I remember that feeling. There were times, after spending all day and the early eve at the War Department looking for any hint of some military victory that I would return to one of Mary's dinners at The White House bone tired and all out of sorts. And sure enough, Mary's food—including her Almond Vanilla cake—our visitors, and my stories returned me to a joyous equilibrium."

"Sure enough, Mr. Lincoln," I replied. "We will be enjoying our camaraderie, I pray, and our very favorite food."

So delighted was I by the arrival of President Lincoln that when I heard another knock I almost jumped with daring anticipation as I moved toward the door a second time. After all, what I had only imagined was now taking place.

"Mr. Lincoln," I shouted out, "we are in for a wonderful treat, a Biblical one at that." I opened the door and there from ancient Judea, as Scripture had revealed him to me, with his twenty-seven-hundred-year-old soul now facing me, was my favorite ethical teacher—the Prophet Amos of Tekoa in Judea.

"Oh, Amos," I blurted out, "'*baruch ha ba*, blessed is your coming!'"

"You speak Hebrew," he laughed with a twinkle in his eye, "a Reform Rabbi?"

Appreciating his tease on a 20th century joke about being a Reform Rabbi, I replied, "How else would I know except from our people's original tongue that Amazaiah, the High Priest at the shrine of Beth El, sarcastically called you '*chozeh*, a mere seer.' For us social activists, however, you are a revered '*n'vi tsedek*, our Prophet of righteousness.'"

"Even though I once informed my adversary, the priest hypocrite Amaziah, 'I am not a prophet, nor the son of a prophet,' I am honored to be invited to your home as your '*n'vi tsedek*.'"

Again, I could not contain my enthusiasm and said, "When visiting modern Israel, I have often wanted to travel to your birthplace near Jerusalem in Palestinian territory but have been afraid. Now you are visiting me.!"

"Do you believe, rabbi, that all God's children should live in freedom," asked Amos, "'each under his own vine and fig tree' in peace—both Israelis and Palestinians?"

My mind raced ahead inundated in a reservoir of joy I had not anticipated. And the words, "You are still our greatest universal prophet," surged from my lips as had Amos's words when he pleaded, "…Let justice well up like water, righteousness flow down like a mighty stream."

Then with a calming tenderness, a prophetic quality Amos did not exhibit in Biblical times, he replied, "You should not have been afraid to visit my birthplace! My soul would have accompanied you."

"As it is now, I should have known then," I replied. "Now dear soul, please come in."

As he crossed my threshold I saw him glance up at the *m'zuzah* on the *doorpost* of my house. Looking at it he mumbled, "How creative of my spiritual descendents, the Pharisee rabbis, to have thought of putting the biblical commandment, 'and you shall write them on the doorpost of your house' in that little box."

As he continued looking at the *m'zuzzh* I wondered if his soul had already encountered Abraham Lincoln's in the eternity of time that encompasses all ethical—character? I couldn't wait to ask them. But as I started to introduce them, Lincoln spoke:

"Dear Rabbi, first, may I, and I am sure I speak for this great Prophet as well, express delight in our return to this world. What a personal pleasure for me to reconnect to the land I called home."

"Yes, indeed," said Amos, "I heartily agree with Mr. Lincoln's delight in our being here. It took great spiritual courage for you to believe that we would come, and we rejoice in this opportunity to be with you."

"So tell us who else from this world have you invited to dine with us?"

"Mr. Lincoln," I replied, "there are so many individuals who personify the reason for our being here—the courage to do what is right—that it was no easy task. I invited Presidents Jimmy Carter and Nelson Mandela. As were you in your century, these two men have been giants for advancing what is right in our time, even when it has been difficult and unpopular."

Then, as these words barely left my mouth, I opened the door to welcome the thirty-ninth President of the United States, Jimmy Carter, and the first President of a new South Africa Republic, Nelson Mandela.

"A marvelous choice of comrades, I have looked forward to meeting you," Mr. Lincoln said as he stepped forward to greet Carter and Mandela.

As I invited my guests to be seated, I experienced a wonderful sense of expectation and excitement as each of us said a few words about ourselves. Then, while Mandela and Lincoln were involved in an animated discussion about politics and the oppression of individuals because of their race, Carter and I looked at each other with smiles that radiated astonishment. We were both marveling, I am sure, at how history and the present were colliding in a celebration of time and place.

As I was about to mention the topic for our dialogue, my wife came in to introduce herself. Listening to what was being said and not said, she rightly pointed out to everyone that we would all feel more comfortable experiencing the past and the present if we understood how this was about to happen. With that she said, "But honey, I almost forgot, I better go shopping as I promised you I would get the other things for dinner."

"Thanks honey, see you later." Then I asked, "Amos and President Lincoln, are we about to experience what people who have momentarily left this world describe as their life intensely flashing by—like a film speeded up—months condensed into microseconds?"

"In a way, yes," Lincoln answered. "When those of us on the other side communicate, our dialogue is compacted, as you said, like a film speeded up. Because on our side, understanding of each other is so natural, our past and present merge, and yet we easily understand each other's events. Our histories become one with our souls."

Amos added, "That is why we call it soul talk." One of us must have looked confused because Amos explained, "Perhaps it will help you understand how the past and the present can come together if you imagine us on a boat at sea sharing stories and memories, as I once did on the Sea of Galilee. The sea is our memory, carrying our individual character collectively as the boat carries us through time on a different plane of consciousness. On our voyage, any separation between us in the boat and the sea below ceases to exist, even though the boat and the sea continue to exist as individual entities. With soul talk we, the boat, the sea and time between past, present and future all merge into the oneness of eternity."

"Usually this form of dialogue," Amos continued, "only happens after one's mortal death, but because you invited us from the other side, we are able to experience it with you."

"So, if I may add flavor to the scene," said Lincoln pointing to the salt next to Carter, "we eternal souls and you transitory souls are here together, you in your physical bodies and us as non-material souls. When we share our experiences with righteousness, compassion and other ethical values, we not only obtain a better understanding of character for our own lives, but our dialogue actually helps perpetuate these values in the universe itself."

"Kind of like therapy," interjected Mandela.

"An eternal therapy," expounded Amos, "because character dialogue connects all souls in a greater understanding of what motivates us to do right."

"However, our discussion of character," laughed Lincoln, "is not bereft of the continuing good taste of meat off the hoof. I don't know about Amos, but I look forward to that lamb."

"Is our character discussion similar to what the philosopher Martin Buber describes as I–Thou dialogue, only this dialogue crosses the boundary of time?" I asked.

"Yes," answered Amos, "It is also what my successors, the rabbis, called 'holy time,' meaning special time. But, you should know, such dialogue is not limited to any one quality of character or ethics. As for the lamb, will it be a kosher one, Mr. Lincoln?"

To which Lincoln, obviously enjoying Amos's Jewish jest, responded, "Come now dear Prophet, you know very well that lamb is kosher, and that the laws of how kosher animals are to be slaughtered came much later than when you lived."

"Mr. Lincoln, you have obviously read our Torah," responded Amos. "I shall indeed look forward to the lamb."

"Amos, you said that dialogue is not limited to any one quality of character or ethics. Is that why ethical qualities like compassion, forgiveness, moral courage, social and economic justice, kindness, peace and empathy are other opportunities for soul talk?"

"Exactly," answered Amos.

"I was hoping you would say that," I said smiling.

Then, turning to Carter and Mandela, Lincoln said, "What I find fascinating is that on our side when we discuss the ethical character of our lives there is no separation between us. President Carter, some day when you join us, you will be surprised to discover as were we that there are no barriers between what you call good and evil."

"Dear Mr. Lincoln, remember now," his Carter smile ascending, "you are addressing a Baptist. How will those of us on this side be motivated to act ethically if they find out that good and evil are not as clear cut as heaven or hell?"

"And I of whom my wife Mary said, 'He was not a technical Christian, but he was a religious man always,' [7] mean no offense," replied Lincoln. "The fact is, saint or sinner, 'saved' or not, there is no heaven and hell on our side. Instead our reality is an eternal consciousness of the things we have done that have brought pain or joy to ourselves and others, and how we have grown from such awareness. In this exploration of our character we receive great help and encouragement from all the others here—part of the divine gift that is ours."

"Yes indeed, Mr. Lincoln, your view of our eternal reality is the same as mine," interjected Amos. "However, as you know now when we recall ours or others' evil behavior, it no longer divides or causes acrimony between us. And, as I am among friends, I confess that centuries ago I was a ruthless judge of evil and good. *Mah tov—how good* it is that now I am delightfully free of that awful prophetic necessity. On 'this side' I know the nature of tranquility."

"Yes, Amos" continued Lincoln, "what you describe as your 'tranquility' is true for me as well—part of our eternal reward. For example, my own vice president, Andrew Johnson, was persistently vocal about punishing the Confederates after we had defeated them. [8] But as the rabbi might say, my present *shalom*, peace, comes with the truth as was said of me.

It was not unpleasant for Lincoln to look back and consider that in all his speeches and papers no one could find a phrase of hate or personal evil wish against the head of the Confederate Government. [9]

"However, unlike this esteemed biographer of mine, I would have declared my distaste for retribution as more than 'unpleasant.' Rather it was most satisfying to be free of such evil or hate against my adversaries.

Such satisfaction on this side survives because in our eternal realm we are able to fully acknowledge the character of our behavior and to know that to hate another only contributes to our own suffering. With that knowledge there is no desire or need to behave in a way that causes others pain and separation."

"On your side," asked Jimmy Carter, "what then is your relationship with one who while on earth caused horrendous pain and suffering to others?"

"Admittedly there is evil in the universe," answered Amos. "But we would have no contact with such a soul unless, to use a phrase from my days as a prophet, 'he turned from his evil ways,' acknowledged the pain and suffering he had done, or permitted, and felt genuine remorse."

"Could you expand on what that means?" I asked.

Replied Lincoln, "Leaving the earth is like being born again; we arrive on this side with an expanded sense of empathy that prevents us from excluding anyone unless he or she excludes us. However, one whose soul does not take advantage of this newfound freedom to accept others with an understanding heart will find this environment of real empathy—love—intolerable."

"Perhaps," I interjected, "the real punishment for someone filled with hatred and exclusion is discovering that superiority or inferiority is non-existent once we leave this earthly domain, and that he can no longer separate himself from any other—including a Jew, an emancipator of slaves, or a President of an African Republic."

"You are correct. Such a person must endure our eternal harmony," replied Amos. "Here it is not possible to deny that we are all God's creation. Because nothing sets us apart, there is no one to hate, no one either free or enslaved for us to fear. Here even language is universal. And because love is expressed unconditionally, its embrace is the very breath of our being."

"So in meeting such a previously evil person," I asked, "nothing destructive would happen?"

Lincoln answered, "Nothing divisive would separate our soul talk, unless one attempted to disturb our oneness with one another and with God."

"This is what Jews living after my time," added Amos, "mean when they speak of 'the profanation of God's name.' Here, profaning the Creator is negating his/her children, by treating them as objects."

"I have been the 'zithulele, the quiet one,'" Nelson Mandela interjected. "True, it was I who proposed to our new nation that we should have a Truth and Reconciliation Commission to facilitate justice and forgiveness for all our citizens who had been part of a vicious cycle of violence. But are not you on the other side giving a truly evil individual a second chance?"

"Sounds properly Christian to me. After all, our Savior taught that we must not hate our enemy," proclaimed Jimmy Carter.

"As you know, Christianity wasn't around when I prophesied so I can not respond to that part of your question. However, my colleague the Prophet Hoshea…"

Carter interrupted, "You mean Hosea."

"No," Amos continued, "I mean Hoshea. His name comes from the Hebrew verb Y-*Sh*-A, and I have no idea why he is now called Hosea. He whose name comes from the verb for salvation taught that forgiveness is an antidote to alienation and separation."

"Separation and isolation," I said, "is always destructive. That is why it is especially deplorable to realize how often food has been used by those in authority to isolate classes of people. And/or, to deprive others of their natural right to be sustained physically or socially at the dining table."

"So, to answer your earlier question, if a truly evil soul attempted to negate, isolate or hurt another," added Lincoln, "that lonely soul would immediately realize it could not survive in our environment. It would leave our eternal time and return to your side where hate and apathy survive in tension with compassion and love—a miserable partnership."

I must have looked confused, because Amos added, "Rabbi, as you know, on earth we are linked and judged by those whose lives were affected by our behavior. With death, however, we discover true re-demption—the freedom to embrace life for the sake of goodness. Here judging others ceases and the power to control others is replaced with dialogue—eternal soul talk.

With death, everyone is equal; each person free to ascend as if on a ladder moving the soul to its higher, better self.

In fact," continued Amos his soul appearing to rise, as if he were reliv-ing the experience, "I can still see the ladders, like thousands of redwood trees soaring upward, as earthly judgments seemed to fall from the lad-ders' rungs, and only our character ascended."

"That is why, when individuals on earth sincerely listen to each other," said Lincoln, "the memories and the stories of their character nurture healthier lives and contribute to a greater ethical awareness and more harmony. And when they don't, there is disharmony, confusion, hatred, even violence. On our side, however, when our souls ascend into this environment of universal acceptance and *shalom*—internal and external harmony—the kiss or sting of feelings associated with good and evil are absent because judgment is replaced with a real and abiding empathy for each other."

"Now I better understand the temporal and the eternal significance of Rabbi Tarphon's ethical saying, 'Do not judge your fellow human being until you reach his place,' "[10] I said. "On earth, our empathy for another's situation encourages us to try to suspend judgment while we examine our own place in the scheme of things. We may try, but our effort does not always meet with success. On the other side, 'his place' literally becomes our place, as judgment is replaced with true empathy and unlimited opportunities for everyone."

"Yes, rabbi, "answered Amos, "but there are still consequences. Everyone ascends on their own ladder toward the opportunity for a higher, more spiritually aware self. Whether they, or even us ancient ones, remain here depends on whether we remain in harmony in this environment of empathy and love where character soul talk sustains us, as food once did, for our eternal salvation."

"Does that mean," I started to ask, "that those who do not remain in the environment you just described go to…?"

My question remained unanswered, as immediately after Amos said the words "eternal salvation," our earthly dialogue ceased. And, as if upon some divine cue, with no baton in sight, the doors and windows of my house opened wide. And all of us broke out in harmonious song: "Our residence—our goodness—now and future bound!" Then, someone said, "We have character and soul, forks and spoons; it's time to feed each other!"

And with that, we heard what sounded like a voice from everywhere say, "They are experiencing eternal redemption on earth," and the whole house rang with a very loud and joyous laughter.

RECIPES

President and Mrs. Carter are Baptists. A Baptist blessing for food in their honor may be found on page 236.

ROSALYNN CARTER'S CHEESE RING

Makes a delicious hors d'oeuvre. Serves 6–8.

Ingredients:
1 pound sharp cheddar cheese, finely grated
1 c. mayonnaise
1 c. chopped pecans
1/2 c. finely chopped onion
6 twists freshly-ground black pepper
Dash of cayenne pepper
1 jar (12 ounces) strawberry preserves
Whole-grain crackers or Melba toast

Directions:
Combine cheese with mayonnaise, chopped nuts and onions. Mix in black pepper and cayenne, and blend thoroughly. Press into 3-cup ring mold. Refrigerate for at least 2 hours. To serve, dip mold into a pan of very hot water for 20 to 30 seconds before turning out onto a serving platter. Fill center with strawberry preserves and serve at once with whole-grain crackers or Melba toast.

BABOTIE—A SOUTH AFRICAN MEAT LOAF *

President Mandela is an Anglican. A blessing for food in his honor may be found on page 240.

Ingredients:
2 onions, thinly sliced
1 apple, peeled and chopped
2 tbsp. butter

2 lbs. ground round*

2 c. milk

2 eggs

2 slices bread

3 tsp. curry

2 tbsp. sugar

2 tbsp. vinegar

2 tsp. salt

1/4 tsp. pepper

1/2 c. raisins (set aside ¼ c.)

2 tbsp. almond slivers

6 bay leaves

1 tsp. turmeric

Directions: Soak bread in 1 cup milk. Sautee onion and apple in butter. Mix meat, bread, milk, onion, apple, curry, sugar, 1 egg, vinegar, salt, pepper, raisins, almond slivers and turmeric. Put in casserole, garnish with bay leaves. Beat 1 egg and the other cup of milk. Pour over top of casserole. Bake at 350 degrees for 1 hour.

Follow directions for 1 cup rice. Add 1 ½ tsp. cinnamon, ½ tsp. turmeric, ½ cup raisins, 3 tbsp. butter, 1 ½ tbsp. brown sugar, salt to taste.

*Babote in South Africa is not made with chicken, but substituting cubed chicken thighs for the beef works very well, as the chicken nicely absorbs the seasonings.

LEG OF LAMB

The **Prophet Amos** was a Judean. A blessing in memory and honor of his passion for righteousness may be found on page 235.

Amos was a shepherd who spoke up against injustice at Beth El, one of the early, religious cultic sites. Some scholars believe Amos prophesied at Beth El during the New Year festivities.

So this would be a nice dish to serve in his honor on *Rosh ha Shanah*, the Jewish New Year that usually falls in September, although in his time it was observed in the spring of the year.

Ingredients:

4–5 lbs. leg of lamb

2 tbsp. minced garlic

1 ½ tsp. salt

1 tsp. ground black pepper

4 c. fresh or frozen spinach

4 c. fresh mushrooms sliced

2 tbsp. butter

½ c. chopped onions

½ c. finely diced red pepper

1 ½ c. chicken stock

½ c. dried chopped apricots

¼ tsp. cinnamon

¼ tsp. ground ginger

1 c. quick cooking couscous

½ c. toasted pine nuts or toasted almonds

¼ c. fresh minced parsley

olive oil

Directions:

Have the butcher butterfly a 4–5 pound leg of lamb, trimmed to an even thickness of two inches.

For stuffing, sauté the fresh or frozen spinach and mushrooms in the butter and add the finely chopped onions and the diced red bell pepper. Stir in chicken stock, the apricots, salt and pepper, cinnamon, and ginger. Add and stir in the couscous. Remove from heat and let stand five minutes and stir with fork. Add the toasted pine nuts or toasted slivered almonds and the parsley. Mix well and starting from the longer side, spoon and roll the stuffing into the lamb and tie with string. The lamb should be longer than it is wide. Rub the boned side of the lamb with olive oil, the set aside one teaspoon salt, minced garlic and ½ teaspoon black pepper.

Place the stuffed leg seam side down on a rack in roasting pan 1.5–1.75 hours or until an internal thermometer reads 130–135 degrees. Remove from the oven and let sit for 10–15 minutes covered loosely with foil. Before serving remove string and cut meat into ½–¾ inch slices.

President Abraham Lincoln

John Hay, one of Lincoln's private secretaries, who occasionally ate with the President, is reported as saying, "He ate less than anyone I know. One day Dr. Henry Whitney Bellows of the Sanitary Commission said to Lincoln, 'Mr. President, I am here at almost every hour of the day or night, and I never see you at the table; do you eat?' 'I try to,' the President replied. 'I manage to browse about pretty much as I can get it.'" [11]

Lincoln did have one culinary obsession: he was inordinately fond of all kinds of fruit and fruit pies. One of his biographers, Ida Tarbell, told how the ladies of New Salem, where he had lived as a young attorney, knew that he loved fruit pies so much that when he was the President they would bake and ship fruit pies to him in homemade wooden boxes.

For home consumption such pies were baked with lattice tops, but for protection in shipping, two crusts were generally used. The steam gashes were often made in the shape of the letter L for Lincoln, or B for blackberry or C for cherry. [12]

If I could send President Lincoln a pie, I would send him this

RED AND WHITE RASPBERRY CHOCOLATE CHEESE PIE

President Lincoln was a Protestant-Deist. A blessing in his honor and memory for what he saw as right—a United union of States—may be found on page 239.

Pie crust:

   1 c. white flour and 1/3 wheat flour
   1/3 plus shortening or butter or combination.
   4–5 tbsp. cold water

PIE FILLING:

Ingredients:

   4 ½ c. raspberries
   1 c. plus 1 tbsp. sugar
   ¼ c. tapioca
   Dash of salt
   1 tbsp. butter

Cheese mixture:
1 ½ large packets (227 grams) cream cheese
¼ c. plus 3 tbsp. sugar
1 c. sour cream
Zest from large orange, about 3 tbsp. (reserve 1 tbsp.)
4 small Hershey bars, broken into small pieces
Spray pie plate with Pam or other non-stick product.

Directions:
Heat berries to a soft boil add tapioca, salt and butter

Let berries cool. Pour berry mash on a plastic bag on top of 9" pie plate and freeze until solid

Beat cream cheese, sugar, and sour cream. Add zest. (Should equal about 2 1/4 cups.)

Heat mixture in a microwave for 2.5 minutes, covered so mixture doesn't splash, and mix well.

Remove frozen mash from freezer and from off the plastic bag. Place it on a hard surface and with a good size knife slice the mash into quarters and then into thirds to make twelve slices. Place slices on a plate and return to freezer for about 15 minutes.

Preheat the oven to 375 degrees

Arrange pieces of chocolate on crust and with a spatula spread the cheese mixture on the crust. Remove the berry slices from the freezer and press one down on the cheese mixture, thus creating a slice of the cheese next to the berry, do the same with the other 11 slices. The result will be 12 red and white slices of pie for serving.

Bake pie for 40-45 minutes.

Chapter II

Compassion is the basis for all morality. —Arthur Schopenhauer

This is a work of creative non-fiction. Within this chapter, the author uses creative license to expand upon biographical and autobiographical information. The actual participation of living persons or historical figures as role models in any particular setting or scene is entirely fictional. Therefore, it should be noted by our readers that any reference in this chapter to Craig Kielburger being arrested in Mexico is pure fiction, and is only meant to enhance the story itself.

L A MESA PENITENTIARY, in Tijuana, Mexico, which houses over 5,800 prisoners, has been described as "one of the toughest in Latin America."[13] Shootings, stabbings and crimes too brutal to describe are not unusual. But that is where Mother Antonia has lived for over thirty years. Mother Antonia, however, doesn't just live in the penitentiary. She once said, "It is more different to live among people than it is to visit them." [14]

"The people" she is talking about are the inmates of La Mesa; some would say the "dregs of the earth." But to Mother they are her *hijos*, sons, God's people just like you and me. "I have to be here with them in the middle of the night in case someone is stabbed," she says, "in case someone has an appendix [attack], in case someone dies." [15]

So you can imagine Mother Antonia's surprise late one afternoon when making her rounds. In one cell she found three new residents. And these *hijos* were different from any other inmates that she had ever met at La Mesa, because like her they had chosen to be there. Well, almost.

You see the Mexican authorities had found these particular *hijos* holding signs in the main plaza that said, *Estamos buscando para compassion en Mexico.* (We are looking for compassion in Mexico.) Not impressed with their signs, the *policia* questioned them and then decided that their statement was an insult to the good people of Mexico. Of course, the three protested their innocence, meaning no disrespect, but to no avail. Looking for compassion they were instead taken to the local jail and accused of "slandering the nation."

Yes, imagine, Mother Antonia's surprise, not just for the innocent question about compassion that had led to the three individuals' incarceration but her utter shock and delight when she realized who they were.

Of course, these new inmates were themselves surprised to meet a Catholic nun in the penitentiary, especially when they heard other inmates calling out to her with such solicitude and affection. "Mother, how have you been?" "Mother, you look pale. Are you eating?" "Mother, my wife is so grateful for what you did." "Mother, you are our Teresa of Mexico...."

Of course, she would always deny that she walked in Mother Teresa's shoes, but in fact, as Mother Antonia's work became better known over the years, her Indian colleague in compassion visited her on several occasions.

If you want to be happy, practice compassion. [16]

"Mother Antonia was born Mary Clarke and raised in a wealthy Beverly Hills family surrounded by the glamorous stars of 1930s Hollywood. At the age of fifty, she left her comfortable world... to dedicate her life to caring for the poorest of the poor—the inmates in one of Mexico's most notorious jails."[17]

Five foot two, with a black-and-white habit and a crisp white veil that frames a face radiating joy, she is a bundle of energy and enthusiasm. Seeing her at home in La Mesa Penitentiary, with its large, imposing, high walls and lookout towers, manned by armed guards, you say to yourself, "A Catholic nun could not live there—impossible."

New World beans [refer] to dried beans, and the fresh pods are known as French, kidney or green beans. You might have supposed I [the author of the History of Food] was saving them until last as a particular delicacy. The fact is that they did not reach Western tables until... 1528 when Canon Piero Valeriano was given some large, kidney-shaped beans by Pope Clement VII. In a spirit of respectful curiosity, he sowed them in pots.[21]

Reading her wonderfully descriptive biography by Mary Jordan and Kevin Sullivan,[18] you not only feel their love and admiration for Mother Antonia but are quickly exposed to what La Mesa was like when she first arrived.

One morning in 1989, the state judicial police conducted one of their periodic raids on the prison, in which they confiscated the money, jewelry, and drugs so many prisoners kept in their cells. This time the fed-up inmates decided to rebel and started throwing empty Coke bottles at the police. As the rain of bottles pelted down, guards opened fire, two prisoners fell dead and many others were wounded.

Then Mother Antonia walked through the gate. With her arms held up high over her head, she walked into the middle of the flying bottles and bullets. Inmates and guards screamed at her to stay away, but she just kept walking, saying, *"Mis hijos, mis hijos.* Stop this. You must stop this now."

Mother's indomitable spirit, faith and courage were so powerful in the face of the violence around her, "the scores of police and guards and hundreds of rioting inmates put down their weapons. The yard went quiet. The fighting ended.[19] Today, La Mesa is much better run than it was when Mother Antonia "with little more than a Spanish dictionary and a toothbrush moved into a cell to live among prisoners who ranged from petty thieves to some of the most powerful drug lords in Mexican history."

In fact, she no longer even noticed when dinner was a *delicacy*—"a can of green beans warmed with hot water from her little coffeepot." [20]

The fact that La Mesa Penitentiary has been

modernized and is less violent in recent years is probably one of the reasons that when I had the honor of visiting in the summer of '06, Mother Antonia agreed to help me with this chapter on compassion. In fact, she said we could meet in her prison cell. We also talked about the two other compassionate souls who would be with us.

Imagine my surprise when a few months later I got a call from one very excited Sister Anne Marie, her administrative assistant: "Rabbi Philip, Mother wants you to come immediately. The other three have arrived."

"What do you mean, 'The other three have arrived?'" I asked incredulously.

"*Ven, ven*, come, come now and you will see."

"But, but..." I started to tell her about my difficulty in getting there so fast. I had already learned on my first visit, however, you don't easily refuse the indomitable, engaging Mother when she tells you what she wants. So I made a few calls, packed and drove to the airport. Less then three hours later I arrived at the Tijuana airport, where I was embraced by a smiling sister Anne.

"Rabbi," Sister Anne, whispered to me after we signed in at security and passed through the large iron entry way door, "Mother Antonia has told some of her *hijos* that a rabbi is visiting. But if some call out to you when they see your *sombrerito*, little cap, do not stop to talk. Mother and the others are waiting for you."

As we walked through the corridors I immediately experienced that same feeling of loss of freedom and too many bodies for one place that I remember from my own prison experience in the 1960s. The sights, sounds and smells of La Mesa were strangely similar to Parchman Penitentiary in Mississippi. Only the language was different—but more about that later.

Arriving at a cell a little larger than the others, I gasped with astonishment as I saw who was seated with Mother Antonia. There was Albert Schweitzer, the famous humanitarian, looking like he had just stepped out of Africa with the safari hat and imposing white moustache. It was clearly his soul visiting us from the beyond. And with him was Craig Kielburger, who founded the organization Free the Children, when he was twelve years old. It was a thrill to see them talking with great enthu-

Sharing bread in the course of ceremonies or simply at ordinary meals forges bonds which, in principle, will never be lost or forgotten. Your companions... are those with whom you have shared bread; the word is derived from Latin com-, "together," and panis,"bread.[23]

siasm, as Mother stood up to welcome and introduce me. Shaking Craig's hand I reminded him that we had met some years ago at a social action conference.[22]

I started to shake the hand of the famous musician and physician who left everything in Europe to go to Africa, but wasn't sure if it was proper to touch a soul. So I just bowed. Then, as I was about to say to the two of them, "I am so pleased that you joined Mother and me," she disappeared. She returned, with Dr. Viktor Frankl, the author of *Man's Search for Meaning*, about whom Mother Antonia had said to me at our original meeting, "Dr. Frankl is my saint. I want him to be in jail with us."

Now looking rather victorious, her face was one gigantic smile. "Rabbi, I told you that if we were going to talk about compassion we had to have Dr. Frankl."

"I am delighted to be here, even though Mother Antonia shared with me that I was not on your original list of guests," said Dr. Frankl.

I started to give Mother a disapproving look for her telling him what I had said, but even at 80 she is so cute and innocent looking, I couldn't. And besides at that moment one of the sisters came by with a large tray of *pan dulce*—bread pastries—and tea. "Mother," she inquired with the same devoted concern for the head of her order that I had witnessed during my earlier visit, "Have you had some tea this morning?"

"Dr. Frankl, I am really thrilled that Mother insisted you join us. In fact, I once had the honor of hearing you speak at a board of rabbis meeting. Truthfully, my only concern was that your wonderful book is more about meaning than compassion."

"The two cannot be separated," pronounced Mother Antonia, rather triumphantly.

"And now that I have reread your book, I quite agree. But tell me," I asked, turning to Schweitzer, Craig and Frankl, "what did you three mean by your signs in the plaza, and did you purposely display them to get arrested-a kind of compassion demonstration?"

"Rabbi, it is a delight for me to be here in the New World as well," said Schweitzer. "Mother so kindly has already taken me to a Bach organ recital at the main cathedral, and I was impressed. As for our intentions, speaking for Frankl and myself from the other side, we convinced our new friend Craig that a most interesting way to embark on a discussion about compassion, though admittedly a bit provocative, was to issue a search for its presence, even if it led to Mother Antonia's jail cell here in Mexico."

"So in a way, I guess you can say we were predisposed to the possibility of confinement, though we hope not as long as Mother's," Frankl laughed.

"Yes, they convinced me to come with them, particularly since I am the only one of the four of you who has never been incarcerated in a jail cell like this one," said Craig. "Although, on that first visit to Pakistan in 1995–'96 there were times I thought I might get arrested for merely meeting the press to address the issue of child slavery. For a 13 year old, it was scary, especially as I knew what had happened to Iqbal."

"Who was Iqbal?" asked Schweitzer. "It sounds like an African name."

"Okay," said Craig, "I can see I will have to tell you the story:

"In April 1995, when I was 12 years old, I stumbled upon an article on the front page of the *Toronto Star* which forever changed my life. It was titled, 'Battled child labour—boy 12—murdered.'[24] Completely gripped by the reality that a boy my own age had just been murdered, I dove into the article, never dreaming that I would become so completely linked to his story.

"I read about Iqbal Masih, a young boy from Pakistan who was sold into slavery at age four to work as a carpet weaver. After many years of gruelling labour, Iqbal escaped and found his way to an organization much like our Free the Children. Iqbal started speaking out against child labor, becoming the voice and face of 2.5 million child laborers. After several years, Iqbal was reunited with his family. Tragically, at age 12, while riding his bike with his friends near his home in Eastern Pakistan he was callously murdered for speaking out against child labor.

"I was outraged. In fact, when Rabbi Posner first contacted me about being part of a discussion about compassion, he asked if it were a matter of unconsciously empathizing or identifying with the suffering implicit in child slavery that moved me to tell my class about Iqbal.

I answered, "'My immediate reaction was not identification with his plight, but rather with his age. I could not understand how someone my own age had not only had such a miserable life, but had been killed for speaking out against child labor, something that I didn't even know existed at the time. I wanted to get to know these kids who were experiencing forced labor, how they felt, what they thought and their hopes and dreams.' [25]

"So, with a group of eleven friends, we formed 'Free the Children.' We met over pizza and pop and dreamed of changing the world. We started with small fundraisers, petitions and local activities. That was 10 years ago. Our goal remains the same today: to free children from abuse, exploitation, and the idea that they are powerless or incapable of making a change in this world."

"You know, Craig, what you did," interjected Mother, "going to South East Asia to get to know such suffering, how they felt… their hopes and dreams, really places you here in this cell with us. In fact, when the rabbi told me you were going to be with us, I said to him, 'This boy amazes me. At such a young age he had the courage to stand up and be horrified at evil and do something about it.'

"And Craig, as the others will tell you, prison is a place where the loss of freedom, like child slavery, makes it very difficult to maintain one's hopes and dreams, one's conviction that there is meaning in life. In fact, all the things like food that we take for granted on the outside, become immeasurably more important when we lose our freedom."

"Mother," I continued, "I only served a mere thirty nine days in the penitentiary in Mississippi in 1961 for sitting in the segregated train station in Jackson, but you are so correct. We 'Freedom Riders,' as we were called, kept our faith by singing and sharing with each other various aspects of life, especially our favorite foods. One of us would shout from his cell so everyone in the cellblock could hear, 'When I get out, the first thing I want is a cheeseburger and fries." Another would say, 'It will be a hot fudge sundae for me,' and on it went."

Then Frankl said, "In the concentration camp at Auschwitz…" and it seemed like the whole Mexican jail around us went totally quiet. He continued:

"Because of the high degree of undernourishment—the daily ration consisted of very watery soup given out once daily and the usual small bread ration—it was natural that when we were not being closely watched we would immediately start discussing food. One fellow would ask another working next to him in the ditch what his favorite dishes were. They would exchange recipes and plan the menu for the day when they would have a reunion[26] even though they knew that the discussion of food was only a hopeful antidote to the likelihood that there would be no such 'reunion.'"

"I have to say that all this talk about food helping to keep one's spirit alive in confinement is not something I experienced," said Schweitzer. 'As a German in French-controlled Africa, I was interned during World War I for a period of three years. But because of the protests of the tribal chieftains and the overall popular demand of medical services, I was kept under house arrest for only a short time and was then allowed to resume my normal activities at the hospital that I had built in Lambarene on the Ogooue River (now in the country of Gabon) for the native Africans. [27]

"As a matter of fact, my earliest recollection of food is not a pleasant one. Perhaps that is why during my internment what sustained me emotionally was not the thought of food, especially what you now call soup, but my passion for Bach and the book I was working on, my third, *A History of Ethics*."

"Will you tell us," Craig inquired, "about the soup?"

"I will, but only because the incident made me realize for the first time how wealth and poverty can influence our compassion for others.

"One day on the way home from school I had a wrestle with George,

Soup derives from sop or sup, meaning the slice of bread on which broth was poured. In the eighteenth century gruel was not only for small children, who had just been weaned, or porridge only for poor peasants: "If it rained porridge," said Goethe, "the poor peasants would have no spoon to eat.[29]

who was bigger than I, and was supposed to be stronger, but I got him down. While he was lying under me, he jerked out, 'Yes, if I got broth to eat twice a week, as you do, I should be as strong as you are!' With cruel plainness, he had declared what I had already been obliged to feel on other occasions. 'I was to them one who was better off than they were, the parson's son, a sprig of the gentry. The broth became nauseous to me; whenever I saw it steaming on the table I could hear George Nitschelm's voice.'"[28]

"Mother Antonia, your kind words about me are appreciated," said Craig. "But surely your compassion for the prisoners with whom you live must have come from experiences similar to Dr. Schweitzer's. After all, you were raised in Beverly Hills, California, not exactly a den of poverty."

"Craig, you are correct. I am sure there are similarities between Dr. Schweitzer and myself. However, the greatest influence in my young life was my father who had a great sense of compassion for the poor, the result of his connection to the dispossessed and rejected who slowly starved to death by the thousands during the potato famine in Ireland. So yes, I grew up in a well-off family, but in order to go from there to here I don't think I had to reach out to find some dispossessed and hungry souls. It was in my veins. I guess that is why so many in this part of Mexico call me," she laughed, "'the Irish nun.'"[30]

"I wish I knew, what precisely in my background prompted my decision to go to Southeast Asia. I only know that my empathic feelings for the plight of the children there only became stronger because I was seeing with my own eyes the tragedy of child slavery.'" [31]

"You know, my new friends," said Frankl with great sadness, "'seeing tragedy' is not always a catalyst for compassion. Dr. Schweitzer's broth and my recollection of soup in the camp moved us to very different emotions. His was an example of greater sensitivity to the outside world, 'mine to my inside apathy.'"

"How so?" I asked.

"In the camp, staring death in the face was a daily occurrence. Once while my cold hands clasped a bowl of hot soup from which I sipped greedily, I happened to look out the window of the hut. A corpse that had just been removed stared in at me with glazed eyes. Two hours before I had spoken to that man. Now I merely continued sipping my soup." [32]

"That's not fair. You had to continue eating your soup," said Dr. Schweitzer, sounding a bit indignant. "In Africa, there were thousands of times in the course of our caring for terminally ill patients and starving natives when we made decisions that meant they died and we lived. Viktor, did you yourself not write of your situation? 'Apathy was a necessary mechanism of self-defense. Reality dimmed, and all efforts and all emotions were centered on one task: Preserving one's life and that of the other fellow.'" [33]

"Thank you. May I call you Albert?" replied Viktor.

"Of course, We have been calling you Viktor."

"Albert, your kindness in attempting to ease the guilt I have occasionally felt for continuing to eat my soup in the face of another's death affirms my view that we were right to come to Mother Antonia's jail, looking for compassion. Mother," continued Frankl, "you call me your 'saint.' But everyone knows that you chose to come here, to live in this prison to give hope and succor to the prisoners around us in this penitentiary."

"Yes, indeed, Viktor," interjected Albert. "Mother Antonia in her prison cell is a powerful example of how compassion and hope can become partners for meaning. But," he continued, "in that Nazi dungeon in which you found yourself, where could you find hope? As you wrote:

Under the influence of a world which no longer recognized the value of human life and human dignity, which had robbed man of his will and

The pleasure of food is the sensation of well-being that derives from the fulfillment of a natural instinct. Two essential elements are involved in food pleasure, the emotional and psychological tension created by the initial impulse of that inner need. [Therefore] eating acquires enormous existential importance when confronted by the problem of the sensation or experience of living.[35]

had made him an object to be exterminated… under this influence the personal ego finally suffered a loss of values.… Driven like a herd of sheep, incessantly, backwards and forwards, with shouts, kicks and blows… we the sheep thought of two things only—how to evade the bad dogs and how to get a little food. [34]

"So, of course, you did not throw away your soup, though I am sure there were times when you were tempted," continued Albert. "And just as important, even in your fear that apathy would deprive you of your humanity in order to survive, did you not say the task was 'preserving one's life and that of the other fellow'?" [36]

"Yes, I, a Catholic nun refer to you, Viktor, a Jewish psychiatrist as 'my saint,' a term," she blushed, "which some call me here as well. Indeed, as Albert just suggested, you maintained a compassionate concern for 'the other fellow' even when you yourself were close to starving."

As Mother said that to Viktor, her voice rose and reverberated throughout the prison's corridors, as she shouted, "*Oigan mis hijos*, listen my sons, this man who resides with us now, this Viktor Frankl has taught us all that compassion and kindness are possible even in the hell of a German concentration camp. How much more so even in this penitentiary?

"So yes, of course," she continued, "Viktor *y mis hijos*, there are times when apathy takes hold of us but in our very suffering we can use it to prompt our native compassion and find peace."

At Mother's outburst of emotion, Frankl started to protest what he perceived was her exaggeration. They were both standing tall as if memory was making them taller than they were. He started to say, "It's not that simple, you exagg—"

But Mother cut him off, "Viktor, remember the time you and a friend had planned an escape from the camp? You wrote, 'I came to my only countryman, who was almost dying, and whose life it had been my ambition to save…. [He] seemed to guess that something was wrong… that I was abandoning him… I ran out of the hut and told my friend I could not go with him.'[37]

"And then what happened?" she asked

Frankl replied, "As soon as I told him with finality that I had made up my mind to stay with my patients, the unhappy feeling left me. I did not know what the following days would bring, but I had gained an inward peace that I had never experienced before."

Their emotional encounter left Frankl and Mother looking exhausted. They had both sat down on one of the cots, when one of Mother's sisters arrived in front of the cell,

"Mother, have you eaten this morning?" the sister inquired, with the same caring devotion as the earlier one. And before she could answer, another sister arrived with a whole tray of food for us all.

"Oh, sister, you know I cannot eat," said Mother in a whisper, "*Cuando mis hijos estan comiendo solamente frijoles*, when my sons are only eating beans."

But then to our astonishment, more sisters arrived with enough food to feed all the inmates in the surrounding cells. "*Si, si, para los gringos*, yes, yes, food for the gringos," the inmates shouted approvingly, "*y para nosotros*, and for us!" They shouted with laughter.

There was freshly baked pumpernickels in honor of Albert, whole trays of Craig's favorite, phad thai, goulash in honor of Viktor, and chopped chicken liver sandwiches in honor of, believe it or not, Mother Antonia.

After we ate, the prisoners on the cell block shouted out their thanks. Quietly, almost as if he was whispering to himself, Schweitzer said, "This wonderful food reminds me that in Europe, Bach and my organ were my celebration for life and sustained me later at difficult times, like my imprisonment."

"And in Africa, at the hospital?" asked Craig.

"In coming to Africa I found an opportunity for compassionate caring that liberated me from a prison-like existence that perhaps I had sometimes felt in Europe, even if it was an artistic one."

"I was too young to feel that kind of meaninglessness," added Craig. "I had yet to feel a woman's warmth, or the loss of it as when love appears quickly. I was still discovering meaning with my mates in the course of a soccer game, yet the same year we started the organization I went off to Southeast Asia."

"You went to Asia by yourself, when you were twelve?" asked an incredulous Albert.

"Yes, my parents would not let me go at first. They thought I was just 'going through a phase` and that I should stop my involvement in this cause. But I felt impelled. 'No, I can't,' I said to my mother, 'I have to continue,' Luckily we found a friend, Alam Rahman, an activist at the time, who at twenty-five ended up taking me to India, Pakistan, Thailand, Nepal and Bangladesh.

"As I look back on it now," continued Craig, "I have a hard time believing I did it. Because for nearly eight weeks we traveled, investigating child labor abuses, even going on raids with groups to literally free indentured children from factory owners and pimps. But surely, seeing them, meeting them and witnessing their plight became my fuel for the work that with my brother Marc our organization continues to do to help break the cycle of poverty and end the practice of child labour." [38]

"Amazing," declared Albert. "I was thirty-eight when my wife and I went to Africa."

Looking at Mother, Craig asked, "Mother, had you read Viktor's *Man's Search for Meaning* before you decided to move to this prison? Were you, perhaps, looking for the meaningfulness that you were not finding in suburbia—the valley in Los Angeles—the raising of your three children—in the midst of Sunday afternoon barbecues?"

"When I made the decision it was hard. My youngest children, though teenagers, were still living at home. I loved being with my kids, trying to be a loving role model. But I also loved my Savior. Remember, I grew up during that time of Nazi terror, when Viktor was suffering from that very evil. I used to cry—it was a terrible time. I always saw Jesus as my Jewish messiah, and to see the hatred against his people was very frightening and sad. Perhaps there was a connection between what I heard was happening in Europe, but I found myself empathizing with everyone. Someone coughed and I coughed. But that weakness was my great strength—to stand up for the suffering wherever it was. [39]

"To answer your question, Craig, I think because I was becoming one with the suffering Christ, I felt the suffering of others. And, as you said, that suffering became my 'fuel,' which energized my compassion for the work I do, and which has given my life such meaning. In fact, it was on Easter Sunday 1976 when I told my family. I was all of fifty years. I remember so clearly, as if it were yesterday. I began with a prayer, 'Thank you God. You've given me so many years and so many feasts like this. But this is the last one for me. I am going to be with you next year. I am going to the prison. I am going to where I am being led.'

"And you know what," Mother continued, "my children weren't the slightest bit surprised. My daughter Kathleen said, 'We had seen it coming our whole life,[40] and when she began giving away her possessions we knew she meant business.'"

"Dear friends," laughed Albert, "I must say, Mother's story has made me feel like I was back in my hospital in Africa — all manly vigor with idealism in my flesh and bone. It is as you Viktor once suggested, 'So imagine first that the present is past and, second that the past may yet be changed and amended.'

"As for me, such a merger of present and past, with values like compassion and kindness, comes to us in our ideals. As this discussion so beautifully exemplifies, especially in what you my new friends have accomplished, 'the power of ideals is incalculable.'

"However," Albert asked rhetorically, "would you agree that 'the power of ideals remains ineffective, however great the enthusiasm,... [and] only becomes effective when [our ideals] are taken up into some refined human personality'?"

"Yes, 'the present and past may be changed and amended' through the quality of our ideals. But they only become real by the human personality when it finds meaning in life by 'looking for the ultimate cause of things' in ourselves.[41] For that reminder of what is breathed into a life of meaning, I am grateful to the three of you."

"Albert, your beautiful comment reminds me of my first meeting with Mother Antonia. Mother," I asked, "do you remember we were talking about freedom, meaning and action? You quoted Martin Luther King, 'One dies when we are unwilling to stand up to evil.' And I used the phrase 'the good old days' to make the point that there seemed to be so much more evil to stand up to today. And you Mother appeared to rise off the floor, bristling with a wonderful and passionate indignation, said to me, 'They were not good old days for the many people who lived in the tenements, who suffered poverty, disease and hunger.' And I quietly agreed. Do you remember that?

"What moved me then and still does was that after I said, 'Mother, your passion for the suffering reminds me that in my Mexican village there is so much I could be doing, and instead I spend almost all my spare time working on my book.' You replied, 'But God didn't call you to do it now! You are doing it now with your book.'[42] 'How kind of you,' I remember thinking to myself, and I hope that's what I said to you."

"Yes," said Frankl, looking at me, "One should not search for an abstract meaning of life. Everyone has his own specific vocation or mission in life; everyone must carry out a concrete assignment that demands fulfillment. Thus everyone's task is as unique as is his specific opportunity to implement it."[43]

"But Viktor did you not also write," asked Craig, "that real meaning is found in three ways: by 'doing a deed, by experiencing a value and by suffering'?"[44]

"I worry that such a quest for 'real meaning' lacks, as I suggested earlier, an ethical anchor, an ideal turned into moral action," interjected Albert.

"Albert, your worry is a valid one. A 'deed,' a 'value' experienced, and 'suffering' are helpful in terms of therapy, which I called Logotherapy. I agree with you, however," continued Viktor, "that from an ethical standpoint, as I wrote out of my concentration camp experience, 'We needed to stop asking about the meaning of life, and instead to think of ourselves as those who were being questioned by life—daily and hourly.'

"However, I want to make it clear that as a Jew I do not view suffering as meaningful in itself. Rather, it is a humane and meaningful achievement if one shoulders an unavoidable suffering in a courageous manner."[45]

Then, just as Viktor continued, "Our answer must consist, not in talk and meditation, but in right action and in right conduct," another sister arrived in front of our cell with a huge cake.

"Mother, have you had something this afternoon," she said with a sweet solicitation that sounded as delicious as the cake looked.

Laughing, while also trying to look angry, Mother turned to me, "You, you, you rabbi are responsible for this delicious looking temptation that you know, based on our first meeting, I cannot eat."

"*Moi, moi,* me, me?" I tried to protest, with a look of innocence.

"You know I won't eat that cake both because of my diet and the vow I once made to God that if He saved the life of one of my *hijos* in this very prison, I would give up this very kind of a white cake with a beautiful wonderful, thick, chocolate icing, the kind I so like."

"Yes, yes," I admitted, "but you also said, 'I would eat a lemon cake, once in a while,' and under that frosting, so it is—a lemon cake! Besides, do you remember what you told me when we spoke by phone, after I had asked you what your favorite food was? 'My favorite food,' you answered, 'is watching others eat.' So, as Viktor

The overwhelming majority of rescuers [who saved Jews in Nazi occupied Europe] cited at least one reason that was founded in their ethical beliefs. Their ethics included justice and fairness, and the belief that persecution of the innocent could not be justified, but the ethic that mattered most was the ethic of care and compassion.[46]

suggested earlier, suffering gives sustenance to meaning, and now I say," I was clearly teasing her, "a delicious cake like this one sustains our collective sweetness."

"Oh, well," sighed Mother, with a slight smile, "it is hard to be a suffering Christian."

To which I replied, "Funny that's what we say, '*s'iz shver tsu zayn a yid*, It's hard to be a Jew.'" I laughed. "Pass the cake, and thank you sister for bringing it."

"And you, Craig and Mother Antonia," continued Viktor who had not finished his comment, having been interrupted by the arrival of the cake, "personify that right conduct and action in life. By your lives you challenge us all to act ethically, as much as we can, daily and hourly."

"Thank you for that clarification," said Albert, "and for your kind words."

Just then as Viktor and Albert were concluding their dialogue the prison corridor reverberated with the sound of shoes. It was Sister Anne walking toward us with the official bearing of an administrator, yet with a cute look of amusement. She handed Mother an envelope.

We watched as she opened and read it, a large smile filled her face, "Well, it seems you three have been released. As you can see," holding up the letter, "the warden says that you were imprisoned illegally as the local court has determined that the search for compassion is everyone's responsibility 'daily and hourly' and that in truth our compassionate deeds liberate us from our indifference to suffering." Mother then broke out in laughter, "And our warden concludes, 'compassionate ones, we hope your confinement did not cause you too much suffering!'"

Looking at each other and with a pleasure that comes from a special shared experience, we anticipated the warden's concluding words and said together, "'You are invited to stay with Mother, as our guests, any time!'"

RECIPES

In July 2006, **Viktor Frankl**'s son in law, Dr. Franz Vesely, sent me some favorite dishes that Dr. Frankl "was fond of" and wrote, *Dear Rabbi Posner, my wife and mother-in-law have commissioned me to respond to your charming request regarding the favorite meals of selected persons. First of all, the ladies send you their regards. We all found the idea truly original, and of course we gladly provide input.*

One of Viktor Frankl's favorites was:

Ungarisches Gulasch mit Kartoffeln—
HUNGARIAN GULASH WITH POTATOES.

A few days after I heard from Dr. Frankl's family, I made an appointment to have my dog clipped, here in my Mexican village of Ajijic, and met Maria. Her accent was not Spanish and I asked the usual, "Where are you from?" "Vienna," she replied with a proud smile. "Do you cook?" "Of course," she pronounced as if she was surprised I would even ask such a question.

Viktor Frankl was Jewish. A blessing in honor and memory of him for his understanding of compassion and meaning can be found on page 237.

Ingredients:
- 2 lbs. stew meat
- 2 tbsp. oil
- 3 yellow onions, chopped
- 2 peppers, red and green, chopped
- 1 10-12 can beef stock, reserve 8 tbsp.
- 1 liter red wine
- 3 ½ tbsp. paprika
- 1 tsp. thyme and pepper
- 1 tsp. salt
- 2 tbsp. cider vinegar
- 3 bay leaves
- 5 tbsp. tomato sauce or paste

6 tbsp. sour cream
2 chilies
3 tbsp. flour
3 potatoes

Directions:

Sauté onion in oil and paprika and cook for 3–4 minutes.

Dredge meat in 3 tablespoons flour, then put into pan; add salt, peppers, chilies, thyme and bay leaf.

Cover meat with wine and stock; simmer for 1 ½ hours uncovered, then an additional 1 ½ hours covered.

Make a paste with reserved stock, tomato paste and vinegar. Add to meat and cook for 15–25 minutes more.

Add sour cream

Serve over sliced boiled or mashed potatoes.

PHAD THAI

Serves 5

In personal correspondence, Craig Kielburger wrote, "I am huge fan of phad thai." (Personally I don't eat shrimp and other Biblically non-kosher foods, but this recipe is in honor of Craig, not me, so I decided to include it. One can substitute a vegetarian Sumi Crab for shrimp, or make Phad Thai with chopped chicken.)

Craig Kielburger was raised as a Catholic. A blessing for food and for his compassion may be found on page 238.

Ingredients:

1 pkg. med. rice noodles
Vegetable oil
3 eggs, beaten
2 c. fresh bean sprouts
1 bunch scallions, cut small
1 clove garlic, crushed or minced
½ tsp. fish sauce

1/2–1 c. chopped dry roasted peanuts
Parsley or cilantro
Cooked shrimp, or a vegetarian option

Directions:

Bring water to a boil. Add noodles. Let cool for 3 minutes; drain and set aside.

Heat a little vegetable oil in a wok or frying pan. Pour in beaten eggs and cook until firm. Don't stir. Remove from pan and cut in thin strips. Set aside.

Heat a little oil in pan again, then add garlic, scallions and bean sprouts. Sauté until translucent Add fish sauce and mix well. Add drained noodles and mix again. Add strips of egg and mix.

Put on a serving plate and garnish with chopped peanuts, parsley or cilantro and, if desired, cooked shrimp or a substitute.

RABBI POSNER'S GERMAN PUMPERNICKEL BREAD

The traditional kind of German pumpernickel that Dr. Albert Schweitzer enjoyed contained no coloring agents (such as molasses, chocolate etc),and required 16–24 hours of baking at a low temperature (about 250 degrees F) in a steam-filled oven, without a baking pan, resulting in a round loaf. Our recipe is for a modern oven or bread machine and includes caraway seeds, providing an alternate flavor that is now characteristic of many commercial pumpernickel (and light rye) breads.

Albert Schweitzer was a Lutheran, the son of a Lutheran pastor.

A blessing in honor and memory of his universal compassion may be found on page 242.

Ingredients:

For a *bread machine*, ingredients for a large loaf:
1 ½ c. warm water, add more if needed
2 tsp. instant coffee
2 tbsp. vegetable oil
2 tbsp. molasses

1 tsp. salt

2 tsp. baking soda

1 ½–2 tbsp. caraway seeds

2–4 tbsp. gluten, optional

2 tbsp. unsweetened cocoa

1 c. rye flour

2 ½ c. whole wheat flour

½ c. corn meal

2/3 c. raisins (optional), add according to directions of type of bread machine used

3 tsp. yeast (1 pkg. = 2 ¼ tsp.)

1/8 tsp. honey

Directions:

In small bowl mix 2 tablespoons of warm water with 1/2 teaspoon sugar and add yeast.

Mix flours, baking soda, corn meal, seeds and salt.

Heat water to hot and add molasses, cocoa and coffee.

Add vegetable oil and stir well.

Add ingredients according to the directions of the make of bread machine used. (I put dry ingredients in first, the oil and then most, but not all of the liquid.)

Add yeast when bubbly.

In bread machines, pumpernickel uses the wheat cycle and the mixture sets for about 25 minutes before the mixing starts. I then slowly add the remaining liquid until the dough is moist but no longer sticks to the side of the pan.

Or dough by hand:

Same as above and mix well until dough is firm and moist but does not stick to the bowl or hands, then add raisins (optional).

Flour a large bowl. Add dough and cover with a towel if dough is to rise in warm oven. Or, place bowl in a large plastic bag and let dough rise in a warm place, outside in the sun or on a warm day in a car with the windows closed, for about 45 minutes.

When dough has almost doubled in size, remove it from bowl and with a fist punch the dough down until it is back to original size.

Shape dough and again let it rise for about 45 minutes in a warm place.

Preheat the oven to 350F or 180C.

Dip a fork into honey, then beat the egg yolk with it. Using a pastry brush, paint the bread with the egg-honey mix.

Bake for 30–35 minutes or until brown.

Cool on a cooling rack.

RASPBERRY LEMON CAKE WITH
A CHOCOLATE FROSTING

Mother Antonia is a Catholic. A blessing in honor of her amazing dedication to the values she holds sacred may be found on page 235.

Ingredients:
3 c. cake flour, sifted
1 ½ tsp. baking power
1 tsp. baking soda
1 tsp. ground ginger
¾ c. butter
2 c. sugar
4 large eggs, separated
¼–½ c. fresh lemon juice, strained (depending how tart you like
    your lemon cake)
1 tsp. vanilla
1 1/3 c. buttermilk
1/3 c. raspberry preserves
2 9" round pans or one large 9 x 13 pan, buttered and dusted with
    flour

Directions:
Butter cake pan(s)
Pre heat oven to 350 F.
Combine dry ingredients.

Cream butter and sugar in large bowl.

Add egg yolks, lemon juice, and vanilla, and beat until blended.

Then alternating, add flour and milk, using 1/3 of each at a time, beginning with the flour.

Beat egg whites and gently fold into batter.

Bake cake on middle rack of oven for 50 minutes or until knife inserted into the center of the cake comes out clean.

Cool for 10 minutes, then take cake out of pan(s). Put on a cake rack until completely cooled. Spread raspberry preserve between the two rounds, and if the cake is baked in large pan, cut it in two halves and spread raspberry preserve between the two halves. On the first half, Pipe a 1 inch border of chocolate icing on the rim of the cake. Put other half on top, and frost cake with chocolate.

Frosting:

1 c. semi sweet chocolate chips

¼ c. butter

½ c. sour cream

1 tsp. vanilla

¼ tsp. salt

2 ¼ to 2 ½ c. confection sugar – to taste

Melt chocolate with other ingredients and slowly beat in sugar.

Chapter III

The Forgiving Place

No matter what happens in the kitchen never apologize"
—Julia Child

ORGIVENESS IS IMPORTANT wherever it takes place. However, this is also a book about food. And what cook would dare ignore Julia Child? So when President Bill and Senator Hillary Clinton, Archbishop Tutu and Joseph of the Bible arrived at my home the following discussion about apology and forgiveness did not happen in my "kitchen."

Rather, with my guests seated in my living room, I said: "President Bill and Senator Hillary, when I wrote asking you to join me in a discussion on repentance and forgiveness it was as if I too saw Hillary's pain when you told her the truth about what you did. As you said in your book, 'She looked at me as if I had punched her in the gut.'[47] I could feel her anger like hot coals.

"Archbishop Tutu when I put a stamp on your letter I felt the crush of your pain, the trampling of bloody feet as described by the bomber, one of so many terrorists who came before your South African Commission to confess and ask forgiveness.

"And ancestor Joseph, thinking of you across the pages of time was like hearing your brothers' shame and despair, seeing the rotten look of guilt and fear on their faces when you told them 'I am Joseph your brother, whom you threw in a pit to die.'

"So please know how very grateful I am to you all for agreeing to come and discuss the issue of repentance, forgiveness and reconciliation.

"Also my colleague Chef Rollo and I hope you will enjoy the food we have prepared for you."

"Rabbi, you tempted me with salmon, cucumbers and leeks," responded Joseph. "I hope

This is a work of creative nonfiction. Within this chapter, the author uses creative license to expand upon biographical and autobiographical information. The actual participation of living persons or historical figures as role models in any particular setting or scene is entirely fictional.

I won't hurt the feelings of modern Egyptians, but I remember Egyptian palace food as dry, like something from a mummy's tomb. Even the meat tasted hard. I look forward to something moist and delicious."

"I think you will be pleased, Joseph," I replied, "and I gather from what you said about my tempting you 'with salmon,' that while you may have been pharaoh's chief adviser, in the case of fish you were able to partake of what he could not."

"Correct," said Joseph, "and as you can imagine pharaoh did not appreciate us enjoying fish in his presence."

"Just how long has it been, Joseph," asked Archbishop Tutu, "since your soul has been nourished by food?"

"You know in our divine residence, we have the joy of being nourished by many things, especially the beautiful character qualities that bless us, so food is a low priority. However, I think the last I ate was something special that the philosopher Baruch Spinoza brought with him when he arrived—a Dutch-Jewish stew called *cholent*. He arrived in 1677 so what was that about a mere 330 years ago," he laughed, "And now I will need some time to restore my appetite."

"And how long did the *cholent* last once you got to the other side?" I asked, hardly able to contain my laughter. Then I explained, "As you may know traditional Jews don't cook on the Sabbath. *Cholent* is a favorite Sabbath dish because it remains warm, in a kind of crock pot. In fact, the word is a wonderful example of the origin and relationship of Yiddish to the old French-German spoken by 10th century Jews of

While the common people of Egypt ate plenty of fish (which was found among the provisions buried in a number of tombs), neither the priests nor the Pharaohs were allowed to partake of it. [48]

the Franco Rhineland area of Europe. Think of the more modern expression from French: non-chalant, or one who remains cool, relaxed, literally not *warm*, i.e., non*chalant*." [49]

Joseph laughed as he said, "That is funny. My Spinoza *cholent* has remained warm for these 330 years."

"Well, Joseph," I said, "it's good that you need time to regain your appetite because before we eat I want to tell you that when I was planning this gathering to talk about forgiveness, I remembered a previous experience I had with you."

Joseph said, "Remind me."

"It was the week before Yom Kippur, the Day of Atonement, some years ago when I wrote my ex-wife asking her forgiveness for a serious sin. As I typed my letter to her, I felt a gentle hand and heard the supporting voice of conscience: 'Rabbi Posner, you are not alone. And what you are doing is the right thing.'

"Who are you?" I asked. "And you answered, 'I am Joseph the son of Jacob, the grandson of Isaac and the great grandson of Abraham.' Then you said that a long time ago, you too had pleaded for forgiveness. You reminded me that you were, to use your words, 'such a spoiled brat to my older brothers' that they threw you into a pit to die. And only many years later when you were the viceroy of Egypt were you and your brothers able to forgive each other.

"And then, Joseph, you made a startling invitation to bring me to what you called the 'Forgiving Place.'"

"Ah, yes, Rabbi, I remember that occurrence well and how surprised you were. I told you that

It's a shame to be caught up in something that doesn't absolutely make you tremble with joy.
— *Julia Child*

very few who still walk the earth are so invited, but that we on the other side know better than you how ethical qualities like forgiveness are eternal in time."

"Yes, remember I asked, "why me?""

"And I answered, because we want you to visit our Forgiving Place before you join us full time. Perhaps then you and others won't be so afraid to admit sins or mistakes, and ask forgiveness."

"So, Bishop Tutu, Senator Hillary and President Bill, imagine my surprise when Joseph contacted me again: 'Rabbi, I understand some others who have had to deal with forgiveness will be joining you in a discussion at your home. May I join you? And, perhaps we can even go to the same Forgiving Place to which I invited you years ago.'"

"'It will be an honor,' I replied, 'for you to participate with us.'

"'Thank you,' Joseph continued, 'because we on the other side want you to know that we appreciate all dialogue that bridges the past, the present and the future.'"

Then, turning to Bishop Tutu, and the Clintons, Joseph said, "Yes, if you three consent to go we will learn how the Forgiving Place on our side is connected to your life on earth."

"So now my friends," I said enthusiastically, "if you agree, we will experience together the surprise that awaits us."

Looking amazingly comfortable, as if unusual surprises were everyday occurrences, Bishop Tutu simply inquired, "Will we be able to return to this side after our visit?"

"I hope so," I replied, looking to Joseph for

Food is often the central focus of another side of sinning, the failure to consider the needs of others as well as one's own. Greed, closely associated with gluttony and lust, is railed against in all of the world's major religious traditions. [50]

confirmation. "But, Bishop Tutu, as you have suggested in your wonderful book, *No Future Without Forgiveness*, 'When you embark on the business of asking for and granting forgiveness, you are taking a risk.'" [51]

"Rabbi Posner, you and Joseph are asking a lot," interrupted Senator Hillary, as she started to point a finger at me, but apparently changed her mind. "Bill and I... well, we almost backed out of coming. I know you may see me as a politician, but I am a fairly private person... much more than Bill. I also had to consider whether being in your book would be good for my career... if you know what I mean. And now you and Joseph are asking that we trust you with something rather personal. That's a risk," she drew out the words, "I'm... not sure... I want to take." Then, she paused, smiled warmly, as if amazed at herself for even contemplating the possibility of remaining and said, "Please call us Hillary and Bill."

"Hillary and Bill, thanks, I understand your feelings and am sincerely grateful for your both coming, and now remaining. And honestly, when I think about how as a couple you so courageously bared your souls in the eyes of the whole world, I think this trip will be for you like a walk in the park holding hands. Joseph has promised me that it will be a wonderful experience for us all."

"Yes, a wonderful and interesting experience," Joseph quickly backed me up.

"Hillary, I admit when I wrote you, I did not believe I would succeed in getting your attention, let alone your agreement to be here. And now I continue to believe what I said in my invitation letter to you and Bill, that a rabbi's book about ethics, which in a candid way reminds us of the importance of repentance and forgiveness, will help personalize you in a positive way by reminding us all that few marriages are perfect. We all make unwise, occasionally reckless, choices. In your case, with the whole world in your face, your relationship survived the heat of pain, repentance and forgiveness in a way that had to leave you singed. But, with tenacity, some evidently good counseling, close friends and love you survived the incredible challenges, and now it is to be hoped that you have a better marriage for it."

"You are most kind, perhaps a little naïve as well, rabbi. Let's hope you are correct. However," laughed Bill, "you should have seen my face when I read that you were inviting me to participate in a book on ethics. Fortunately, my correspondence secretary urged me to read your whole letter before I tossed it aside."

"Please thank your secretary, because as I said, I really believe that many, perhaps even most Americans admire and respect the way you as a couple dealt with your unethical behavior. I mean you… ," pausing to find the right words, "well… you didn't exactly run away."

"May I say," interrupted Bishop Tutu with the right air of authority and politeness, "when Rabbi Posner wrote me that he was inviting you Bill, I was at first rather surprised as well. But when I, thought of all the incredible courageous individuals who came to our Truth and Reconciliation Commission to ask for forgiveness, it occurred to me that you two were even more in the world's spotlight than we were for what we accomplished in South Africa."

"Thank you, Bishop Tutu, for you understanding," said Bill. Sitting erect, he continued in that calm deliberate way Bill Clinton has of saying something serious that comes out sounding casual, "I still can't get over how much has been written or said about our marriage… probably, I reckon, more than any other in American history."

Then looking at Bishop Tutu, and with a glance at Hillary, he said, "Our relationship and my personal failure aroused curiosity everywhere. Even in Japan at a televised town hall meeting I answered a variety of questions including, how I was coping with all the pressures of the presidency, and how I had apologized to Hillary and Chelsea."

At that point Hillary looked at Bishop Tutu and said, "With all our insecurity about this adventure Bill and I are delighted that we are with you now. When I was recovering from our marital troubles, visiting South Africa, meeting you and Nelson Mandela gave me hope.

"Remember, Bishop Tutu," she continued, "I had the honor of meeting you and members of the Commission in Cape Town when you were taking testimony from victims and perpetuators of violence as a means of exposing the truth and encouraging reconciliation among the races after generations of injustice and brutality.[53] Now that I look back on those terrible months and what a challenge it was to forgive Bill,[54] I remember sitting in that courtroom, admiring how you and President Mandela understood the challenge and the importance of institutionalizing forgiveness.[55] I know your example contributed to my ability to eventually forgive at a personal level."

"Hillary, you are too kind to me. Yes, I admit I am proud of the part I paid in my country's development of, as you said, 'institutionalizing forgiveness.' But it would never have happened without our former President Mandela who is really such a remarkable man. As I wrote in my book, 'This man, who had been vilified and hunted down as a dangerous fugitive and incarcerated for nearly decades [even]... invited his white jailer to attend his inauguration as an honored guest, the first of many gestures he would make in his spectacular way, showing his breathtaking magnanimity and willingness to forgive... [And he] would soon be transformed into the embodiment of forgiveness and reconciliation.'" [56]

Forgiveness does not change the past, but it does enlarge the future.[52]

Joseph had been most attentive to what Bishop Tutu was saying, but now I noticed that he looked restless. Acting like an anxious tour guide who had to wait too long for his passengers to finish their breakfast, he asked, "Well, now that we are all here, are you ready to go with me to the Forgiving Place?"

Bill asked, "What do you think honey, are we ready?" His emphasis on "we" was clearly intentional and rhetorical as he immediately asked: "Don't we individually have to say 'I am sincerely sorry,' before we seek a Forgiving Place?"

"Certainly, we wouldn't be going there unless we sincerely asked forgiveness of those we have hurt," replied Joseph. "And, Bill, from the remorse that you expressed publicly, don't you agree that being forgiven, like our sins, remains part of our continuing pain and our freedom to grow and learn from our mistakes?"

With his well-known grin and chuckle, Bill replied, "You got that right."

"In fact," I interrupted, "*a'ni mitstaer*—the Hebrew for 'I am sorry'—actually comes from the root word for pain or suffering, *ts-a-ar*, which in Yiddish many know as *tsu-rus*, suffering trouble."

"That is so true. In my case the pain associated with my prostate cancer," volunteered Tutu, "helped me to be a little more laid back, as they say in, dealing with the problems of the Commission, because I realized more sharply that there was literally not enough time to be nasty.[57]And then there was the suffering I felt at hearing some of the testimony. It was at times like a dam broken loose, yet from it flowed repentance, forgiveness and some amount of reconciliation between our people."

When Bishop Tutu mentioned the words suffering and repentance, I could see Bill's face redden slightly and his body grow tense, as he said: "Probably the most painful part, for me, in the whole Monica thing, other than coming clean to Hillary, was the September 1998 speech I made at the annual White House Prayer breakfast, right after I had testified before the Starr Whitewater Committee. I agreed with those who had said, 'I was not contrite enough.'

"When I stated, 'I don't think there is a fancy way to say that I have sinned,'[58] I recall a real swell of empathy for the pain I was feeling. I also knew that there were thousands of our fellow citizens who would be unable or unwilling to forgive me, and I had to accept that. Nevertheless, before those religious leaders, I said, with sadness in my voice and I know with a heavy heart, 'It is important to me that everybody who has been hurt know that the sorrow I feel is genuine.'

First and most important, (the hurt I caused) my family; also my friends, my staff, my Cabinet, Monica Lewinsky and her family, and the American people, I have asked them all for their forgiveness.

"That is why, Joseph, as you suggested a moment ago, I know from my own experience how pain, forgiveness and acknowledging our sins contribute to our freedom to grow and learn from our mistakes, which is why at the Prayer breakfast I also said that:

> To be forgiven, more than sorrow is required—at least two more things. First, genuine repentance—a determination to change and to repair breaches of my own making. [And] I have repented. Second... a willingness to give the very forgiveness I seek; a renunciation of the pride and the anger which cloud judgment, lead people to excuse and compare and to blame and complain.[59]

"Bill," said Joseph, "I appreciate your agreeing with my comments about pain and forgiveness and your honesty in suggesting that your own 'anger' was one of the emotions that influenced your improper behavior. But are we ready now," he was looking at all of us, "to visit the Forgiving Place? They are waiting for us."

"I am feeling less anxious, so I am getting closer to going," said Hillary. "But in order to go, I need to add to what my husband has shared with you. Before Bill offered his 'emotional admission of his sins and a plea for forgiveness from the American people,' as I say in my book, 'for weeks he had apologized to me, to Chelsea and to his friends, Cabinet members, staffers and colleagues he had misled and disappointed.'[60] I admired him for his public candor and especially appreciated his concluding paragraph to the religious leaders at the Prayer Breakfast."

Looking at Bill, she said, "If I remember right, you talked about how, if your repentance was genuine and sustained, then good would come from it for yourself, the country and our family. Bill," Hillary continued, "what I especially appreciated was that when you mentioned 'our family,' you were especially thinking of Chelsea because you then went on to talk about the children of our country; that with forgiveness they too could learn in a profound way that integrity is important and selfishness is wrong, but God can change us and make us strong at the broken places."

Then turning away from Bill, her voice grew softer. "I also say elsewhere in my book, 'It was a challenge to forgive Bill... .'[61] He had betrayed the trust in our marriage, and we both knew it might be an irreparable breach.... [62] In the beginning, he kept trying to explain and apologize but I wasn't ready to be in the same room with him, let alone forgive him. I would have to go deep inside myself and my faith to discover any remaining belief in our marriage, to find some path to understanding.'"[63]

As Hillary was speaking, you could have cut the empathy we all felt for her with a knife. I remember thinking Hillary was expressing feelings we moderns could all relate to, and which Joseph could relate to as well. Hillary's words appeared all the more memorable and poignant because as she spoke Bill's whole body appeared as straight as a pine tree, with eyes that never left from looking at her. Her comments were like branches, reaching out to him with admiration and appreciation. And she wasn't finished: "I knew that people were wondering, 'How can she get up in the morning, let alone go out in public?'[64] But as I said before," her eyes turned to Bishop Tutu, "you and Mandela and so many South Africans went through hell and yet you were able to forgive.

"As a matter of fact," still looking at Bishop Tutu, she continued, "when President Mandela gave Chelsea and me a tour of the prison on Robben Island where he was confined for eighteen years, he explained that he had years to think about what he would do when and if he got out. He went through his own truth and reconciliation process, which led him to say, 'Forgiveness is not an easy task anywhere, anytime… for most of us mere mortals, forgiveness is harder to summon than the desire to settle old scores.' Mandela showed the world how to make the choice to forgive and move forward." [65]

"We were able to forgive and move forward," replied Bishop Tutu, "because time is a great healer. Then there is the truth that in order to move forward one has to stare 'the beast of our dark past in the eye,' knowing that it doesn't take much for us to become the beast—acknowledging 'how each of us has the capacity for the most awful evil—every one of us.' [66] That is why it was so important that the Whites and the Blacks of our nation mutually saw the beast on their side and ours."

"That you could do that," said Bill, "is why South Africa should be an example to the whole world."

"Thank you," said Bishop Tutu, "after all, every country's integrity is measured by its ability to face its truths, and not pretend that things are other than they are." He continued,

True reconciliation exposes the awfulness, the abuse, the pain, the degradation, the truth. It could even sometimes make things worse. It is a very risky undertaking, because in the end dealing with the real situation helps to bring healing. [67]

"Bishop Tutu, before I talked about my transgression and suffering, you were about to share something of the pain and suffering that came before your Commission," said Clinton.

"Yes I started to say that we were often 'shattered at what we heard' and we frequently 'broke down' or were on the verge of it. Fortunately there were mental health workers to help us get through it, but we may never know just how much what we went through has affected us; the cost of it to us and to our families. [68]

"Sometimes," he continued, "I wondered how even the walls where we heard testimony absorbed such stories of terror and suffering. It wasn't like Auschwitz where one sees the walls scratched by those dying in the crematoria. It was like the walls described in a leper's house, in the Book of Leviticus where the 'walls of the house shall be scraped all around' by the priest (Lev. 14:55). I guess all of us who heard were the priests scraping the walls of a terrible plague."

"Was any of it more difficult than any other?" Hillary asked.

"It was particularly rough for our interpreters, because they had to speak in the first person being the victim and at another being a perpetrator:

'They undressed me; they opened a drawer and then they stuffed my breast in the drawer which they slammed repeatedly on my nipple until a white stuff oozed.

'We abducted him and gave him drugged coffee and then I shot him in the head. We then burned his body and while this was happening, we were enjoying a barbecue on the side.' [69]

There was a shocked silence at the brutality we had just heard. Then I asked, "They could enjoy their barbecue in the presence of such suffering, but wasn't it difficult for you and the others to eat, after you had heard such testimony?"

"I often asked that question of myself," answered Tutu. "The truth is that the ingredients of suffering, repentance, forgiveness and reconciliation leave one empty, but like food such ingredients also sustain our bodies and our souls. Without such sustenance, retaliation or, worse still, vengeance takes over. Just as those who endured the pain and suffering I have described had to forgive to have their health restored, so similarly we who were part of the testimony had to eat."

"As you know, after my time there was a new pharaoh who 'did not know' of my contributions to Egypt," said Joseph, "and the new pharaoh made our people into slaves. But hearing you, Bishop Tutu, describe what modern societies are capable of doing to others makes one wonder if we ever learn from our evil past."

"I appreciate your comment, Joseph, because what you Hebrews experienced in Egypt has its similarities with the treatment of human beings in the last three centuries: Slavery in the United States before the Civil War, then segregation, and in my own country under apartheid the same dehumanization and humiliation of the individual occurred. Whether it was Cape Town or Selma, imagine what it is like to take your child out for a walk and see the playground that was not yours.

"Can you imagine," continued Bishop Tutu, his voice tightening with emotion, "hearing your daughter say, 'Daddy, I want to go to the swing,' and you said with a hollow voice and a dead weight in the pit of the tummy, 'No, darling, you can't go.' What do you say, how do you feel when your baby says, 'But Daddy, there are other children playing there'? How do you tell your little darling that she could not go because she was a child but she was not really a child, not that kind of child? And you died many times and were not able to look your child in the eyes because you felt so dehumanized, so humiliated, so diminished."[70]

"It is getting later and later for us to get to the Forgiving Place," interrupted Joseph in a clearly frustrated voice.

But this time Bill Clinton acted as if he had not heard Joseph's frustration and asked him, "Joseph, what about the anger you felt toward your brothers? I know from personal experience no one can be as angry as I was. I was seething inside when I felt so many blameless people were being hounded by Starr[71] without doing himself harm."[72]

"Okay Bill, I'm taking your bait. We will wait a little longer. To answer your question, I clearly held my anger in for all the years I was in Egypt and then when my brothers suddenly appeared I retaliated against them by forcing them to humble themselves before me in my palace. They were, as we said in ancient times, 'sorely afraid' that I would retaliate against them, and I relished the fact that they didn't know who I was.

It was only when I could no longer stomach their suffering that I ordered them, 'Come forward to me.' And when they did I said, 'I am your brother Joseph, he whom you sold into Egypt.' Then we embraced, kissed and wept. [73] And only then were they able to talk to me. We had forgiven each other, but it had taken a long time."

"It often does," said Hillary. "Time may not spring to mind immediately when one thinks of food, but even there time is a factor. After all, cooking preparation involves time and recipes generally incorporate an element of time. For example, 'let rise for four hours,' or 'bake for forty-five minutes.' As time is relevant to cooking, how much more so is time relevant to our emotional ability to forgive?"

"You know what was interesting?" continued Joseph. "In my time, there were those who did not believe that I actually forgave my brothers, even though the Torah clearly described what happened to us. Bill, did the same thing happen to you? Did you have friends who stopped being friends because they didn't believe you?"

"Joseph, you've been there, so you know how cynical people can be. But Joseph," he continued, "what your brothers did to you only became public years after it happened. Hillary and I were constantly in the public's eye. But yes, to answer the question, even though lots of Americans, sad to say, have done what I did, I know that to this day there are thousands who refuse to believe that I sincerely felt terrible for what I did. And while it took Hillary a long time, as we both said in our books, thank God she eventually forgave me."

"You know, President Clinton, I too had friends who advised me not to include you in this chapter," I interjected. "But my religion teaches 'Weigh each judgment for every person toward the scale of merit.' That is, give them the benefit of the doubt."

"Of course," said Bishop Tutu, "Christianity also has similar statements and such a charitable view greatly contributed to my nation's reconciliation process. It let everyone know, especially the cynics, that in the face of torture and evil beyond imagining, there were heroic individuals who repented and even more heroic individuals who forgave."

"I am enjoying this discussion, but am increasingly worried that we will miss our appointment," pronounced Joseph.

"I can imagine how you feel, Joseph, but such a place has been waiting for us sinners for a long time," said Bishop Tutu. "Surely, there is still time and place for our eventual arrival.

"I am sorry Joseph," continued Bishop Tutu, "but before we go I need to speak about 'the resilience of the human spirit.'"

"As politicians," volunteered Hillary, "we see that resilience all the time. In a way," she added, looking at Bill, "it is what keeps us going."

"Indeed, the Sr. President Bush and I were overwhelmed with people's resilience after the tsunami in 2005—the ability of so many to overcome one of the greatest tragedies in history and to go on," said Bill.

"And to see that same resilience in the way individuals can forgive when they choose to is magnificent," said Bishop Tutu. Then, looking at Joseph, he said and asked at the same time, "Just two examples?"

Joseph gave a nod of agreement, "But only two and then I insist we go to the Forgiving Place."

"When a massive car bomb went off outside the headquarters of The South African Air Force, one of the 219 injured or killed was Mr. Neville Clarence, who was blinded. But he told one of our Human Rights Violations Committee hearings: 'I have absolutely no grudge whatsoever to bear, never have and never will, against the per-

People have long associated food with sin. Although a complex concept that varies throughout human cultures, sin is at its most basic a violation of the boundary between the sacred and the profane.[74]

petrators of that car bomb explosion.' [75]

"In fact," continued Bishop Tutu, "when Mr. Aboobaker Ismail, one of those who masterminded the attack, applied for amnesty, Mr. Clarence did not oppose the application. Instead he went over to Mr. Ismail, who had apologized for causing the civilian casualties, shook hands with him, and said he forgave him even though his action had cost him his sight and said he wanted to join forces to work for the common good of all.

"The cycle of violence that almost destroyed our country, however, affected even non-South Africans," continued Tutu. "On August 25, 1993, Amy Biehl, a student from Stanford University who was involved in the anti-apartheid student campaign, lost her life when the car she was riding in was chased by a mob of youths, who then preceded to stone and stab her to death.

"Her family (was) obviously shattered. Yet instead of being embittered and seeking revenge, quite remarkably they did not oppose the amnesty application of those who had killed their child so brutally.

"They not only attended the hearing, supported the entire process of reconciliation and amnesty, they were even able to embrace the families of the murderers of their child. But what is more remarkable is that they have established the Amy Biehl Foundation with the objective of uplifting the youth in the very township where their daughter was killed.[76]

"I could go on and on," said Bishop Tutu, "but Joseph has been incredibly patient with us all."

"Patient yes," interrupted Bill. "But, come on," he said, drawing out the second word, his way of attempting to appear both patient and serious, "Joseph, isn't the truth that you have already taken us to our forgiving place, or shall I say we have been there together?"

Looking a bit relieved for what Bill's question allowed him to reveal, Joseph responded, "In a way yes, Bill, you are correct. But actually there is a Forgiving Place. It exists as a special place in eternity where we can go to visit whenever we need to forgive or be forgiven—past and present. In eternity every individual's ethical assets can be seen, in same way you can turn on a monitor, in your temporal place, and see words."

"We merely have to think," Joseph continued, "place a specific individual's character trait in our conscious soul, and that virtue becomes present for all of us to see and be inspired. For example, we can place in our soul Abraham Lincoln's forgiveness. And an example of his forgiveness immediately appears."

Then looking very determined, Joseph said, "Are you ready now? This is the last time I can ask!"

"Yes," we all seemed to say at the same time. Joseph gave a nod and suddenly we were standing at a slightly open door that read: "War Department."

Speaking in a whisper Joseph said to us, "It is the early part of January, 1861. There, to the right of President Lincoln you see that tall distinguished gentleman? That is Peter Watson. And in three more weeks he will accept the President's appointment to be a new Assistant Secretary of War." No sooner had Joseph pronounced the word "war," than Mr. Watson came out to greet us.

"Welcome to Washington," he cheerfully said. "Sorry for the chilly hallway. No electricity yet, you know. Anyway, our old friend Joseph asked if we could show you something of our President's character, a scene from the past, as it were."

"Thank you, Peter, " said Joseph, "and now my friends listen and next you will hear Watson and Mr. Blair, the Postmaster General, trying to convince President Lincoln he is being unnecessarily conciliatory."

"As usual," said another voice from inside.

We looked into the partially lit room, and there were the three of them. Lincoln was seated in a rocking chair, the text for a telegram on his lap, and Watson and Blair were standing before him.

"Mr. Lincoln," said Blair, "surely there are other fine candidates besides Stanton to replace the present Secretary of War."

"How can you really believe that Stanton will occupy this place and show you the respect you deserve after what he and I did to you in Cincinnati?" asked Watson.

"Gentlemen, he is the best man for the job. True, I admit," Lincoln said, looking at Watson, "I certainly was more then a little vexed at the way you and the others in the McCormick Reaper case treated me, after they had asked me to join them as a participating attorney in the case." (Joseph then whispered to us, "Six years ago Cyrus McCormick sued a gentleman named John H. Manny for infringing on one of his patents for his reaper.")

"A little vexed you say," Blair's tone sounding close to mocking the President, "when you went to work with greater thoroughness on that case than any other ever before? And they didn't even look at your briefs, merely referring to you as '… our necessary Western Counsel,' and other descriptions of your person that were downright insulting."[77]

"Come now, Mr. President," continued Blair, "magnanimity is one thing. Allowing yourself to be bit in the rear is the other end of rank foolishness. You yourself once told me (I can still hear the agitation in your voice), 'They didn't even invite me to go to the Court house with them or to dine with them the whole time we were in Cincinnati.'" [78]

"Gentlemen," Lincoln replied, looking clearly agitated, "we have been all through this these past days. The war is a monstrous open wound without an attending physician for the military. We need someone who can sew it up and be done with it. The top of the barrel is that Stanton 'is terribly in earnest,' and we need the likes of him to seal it.

"True, 'he does not always use the [most] conciliatory language. But he very sensibly feels the need we have of victories, and he would take almost any means to get them. And the fact is, unless we have them soon the war is likely to be prolonged indefinitely,[79] while Lee goes about the field, south of this very place, at his blasted pleasure.

"As for those five year ago feelings, I trust that I can overcome any previous hurt. After all, Mr. Watson I have asked you to be one of Stanton's assistants even though, when you were one of his co-attorneys, as you later admitted, you advised him to 'sideline' me in that very Reaper Case you just referred to. As you say, my forgiveness may be magnanimous but it is also pragmatic and required. Stanton will get the job done."

"But…," one in the war room started to say. "I…" The President cut him off.

"I've made my decision. Ready the telegram. Come now, it's late, Mary Todd awaits us with a fine leg of lamb."

We watched them disappear, not sure if they noticed us, but honored to have witnessed a fascinating moment in history.

When we returned to our side of the Forgiving Place, the dining room table had a center piece of freshly cut flowers and everyone's favorite food: Tutu's chicken, salmon in honor of Joseph, and Hillary's peach pie for Bill.

I thought of the 23rd Psalm, "... Only goodness and steadfast love shall pursue me all the days of my life, and I shall dwell in the house of the Lord forever." And so it is, thought the preacher in me, when we pursue our faith with the eternal values of repentance and forgiveness.

Joseph must have read my mind, as he quietly said,

"And yes, the only tigers we face are those we remember in the zoo."

Seated at the dining table, Joseph said, "Rabbi, the Salmon looks wonderful.

Bill added, "And how did you know one of the things I missed most when we left the White House were the freshly cut flowers every day?"

Then Hillary said, "And now that we are safely back I have to say the whole Forgiving Place experience was a real revelation, one I shall long remember and hopefully be of benefit if I should become,..."

"Indeed, I had heard that your President Lincoln was amazing," Bishop Tutu interrupted her, "but such forgiveness was breathtaking."

"Like my hunger," laughed Bill.

"And Hillary, would you now agree with Bishop Tutu and me," I asked, "that asking for and granting forgiveness can be a risk, but our recent adventure was risk free?"

Before Hillary could answer, there was a loud knock from the outside. Going to the door, I probably sounded more irritated by the interruption than I was. I shouted, "Who is there?"

Opening the door, there stood the answer:

The peach tree of the Garden of Immortality is vast. It takes a thousand men holding hands to encircle it. At the first fork in its branches an invisible gate opens, and the spirits of the dead can slip out. The guardians of this gate let only souls of good-will pass them. The others are seized and thrown to the tigers.

Two souls confronting each other. They were arguing. The one who wore the image of a face I had seen before said to the other, "I only want to ask Bishop Tutu and the others if they will talk to me?"

"I am Simon Weisenthal," said the other man, as he turned toward us, "on earth I was known as 'the Nazi hunter.' I begged him," he looked glaringly at the other man, "not to come to your door. He is not ready to forgive or be forgiven."

"How do you know," asked the other? "I have contacted as many of those who I helped exterminate as I can. Some have looked into my soul, actually empathized with my present agony and guilt and have forgiven me. And, yes, others have refused to forgive me."

"I can barely talk to you myself," replied Weisenthal. "Surely you must know that you are abhorred by those whose lives you affected so terribly, yet you seek forgiveness, and seek the counsel of this Bishop and these other esteemed individuals?"

"Mr. Weisenthal, forgive me, but you are a recent arrival to this side. I have been going back and forth almost daily for many, many years. In that transmigration between then and now, my soul is no longer the same as he who inhabited the earth so many years ago. I am exhausted and I need to know my future, as you seem to know yours."

"I know," replied Weisenthal, "the Bishop believes as he has shown with his Commission that forgiveness and truth can merge for individual and national healing. But for you? There was evil beyond belief. Can it really be wiped clean with repentance and healing? Perhaps you only want to taste once again," he said contemptuously, "some of their earthly food."

"Mr. Weisenthal, who are you to judge my right to ask forgiveness? Does not your religion teach that 'an individual sinner who repents is greater than even the High Priest' (who prayed for the whole people's forgiveness in the Holy of Holies at the Ancient Temple in Jerusalem)?" [80]

"But you—" shouted Weisenthal, as his anger appeared to swell while peering through the open door looking for support from us, "you, you...

Instead there were no more words. Time seemed to stand still as if it had been seized, waiting for some divine revelation to reveal itself.

Mr. Weisenthal and his adversary's question resonated with us: Who can forgive? And the realization that forgiveness is an expression of character in eternal time, hung in the air before us like intermittent strands of mist and sunlight.

"Will you allow me in?" he asked again.

Our food was getting cold. The door remained open, his question unanswered. Surely each of us were reliving the memories of our own sins and repentance, waiting for God to help us answer him, and ourselves.

There was only silence.

RECIPES

In February 2006, I received this nice note from **Archbishop Tutu**'s secretary in Cape Town, including a recipe for Tutu Chicken which was made for him

Dear Rabbi Posner:

I am sorry to take so long to respond. We are overwhelmed here and the Archbishop has asked me to respond on his behalf. [In addition] his favourite foods are curry and rum and raisin ice cream (not together!). Most other foods if they have a good dose of Tabasco sauce.

Archbishop, Tutu is an Anglican. A blessing in honor of his powerful commitment to forgiveness may be found on page 242.

TUTU CHICKEN

Ingredients:

3 medium potatoes

2 large tomatoes, skinned and chopped

1 chicken, cut in pieces

14 oz. can tomato puree

3 oz. seasoned flour

1 tbsp. mild curry paste

2 tbsp. vegetable oil

1 tsp. Tabasco sauce

2 onions, chopped

1 chicken stock cube

1 green pepper, sliced

1 pint water

2 c. sliced, fresh mushrooms (not in original recipe)

Directions:

Boil the potatoes for ten minutes until half cooked. Peel and slice.

Dredge chicken in seasoned flour.

Heat oil in a frying pan until hot, and brown chicken pieces. Remove chicken from pan.

Add onions and green pepper to the pan, and cook until soft, and add the tomatoes. Set aside.

Add 4–5 tablespoons of the remaining flour to the pan and cook for 1 minute.

Add tomato puree, curry paste, Tabasco sauce, stock and sufficient water to make a thick sauce.

Put the chicken pieces in a large casserole, cover with the sliced potatoes and the vegetables.

Cover the casserole and bake at 150C (300F) for an hour and a quarter. Serve with rice.

Joseph of the Torah/Bible

A Hebrew blessing in honor and memory of **Joseph** the son of Jacob and Rachel may be found on page 238.

POACHED SALMON WITH CREAMY BEURRE BLANC SAUCE

It's a bit unlikely that salmon found its way to ancient Egypt but as you just read, I promised Joseph something moist.

Ingredients:
    4 salmon filets, 4-5 oz. each
    Poaching liquid:
    3 c. water
    ½ c. dry white wine
    1 small onion, sliced
    1 rib celery, sliced
    3–4 parsley sprigs
    3–4 dill sprigs or ½ tsp. dry dill
    ½ lemon, thickly sliced
    Salt and course ground pepper

Directions:
    Prepare poaching liquid in a large skillet. Combine all the ingredients and bring to boil. Lower heat and simmer 8–10 minutes.

Add filets, skin side down, cover and poach 8 minutes. Salmon should be slightly translucent in the center.

BURRE BLANC SAUCE

Ingredients:
- 1 c. dry white wine
- ¼ c. white wine vinegar
- 1/3 finely chopped shallots
- 1 ½ c. thick double cream or whipping cream
- ½ to 1 tsp. lemon juice
- 2 tbsp. unsalted cultured butter, chilled and cut in small pieces
- Salt and ground white pepper

And the Israelites, moreover, wept and said,..." We remember... the cucumbers, the melons, the leeks, the onions, and the garlic. Now our gullets are shriveled. There is nothing at all! Nothing but this manna to look to. — Numbers 11: 5, 6

Directions:

In sauce pan combine wine, vinegar and shallots, and bring to a boil; cook until liquid is almost totally evaporated.

Stir in cream and cook over medium heat until mixture is thick enough to coat a spoon.

Wisk in butter, one piece at a time, until well blended; add lemon juice and season with salt and pepper to taste.

Arrange filets on plates and spoon sauce over top.

LEEK AND CHEESE MATZAH PIE

Serves 6 to 8 as a side dish

Ingredients:
- 1 ½ to 2 medium leeks
- 3 tbsp. unsalted butter, vegetable oil, or margarine.

1 onion, chopped

1 c., or ½ lb. ricotta or farmer cheese

1 ½ tsp. salt, or to taste

½ tsp. freshly ground black pepper

1/4 tsp. nutmeg, freshly grated

½ tsp. chopped fresh dill or ¼ tsp. dill.

4 matzahs, softened in water about 3 minutes, but not so much that they fall apart.

1 1/3 c., about 5 oz., grated gruyere cheese

Directions:

Cut the root ends and most of the green part from the leeks and discard. Peel away any loose layers, cut the leeks in half and then cut crosswise into thin slices. Soak the leeks in cold water, stir to loosen any dirt, remove and drain well in a colander. You will have about 3 ½ c. chopped leeks.

Warm the butter or oil in a large sauté pan over medium heat. Add the leeks and onion and cook, stirring often, until the leeks are very tender, 15–20 minutes, adding water as necessary to soften them. Make sure all the water has evaporated, or drain well. Place the leeks and onion in a medium bowl, and mix in the cheese, 2 of the eggs, salt, pepper, nutmeg and dill.

Preheat the oven to 375 degrees F. Oil or spray an 8" square baking pan.

Beat the remaining egg in a shallow bowl large enough to hold a matzah and dip one of the soaked matzahs into the egg and place in the baking pan. Repeat, using enough of the additional matzah to fill in any spaces in the pan.

Sprinkle with 2/3 cup of the grated cheese, and top with the leek mixture. Add the remaining matzahs, and top with the remaining cheese.

Bake the pie until brown, 30–40 minutes. Let pie rest for 10 minutes, cut into squares and serve.[81]

Bill Clinton loves McDonald's Big Macs and Egg Mc Muffins. In fact, he calls Al Gore his Vice McPresident. (Credit Bob Hope)

"No one has ever accused President Clinton of being a slouch when it comes to food: Our president likes to eat—anything. He's a Democrat but his appetite is bipartisan." (Dear Prez, Bob Hope)

Bob Hope's comments were relevant before the President had his heart problem. But before January 2004 when he swore off junk food, there were those pies he enjoyed so much. In fact, when Hillary and Bill were first dating, she baked him his favorite—a Peach Pie.

Bill Clinton is a Baptist, Hillary is a Methodist. A Blessing in the Baptist or Methodist tradition may be found on page 236.

GINGER CUSTARD PEACH PIE

Ingredients
1 9-inch prepared pie shell
Ginger Snaps (optional)
Or your own pie crust:
1 c. white flour and 1/3 c. wheat flour
1/3 c. combination of shortening and butter
4–5 tbsp. cold water
½ tsp. salt
½ tsp. powdered ginger
1 tbsp. sugar

Custard:
¾ c. sugar
¼ c. corn starch, flour or tapioca
1 tsp. powdered ginger
¼ c. melted butter
3 eggs plus one egg yolk.
1 egg white and set aside
4 medium ripe peaches, or, if not available, may use 1½ of two 15 oz.
cans of peaches sliced into quarters and a few eighths.
1 tbsp. brown sugar
¼ c. slivered almonds.

¾ tsp. powdered ginger

1 tbsp. additional ginger (optional): Peel some fresh ginger root, finely slice into small pieces.

Directions

Pie Shell: Use a fork to generously prick the sides and bottom of the pastry. Brush pie shell with a little of the egg white. Bake 10 minutes at 425 F. or until baked to a golden brown.

Peaches: Arrange sliced peaches on the partially baked pie shell with points toward center, using smaller pieces to fill in the center.

Custard Sauce: Mix sugar, flour, salt and ginger in a large bowl (make sure ginger does not have any lumps). Now mix the eggs and add them, with the melted butter, to the dry ingredients, and beat well.

Pour the sauce, but do not totally cover the peaches—the tops of the peaches should be seen. Lightly sprinkle with the nutmeg. Set aside any extra sauce.

Bake at 350 F. for 45 minutes, until a light brown.

Glaze: Mix remaining egg white and brown sugar. After 35 minutes, remove pie from oven and brush glaze over top of pie. Sprinkle with almonds, and fresh ginger pieces, and bake another 5–10 minutes until a toasty brown.

Ginger Snaps: If using, remove pie from oven after 35 minutes, brush glaze, surround the perimeter of the pie with the ginger snaps, and bake for another 5–10 minutes until the pie is a toasty brown. Let pie cool and set before serving.

Chapter IV

The Tabernacle of Righteousness

*"On some positions, Cowardice asks the question 'Is it safe?' Expediency asks
the question 'Is it politic?' And Vanity comes along and asks the question
'Is it popular?' But Conscience asks the question, 'Is it right?'"* [82]
— *Martin Luther King, Jr.*

This is a work of creative non-fiction. Within this chapter, the author uses creative license to expand upon biographical and autobiographical information. The actual participation of living persons or historical figures as role models in any particular setting or scene is entirely fictional.

CCORDING TO THE *Zohar,* the book of Jewish mysticism, "When a person is seated in his/her *sukah* [the booth symbolic of God's beneficence], Abraham and six distinguished mystery guests partake of his company." [83]

In keeping with this tradition, it was during the seven-day fall festival of *Sukkot* that I invited my guests to be sustained with good food and a discussion about righteousness.

So, when Presidents Jimmy Carter and Nelson Mandela arrived I shared with them this tradition of *Ushpizin* (having mystery guests) and suggested that we have our discussion in the *sukah,* where it is also a *mitzvah* (commandment) to eat one's meals.

Seated under the palm branches hanging with fruit, President Carter asked, "Will Abraham be coming? And who are the two other guests?"

At that very moment the sukah rustled as if a slight wind had descended upon us, stirring up both leaves of matter and words of the spirit. And two figures appeared.

"*Shalom a'leychem,* peace be upon you," one of them said. "I am the Prophet Amos. *Avraham avinoo,* Abraham our father, sends his regrets but with so many *sukkot* to visit, he asked me to come in his place. And rabbi, as this is to be a discussion of righteousness, I am sure you will agree I have also brought with me a wonderful exemplar of that virtue."

And with that introduction, President Abraham Lincoln stepped forth, saying, "I've always wanted to be a guest in one of these Hebrew fruit booths ever since I read about them in the Bible."

"*Aleychem ha shalom,* peace and welcome to you," I returned their greeting, and we proceeded to enjoy introducing ourselves.

"Presidents Lincoln, Mandela, and Carter, and Prophet Amos, I am honored to have you in my home, a guest in this *sukah,* though I admit to being nervous about your tastes in food. I can only hope that you, Mr. Lincoln, will still enjoy your wife's almond cake, and that you, Amos, still have a taste for lamb.

"Our dear host," said Mr. Lincoln, "I remember Mary's cake with delicious delight. As for them forks and spoons, as you know I am a bit of a storyteller myself and that there *Midrash* was quite a yarn and not that far off.

Yes, indeed, Amos and I know how to help feed each other, so I will in the course of our dinner and discussion enjoy the almond cake once again. As for your lamb, dear Prophet, we often enjoyed lamb at one of Mary's special White House dinners."

"Now Abraham, you know it's not my lamb," replied Amos. "In fact, dear host," as he looked at me, "I rarely ate it, though yes, I was a shepherd to flocks in Tekoa, near Jerusalem. In my day only the well-heeled could afford lamb. So it is very kind of you to include this delicacy in the meal you have prepared for us."

"As for me," said Carter, "you know the rice and the cucumber salad will certainly go well with the lamb." Looking to President Mandela, he continued, "and I can't wait to taste one of your favorites—*Umngqusho.*"

"Yes, I was delighted that a friend from South Africa sent the recipe to you, Rabbi Posner. And President Carter, once again you and I will be enjoying something we have in common, even if we didn't grow the peanuts."

"Well then," I continued, "*bon appetite,* or as we say in modern Hebrew, *b'teyavon,* with good appetite let us enjoy all these marvelous tastes as we inquire into the nature of our righteousness."

"Or lack of it," interjected President Lincoln.

"On that note of righteous objectivity," I said, looking at Lincoln, "let's begin with what the four of you have in common. Would you agree that each of you personifies the courage to say what was morally right even when others didn't want to hear it?"

"Perhaps, rabbi, your compliment is true for the others. However, I think my reputation for honesty has otherwise confused you." Trying not to laugh, Lincoln continued, "As one biographer wrote of me: 'Lincoln was human... he was not born on Mount Rushmore,... (so) that such moral distinction as he did achieve by deliberate effort over time... never was or would be anything like perfection.'"[84]

"Rabbi," added President Carter, "I too think you exaggerate our virtues, but thank you nevertheless. And, Mr. Lincoln, may I remind you that none of us is perfect. As a Christian my beliefs make me ever more conscious that we all sin. Our ethical virtues are not cut in stone."

"Ah, ah," laughed Lincoln, "That is exactly why I was profoundly amused when I heard they intended to cut me into that there Mt. Rushmore stone."

"Yes," smiled Carter. "But I am sure you will agree, it is so marvelously chiseled, you are in good company. Besides, many possess the virtue of honesty, but not righteousness. Mr. Lincoln, you have always impressed me as having both."

And your observation 'that we all sin,' reminds me about your famous comment in that magazine, Play... something..."

Carter, looking astonished interrupted, "*Playboy.* Are you suggesting, Mr. Lincoln, I could read it on the other side?"

"If it's here, it's there. Remember," Asked Amos, "Marshal McLuen's 'the medium is the message'? The difference is on our side, the message, the encounter, is the medium."

"Nothing censored on high," proclaimed Lincoln. "However those nude bodies in the centerfolds," his soul appearing to blush, "do recall, shall I say, one's ancient passions. Anyway, as I was saying, Mr. Carter, you once said of the famous *Playboy* article during your 1976 presidential campaign, 'It now seems like a humorous incident, but I almost lost the presidential election by attempting to explain... biblical texts like... "all have sinned and come short of the glory of God."'" [85]

"Yes, because I spoke of my lust, within a week I lost 10 percentage points in public opinion polls.[86] I can only imagine what they would have said about you, Mr. Lincoln, if in your day you had spoken so personally about sin."

"Perhaps, President Carter, that's why I rarely went to Church except when Mary dragged me along in the hope that it would make a Christian of me. That way the only sins them preachers could brand me with were straight political."

"Enough about sin, let us return to our ethical virtues," objected Amos. "Let me remind you gentlemen that as God's spokesmen we prophets were not proclaiming our virtues were all perfect, anymore than there is a perfect human being."

"Excuse me for interrupting," said Mandela, "but I have to say, what is clearly perfect is this lamb stew, especially with the saffron rice pilaf."

"It really is delicious. Our ancestors in Egypt certainly knew what they were doing in making lamb so central to the Passover festival," added Amos. "Anyway, as I was saying, our ethical choices are neither all negative nor all positive. But as you, Mr. Lincoln, would say during the days of your terrible war, let us do our duty 'as we understand it.' In my day, what you called 'duty' we understood as God's Torah...."

"Yes, what you Jews call the Law."

"Correct, Mr. Carter. The idea that God and ethical living are one and the same," said Amos. "And while I condemned my own people as being unworthy of the Covenant, the truth is that all of God's children have profaned God's law by not doing 'right' in the face of evil and injustice."

"I am glad to hear you say that, Amos, but if you felt that way," I asked, "why were you so insistent that Israel be punished more severely than the rest of 'God's children'?"

"You know, as I look back on it now," he smiled, "God and I could have used some of President Lincoln and Mandela's patience and magnanimity for those that appeared 'to hate what is right.'"

"You are too kind. Lincoln and I were politicians. We knew that once the fighting had ceased, the 'reconstruction' of our societies would not endure if we retaliated against our enemies with the indignation of a Prophet."

Turning toward Mr. Lincoln, Mandela continued, "Surely, Mr. Lincoln, you must know that your words were like a beacon of righteousness, not just in your time, but to us a century later in South Africa. The words you spoke at your Second Inaugural as President: 'With firmness in the right as God gives us to see the right,' not only gave moral succor to the citizens of your day but to those of ours, one hundred years later, in the grave struggle against apartheid." [87]

"So Mr. Lincoln, do you still think yourself lacking compared to these other gentlemen in the virtue of righteousness? Because if so," I continued, "I have to remind you of an interesting comment you made about yourself before you married Marry Todd, to… ."

"Oh my," interrupted Lincoln, "I feel the presence of Ann Rutledge in this room. How much she and I still suffer from the arrows of our young and innocent love; as much, I fear, as the historians loved to wonder about us."

"So, do you remember saying to Miss Rutledge: 'I want in all cases to do right and most particularly so, in all cases with women. I want at this particular time, more than any thing else, to do right with you'?" [88]

"Before I answer," said Lincoln, beginning to laugh, "will someone pass the cucumber salad?"

"Now," he continued, "you can imagine, my new friends, the words I once said to her are dim with time but as with the sentiment, she still resides. In that sense, one's right behavior, whether affectionately demonstrated toward the belle of one's youth or toward those otherwise oppressed is no absolute. Indeed, such attributes are part of our moral treasury, which like are material ones, ebb and flow. Though, as I once said to my law partner, Joshua Speed, if there be a 'gem' to my character, it was my ability 'to keep my resolves when they are made.'"

"Which is how posterity views you to this very day," added Carter. "Truly, Mr. Lincoln, our nation owes you an enduring debt of gratitude for your tenacious spirit to a righteous cause. As I once wrote, you persisted in your 'resolves' to get elected to political office despite 'a life story that before being elected President was almost an unrelieved litany of failure.'" [89]

"Admittedly so," sighed Lincoln. "But such failures were also mitigated by my tendency to favor others occasionally before my own self interest—a humble trait my dear Mary found most annoying."

"Yes, one of the most famous examples of that humility," continued Carter, "was the Senate race of February 1855, which you really wanted to win. Yet against your wife's wishes, in a very close nomination race you told your supporters, 'You ought to drop me and go for Lyman Trumbull' (the other candidate)."

"Why did you do that?" asked Mandela.

"Because, it was obvious to me that if I did not throw my support to Trumbull who was a Whig candidate like me his opponent who supported Stephen Douglas and the maintenance of slavery in Nebraska would have won."

"And isn't it also true, that Mary Todd held a grudge against Trumbull, including his wife, the rest of her life," asked Carter, "for having taken the nomination (and the Senate seat) that in her view should have gone to her husband?"

"'Fraid so," answered Lincoln, "but as I was to say later, 'The defeat of the Nebraska/Democratic/Douglas forces (who favored allowing Kansas and Nebraska to become slave territory) gave me more pleasure than my own merely personal defeat gives me pain.' What was probably more difficult for my disgruntled wife was the fact that I held no grudge against Mr.Trumbull and the others. In fact, he and I had a good working relationship for the good of the Republican Party the rest of my life.[90]

"But of slavery, I confess most of my friends and associates in my early youth had what I called 'slight pro-slavery proclivities.' As the historian David Potter has suggested there is a real conflict between 'deeply held convictions' and how individuals on the other hand conform to the 'cultural practices' of the society in which they live. The good scholar was right to say:

"'Lincoln was a mild opponent of slavery and a moderate defender of racial discrimination.' But in his heart he possessed a feeling for 'humanity which impelled him inexorably in the direction of freedom and equality.'" [91]

"In fact, President Lincoln, I think it was you who said, 'There are few things wholly evil, or wholly good,' which is why as 'a devout Christian' I believe we are 'called to righteousness,' so that we can make the healthiest ethical choices possible." [92]

"The problem as Amos has suggested, is that "righteousness" has to be finely tempered with a proper mix of reality and compassion," Lincoln added. "In fact, Mr. Carter, though you describe yourself as 'a devout Christian,' you have recently felt the necessity to speak out against the moral absolutists of your own day, who are now called 'fundamentalist Christians.' You have rightly described a characteristic of fundamentalism as 'I am right and worthy, but you are wrong and condemned.'" [93]

"Mr. Mandela, President Carter and I, each in our own way," continued Lincoln, "have had to deal with extremists or 'fundamentalists' in government. For example, Mr. Mandela, did you and your South African liberation movement view righteous morality only in terms of black and white?"

Mr. Mandela smiled broadly, "Mr. President did you purposely use the colloquialism: To see things 'only in black and white' to indicate the true nature of our Liberation Movement? Whether you did or not, your question is on target. Many in our country, on both sides Black and White, those who held power and those who coveted power saw things in the extreme.

"And, your question, Mr. Lincoln, is both interesting and relevant to me because I too had to deal with the extremists in my country. Knowing how, especially in your first inaugural speech, you tried to be conciliatory to the South and were besieged by both the rebels and the radical abolitionists prepared me for my own challenges."

"Thank you, Mandela; is it not amazing how different historical circumstances can be so similar, especially in matters of values? And, you are right sir. In my 1861 inaugural speech I spoke for the maintenance of the Union, yet reached out to 'my dissatisfied countrymen' on both sides. I asked:

In our present differences, is either party without faith of being in the right? If the Almighty Ruler of nations, with his eternal truth and justice, be on our side of the North, or on yours of the South, that truth, and that justice will surely prevail, by the judgment of this great tribunal, the American people....[94]

"And, I concluded with as much down right affection for my Southern brothers as I could muster:

We are not enemies, but friends... Though passion may have

strained, it must not break our bonds of affection. The mystic chords of memory, stretching from every battle-field, and patriot grave, to every living heart and hearthstone, all over this broad land, will yet swell the chorus of the Union, when again touched, as surely they will be, by the better angels of our nature." [95]

"Such eloquent words!" said Carter.

"You are too gracious, however the 'better angels' as we know fled, leaving the field to those of the like of an Iowa farmer who urged me not to yield: 'Give the little finger and shortly the whole hand is required.' Yet, the *Richmond Enquirer* saw in my speech only the '... cool, unimpassioned deliberate language of the fanatic... Sectional war awaits only the signal gun....'" [96]

"How each side sees his own righteousness and the other's trespass is truly what makes leadership such an unrelenting burden," added Mandela. "I discovered that in my prison solitude,' especially toward the end of my imprisonment when I was separated from my ANC colleagues, that the time had come when the struggle could best be pushed forward, no longer with violence, but through negotiations."[97]

"And that is one of the reasons I admire you, President Mandela. As bad as apartheid was, you succeeded in avoiding all-out war with the government by convincing Prime Minister de Clerk that you could both compromise the righteousness of your cause for the greater cause of peace. You and President Carter graciously describe my words as eloquent, but in truth those very words may have contributed to our terrible war."

"In all fairness, Mr. Lincoln, southern slavery had been our way of life for 250 years. The tide of such an inequality was a vast ocean of separation, compared to the 46 years of apartheid that South Africa had brought down upon its citizens."

"President Carter, your reputation for kindness is true indeed," responded Lincoln. "I do appreciate your attempting to ease this old burden. As you gentlemen know as well as I, true leadership is a lonely business."

"Precisely," responded Mandela, "And that is why I chose to tell no one what I was about to do. I knew that my prison colleagues upstairs would condemn my proposal to negotiate and that they would kill my initiative even before it was born."[98]

"Mr. Mandela, your words recall a load of memory and a weight of loneliness that grew ever so heavier as I debated the propriety and timing of what came to be my Emancipation Proclamation. As with you, Nelson, I kept the proclamation to myself, until I revealed it to my Cabinet. And, I must say I had a great joy in doing so. I riled up some of those adviser counselors of mine like a pig in a rut. But that's another story."

"I can imagine, and that is why I suspect we all agree that there are times when a leader must move out ahead of the flock, go off in a new direction, confident that he is leading his people the right way—including his sainted advisers," said Mandela.[99]

"Speaking of 'the flock,'" said Amos, "I am embarrassed to say I am feeling rather rich at this gorgeous table, enjoying it so." He laughed. "Would one of you pass the lamb?"

"Glad to," said Carter; "Mandela, you are right regarding our responsibility to lead progressively. I believe that in this matter of leading the 'right way,' as our friend Abraham suggested, 'the better angels' are not always present. In that context, I have often taught that as Christians, we have an obligation to those in our communities, or other nations who are suffering from either deprivation or persecution. [100] In fact, in one of my poems I wrote of the tragedy of apartheid. If I may, it went something like:

With apartheid's constant shame
Black miners slave for gems of gold
The wealth and freedom are not theirs;
White masters always keep control.[101]

"Mr. Carter—may I call you Jimmy?" asked Mandela.

"Of course. When I ran for president, I always introduced my self as Jimmy. In fact, the Northern establishment loved it: 'I'm Jimmy Carter and I am running for President,' I would say."

"Gentlemen, why don't we make it easier and call each other by our first names?" suggested Lincoln.

"Well, Jimmy, on the road to the presidency, we had different experiences. I went directly from prison to an acclamation that led to my becoming the President of the new Republic of South Africa. That aside, your poem reminds me that you, Jimmy, Abraham, and I all share something more than our connection as one-time presidents." Chuckling Mandela continued, "In fact, Jimmy, I meant to tell you when you spoke about Mr. Lincoln's 'almost unrelieved litany of failure' to get elected to political office. Am I not correct, Abraham, in suggesting that you hated agriculture and couldn't wait to get away from it—perhaps one of the reasons for your uneasy relationship with your father?"

"Correct. I found strength with an ax in hand and a tree to fell but farming inspired nothing but drudgery. Although, the tenuous relationship I had with my father," Lincoln said with a sigh, "was more the result of our dissimilar interests in a variety of matters."

"My point is that yes, the three of us had the honor of being presidents of our nations," continued Mandela, "but unlike you, Jimmy, as I state in my autobiography while I enjoyed gardening and horticulture, when I attempted to grow peanuts and used different soils and fertilizers I finally gave up. It was one of my only failures."[102]

"A real irony indeed," Carter smiled wistfully as he said, "Abraham fled the soil and overcame failure away from it to become one of our most revered presidents. Nelson, you failed with peanuts, but succeeded in helping to build a new nation. And I, an expert in peanuts, am viewed by many as having had a failed presidency, but am honored and admired in retirement for my work in peace, justice and international affairs."

"Peanuts? Not from where I came. While viewed by history as a Prophet from Judea where I enjoyed tending to the fruit of sycamore trees and the flocks, I confess I hated having to proclaim God's message to my people.

"Yes, indeed, you Mandela, and you Lincoln, spoke of how lonely it was to lead for a right cause, to do so even against the wishes of friends. Imagine I who only wanted the tranquility to tend his fields and shepherd the flocks? Hated by those who held power, and despised even by my own class for prophetic dissent, I wore my loneliness oppressively tight like a girdle for a vest.

"Yet I had no choice but to speak of the need for justice and righteousness to the 'enemies of righteousness'—to proclaim that it is impossible to say you love God, but 'sell' brothers and sisters into slavery for 'the price of a pair of sandals,' 'impose onerous taxes on the poor,' 'subvert the cause of the needy at the court,' or 'give bribes to priestly officials.'"[103]

"Amos, you spoke those stirring words so many centuries ago, yet sad to tell, the same evils persist, tainting individuals and society at large much the same," said Carter, without his customary smile.

"Yes President Carter, in that context would you share a few more of the stanzas from your poem?" inquired Amos.

"Amos, you honor me with your eternal knowledge of my poor words."

"Poor words? No my righteous friend, whenever humanity pleads for righteousness its cause transcends time and place. That is why, dear Jimmy, I am familiar with your passionate words, including those that refer to the very land I once tended:

We chosen people, rich and blessed,
Rarely come to ask ourselves
If we should share our voice or power,
or a portion of our wealth.
Hollow eyes in tiny faces,
hollow bellies, gaunt limbs, there
so far away. Why grieve here
for such vague, remote despair?

Bulldozed houses, olive trees axed;
terrorist bombs, funeral wails;
no courts or trials, prison still,
The land is holy, hate prevails.

We chosen few are truly blessed,
It's clear God does not want us pained
By those who suffer far away.
Are we to doubt what He ordained?"[104]

"Amos, we are all grateful and a little amazed for your recall of President Carter's words, but Jimmy," Lincoln said, "I confess I am somewhat confused by the last stanza. As there is a God, I am sure He 'does not want us pained.' Yet, you close your poem, by asking: 'Are we to doubt what He ordained?'

"Is that what 'He ordained,' humanity's pain? Or are you like Amos suggesting that when we know the suffering of others, we have to do what is right to alleviate it? If so, are 'we the chosen few… truly blessed' because we have no choice but to try to alleviate the pain of 'those who suffer far away' or near? Or, are 'we chosen' simply because we 'believe' in Christ; have Mohammed as our prophet; or were 'chosen' at Sinai?"

Amos interjected, "Abraham, you are wise indeed. I hear the truth of what your wife said, 'He was not "a technical Christian," but "he was a religious man always."'" [105]

"A 'religious man,' perhaps? But far more so a lawyer; 'a lover of words' like you Jews," replied Lincoln.

"Abraham, it is a fair question, and as honest as your famous nickname," said Carter. "As I said, earlier, I believe as a Christian we are called to righteousness. In that sense, I may anger my more conservative Christian friends when I say: We are all chosen!"

"I appreciate that clarification," responded Lincoln. "In my day, some accused me of being 'an open scoffer at Christianity.' However, as I said on more than one occasion, 'But for the Bible we would not know right from wrong.'[106] In truth, as stated by friends, my discomfort with 'the apparent injustice of eternal damnation' would most likely place me closer to Amos's community than the community of the Apostle Paul."

"Talking with you now," said Carter, "suggests that any fear of eternal damnation for your universal, vigorous defense of human equality for all races, was an unwarranted concern. As we say in Georgia, truth to tell, were it not for that defense of equality none of us would be here now."

"Abraham, I am interested to hear you suggest that you would have been more comfortable with my community than Paul's," said Amos.

"Rabbi, is it not true that in Amos's time there was no concept of eternal damnation, because there was no concept of life after death," asked Lincoln, "as in the time of Paul?"

"Yes," I answered.

Amos added, "In my day, damnation or reward was of this world and applied more to a whole people than an individual."

"That's what I thought. But now let me declare something which I never made public, because Mary Todd was so opposed. But as has been pointed out, I am evidently the only American president not to have declared himself a member of any particular religious faith, I was not raised in church nor did I ever belong to one.[107]

"My name is Abraham, my great-grandfather was named Mordechai, and my parents were not married in a church but in the home of a Mr. Berry, whom some hold to have been of Hebrew heritage. And there's more. The town of Lincoln, in eastern England, where my father's ancestors came from, has a long an interesting association with Jews, and according to some my cousin, also named Mordecai Lincoln practiced Judaism.[108]

"Friends, in my day these facts gave rise to a great deal of speculation, in fact there were those who believed that the Lincoln side of my family has Jewish roots.

"Further, more recently a professor named Dr. Elizabeth Hirschman and her colleague Dr. Donald Yates have written based on that new fangled stuff called DNA that my mother Nancy was kin to a folk called Melungeon. They were descendents of Sephardic Jews who came to the South Eastern part of the United States in the 16 the century which would make me of Jewish ancestry.'"[109]

"And are you telling us this is the first time that your Jewish heritage has been written about?" asked Amos.

"Well, no, not exactly," Lincoln replied. "As you may know, when I was assassinated there was an awful amount of howling and carrying on, most of it sincere, and that outpouring of grief included the Jewish community. Rabbis from all over the country kindly eulogized my passing, including Rabbi Isaac Mayer Wise, the founder of American Reform Judaism. Rabbi Wise actually concluded his eulogy saying,

> Brethren, the lamented Abraham Lincoln believed himself to be bone from our bone and flesh from our flesh. He purposed to be a descendant of Hebrew parentage. He said so in my presence.

And indeed, he preserved numerous features of the Hebrew race, both in countenance and character. He was a man of many noble virtues which may be our heritage; and God may forgive him his sins, and accept his soul in grace among the righteous men of all nations.[110]

"Now, I can perceive what you are about to ask. All I can say now is that I wasn't around to affirm or deny the good rabbi's statement. I will tell you, however, that Rabbi's Wise's eulogy appeared in the *Israelite*, and one other Cincinnati newspaper,[111] and to my knowledge neither my wife, nor anyone else wrote to rebut Rabbi Wise's comment about my ancient heritage. So," continued President Lincoln with a bemused smile, "it must be true."

President Lincoln, as is well known, was famous for his wry sense of humor, so the rest of us did not know what to make of his revelation. Amos merely said, "How interesting," President Carter said, "fascinating," and President Mandela continued with the point he had started:

"Dear friends, since we all agree that each of us in our own way is held to a divine necessity for such a 'vigorous defense of human equality' and justice, we owe a debt of thanks to you, Amos! You suffered for proclaiming that what God wants of us is not empty ritual, but ethical behavior: '... Just let justice well up like water, righteousness flow down like a mighty stream.'"[113]

"I was not so thanked when those words flowed out of me," responded Amos. "So I am especially grateful for your kindness as I still

Every morning he and his wife set out a meal for Lincoln in (their Thai Chicago) restaurant, next to his statue. "It's a full meal—everything, entrée, dessert, appetizer, drink also," Mr. Esche said. "We change the meal every day, so it's always different. We serve him everything." Mrs. Esche interrupted. "Yes," Mr. Esche said. "Everything but no pork." Oh? "We do not want to be disrespectful." I guess Mr. Esche saw my puzzled look. "He is Abraham Lincoln, yes?" he said, with special emphasis. "Jewish people, they don't eat pork.[112]

see the continuous truth of those words—so much ritual still profanes God's name instead of honoring Him with righteous action!"

"All too true," said Carter. "Now, if I may again return to Abraham's query regarding the last stanza of my poem. Candidly, it has been a long time since I penned the question: 'Are we to doubt what He ordained?' However, as I now remember my summary paragraph, following the poem, I wrote: 'If I am my brother's keeper, it's not enough for me to learn about or even pray about his troubles. I'm called upon to act on his behalf, even when that requires fighting injustice and tyranny.'[114]

"Now, our discussion forces me to wonder why I asked, 'If I am my brother's keeper'? If I, we, are not here to help our brothers and sisters when they need us, as Amos reminds us, of what purpose would be our covenant with God? 'What He ordained' means that through God's revealed word, however we understand it, we are not free to ignore what we know is the right way to behave—at least not without consequences."

"Jimmy, your honest willingness to reexamine with us the nature of what is right is much appreciated," said Amos. "Even more so, you and your wife Rosalynn's amazing work with the Carter Center for the alleviation of human suffering everywhere, your work with Habitat for Humanity, visits to over sixty-five countries, including Israel and Palestine, to foster peace, justice and fair elections, and your decisive role in the Camp David accords, which led to peace between Egypt and Israel, deserve humanity's enduring gratitude.

"Your conviction, all the more so by your example, that we are not free to ignore what we know is the right way to behave reminds me of the truth of a great teacher: Tarphon, one of the Pharisee rabbis, to whom, by the way, I owe a great debt. For it was the Pharisees who were responsible for deciding what books, including the Prophets, were to be included in the Biblical canon.

"Rabbi Tarphon taught: 'It is not up to you to finish an ethical task [responsibility] all by yourself. However, as an individual you are not so free that you are exempt from it [trying to make a difference].'"[115]

"Yes, the rabbis' view of humanity did not include modern man's view of freedom as a kind of pernicious liberty to not act responsibly."

"What the good rabbi just said reminds me that at my presidential farewell," said Carter, "I stated a similar view, 'Our American values are not luxuries but necessities. Not the salt in our bread, but the bread itself.'"

"Jimmy yours and Rabbi Tarphon's statement succinctly describes our responsibility to do what is right," said Mandela. "But Amos, as you prophets proclaimed so often, 'The word of the Lord came to you.' But we politicians, as with most of us who have to make ethical decisions, do not have the luxury of being a prophet."

"Absolutely," President Carter interrupted. "After all what is 'right' is not difficult to know when God is speaking in your ear. Truly, gentlemen, when I wrote *Our Endangered Values* I was very much aware, especially as with our war with Iraq, how easy it is to trap oneself with the misguided certainty that one's cause, or task, is 'right and worthy' and one's adversary is 'wrong and condemned.'[116]

"If you think I am exaggerating," continued Carter, "how war presidents so similarly justify a 'preemptive war,' listen to President George W. Bush's rationalization for the invasion of Iraq:

We had ample cause of war against Iraq, long before the breaking out of hostilities. But even then we forbore to take redress into our own hands, until Iraq herself became the aggressor by... shedding the blood of our citizens [by joining hands with Osama Ben Laden].

Lincoln, looking suddenly puzzled interjected, "Mmm, those very words sound awfully familiar. Except for eight words that statement is exactly the same as I remember President Polk's message of December 8, 1846, regarding our country's invasion of Mexico in the Mexican War, which as a brand-new congressman I strongly condemned."

"That's right, Abraham. Substitute 'Mexico' for 'Iraq' subtract Osama Ben Laden's name and you have the same message," explained Carter. "They are the bad guys, and we are the good guys, who have to invade another country to defend our citizens."

"It is so easy to fall into that I am 'right and worthy' and one's adversary is 'wrong and condemned morality.' I confess," continued Lincoln, "looking back at my attack on President Polk for the Mexican war, I stand guilty of unnecessary hyperbole in addressing what I saw as evil. I said of a fellow President, 'He is a bewildered, confounded, and miserably perplexed man. God grant he may be able to show, there is not something about his conscience, more painful than all his mental perplexity!"[117] Notice, I even injected 'God' into my condemnation."

Carter said to Lincoln, "I admire your candor but I suspect you are being a bit hard on yourself. After all you were a fresh congressman, all of thirty-eight years old, trying to make a name for yourself."

"And I would like to think that I learned my lesson so that under the hell fire of our Civil War, I was much more circumspect. Now Jimmy," continued Lincoln, "as a soldier yourself… "

Carter interrupted: "Yes, except for General Dwight Eisenhower, I spent more years in active military service than any other president since President Grant." [118]

"Well then," said Lincoln, "you well know the bloody chaos, the disease and corpses of war that should more properly lead to a prudent view of absolute 'right' and 'wrong.' Though, truth to tell, there were times when even more sickening to me than the heartbreak of battle was the anguish I felt at having to make the awful ethical decisions regarding right and wrong. For example, as the commander in chief I had to decide whether I must shoot a simple-minded soldier boy who deserts, while I must not touch a hair of a wiley agitator who induced him to desert." [119]

"Mr. Lincoln, we have all had to endure our 'wiley' agitators in politics," commented Carter, "or were you referring to a specific one?"

"Oh yes indeed, I had a barrel full of them, but Congressman Clement Vallandigham of Ohio was an especially sour pickle to the Union cause, as he had outlined a plan for the soldiers of both armies to fraternize and return to their homes."[120]

"Yes, you politicians had to endure the politics of 'right and wrong,' but at least you were elected to do so," said Amos. "Can you imagine how painful it was to possess an absolute sense of righteousness? It so clashed with my usual outlook, what you moderns would call a sense of equality.

"To be honest, when I look back on my indignation at ancient Israel's evil and the terrifying punishment I prophesied for all their wicked behavior, I feel embarrassed."

"It is indeed informative of you, Amos, to shed light on a prophet's lack of moral ambiguity," said Carter. "But as Abraham has suggested, when speaking of the War Between the States,[121] as I experienced during my difficulties with the Iranians and now with today's fundamentalists we—"

Lincoln interrupted: "Now, now, Jimmy, I know you are a Georgian, but let us proceed without acrimonious memory. I spoke of no such War Between the States. It was a Civil War that we fought… .

"Yes, I stand corrected by the very president who helped preserve that U-u-nion," Carter replied, drawing out the word as if he was recalling General Sherman's terrible march through his native Georgia countryside. "But," he continued, "We leaders contribute to discord and an unhealthy breakdown of communal morale whenever we take up the cudgel of moral absolutists, declaring 'the truth' of our own righteousness."

"So what are we to do? Not speak up for what we view as the right? Was I not also a moral absolutist in declaring apartheid 'diabolical'?" asked Mandela. "And you, President Lincoln, were you not equally rigid in stating 'If slavery is not wrong, nothing is wrong'? And, you Jimmy have written that you are 'convinced that every abortion is an unplanned tragedy.'" [122]

"And dare I, a prophet, not add to this ethical dilemma by reminding us that there have always been those who have held that slavery is God's will? In truth, as you Abraham may remember all too well, one of your contemporaries, the Reverend Frederick A. Ross, wrote a book in 1857 that he actually titled, *Slavery Ordained of God*."

"Yes, both my friends and adversaries used God to justify the righteousness of their cause. That is why this issue of slavery goes to the heart of how we appeal to and honor our sense of what is right. In fact, dear Amos, while not referring to you I once said, 'Certainly there is no contending against the Will of God; but still there is some difficulty in ascertaining, and applying it, to particular cases,' especially for we who do not easily apprehend the will of God."[123]

"President Lincoln," I asked, "Certainly you were not suggesting that, as some in your time held, 'it is better for some people to be slaves and in such cases it is the Will of God that they be such'?" [124]

"To the contrary, I held that 'although volume upon volume is written to prove slavery a very good thing, we never hear of the man who wishes to take the good of it by being a slave himself!' [125] In fact, dear rabbi, though certainly not a theologian myself, I once titled a short article about the evils of slavery: *Fragments in Pro-Slavery theology.*"

"Why did you call it such?" Carter asked.

"I was making the point that the advocates of slavery rationalized it as good, because it was God's will. In doing so, their dishonesty showed forth like an unfaithful spouse who claims polygamy is his choice because God's first servant—the Patriarch Abraham—had more than one wife. Further, I also wrote:

'For if it is anything, as a good thing, slavery is strikingly peculiar, in this, that it is the only good thing, which no man ever seeks the good of for himself.'"[126]

"Hearing you say these words now, so articulately stated, reminds me that as much as Mahatma Gandhi was my hero, you too were admired by we who fought apartheid."

"I am honored," said Lincoln," to be mentioned with the incredible Gandhi."

"May I, however, return to Nelson's suggestion that there are times when we leaders have to take positions that are morally rigid," said Carter. "Nelson is correct. Our sense of what is right is based on a variety of moral imperatives, including our perception of what is good. Such use of the word 'good' places us nearly in the same camp as those who now apply the word to such evils as slavery, apartheid, or child slavery in our own time."

"Forgive me, President Carter, but the nature of good," I laughed, "reminds me of the philosophy professor at my seminary, Dr. Alvin Reines, who in the context of a similar discussion suddenly stood up and screamed: G-o-o-o-o-D! Looking into our shocked *punims* (faces) he then declared: 'That's as much as I can say about what good is.'"

"What I knew," smiled Amos, "about philosophy when God sent me to denounce evil, I could have put on a sheep's tail and called it 'not good.' However can we agree that the ethical system we agree to, understands God's goodness as universal and not particular—not for one group of individuals to the exclusion of another?"

"Absolutely, and certainly, not to be used to advocate hurting, or causing unnecessary pain to others," said Carter.

"Jimmy, I agree with you that pain and suffering are very relevant to any ethical system, but I can't stop thinking maybe Israel would have felt less pained and would have listened to me," Amos looked amused, "had I just screamed: *To-o-ov*!

"Indeed," added Mandela, "which is why I repeat, Abraham's expression of what is good, or *tov*" (he smiled at his pronunciation of a Hebrew word) "is so profound, that an ethical sense of good has to apply to all. If one claims this is good for me, as my adversaries said of apartheid, but we know it is bad for others, than it is clearly not a true universal good."

"Does that 'universal good' apply to a broccoli casserole?" I asked.

"Only if it's my wife's," laughed Carter.

"Good," said Amos, "because none came my way. Please pass me some."

"Nelson, Your explanation of universal good reminds me that some folk took me seriously," chuckled Lincoln, "when with irony I condemned the idea that slavery is a good thing 'for some people.' I had said: 'Nonsense! Wolves devouring lambs, not because it is good for their own greedy maws, but because it is good for the lambs!'[127]

"Believers in a true good, what Amos referred to as God's universal good," continued Lincoln, "know better than to believe that the wolves in our human nature are interested in the welfare of us, or our *lambs*."

"Yes, rabbi, we admit to our own ethical prejudices, our own view of righteousness; even your professor's view of good. But as a Christian may I add to what Abraham said. Our love for others precludes our unjustly favoring our own welfare to the hurt of others. Slavery was and is wrong because we are taught the Golden Rule 'to do unto others as we would have them do unto us.'"

"With all respect, Jimmy, and in this I suspect our host, the rabbi, will agree your Golden Rule is valid but also insufficient," stated Amos, "because there are too many, what do you moderns call them: narcissistic persons? Those, whose love of self is so self absorbed—"

I interrupted, "—that such narcissists are incapable of *loving* or doing any good for anybody else. That is why our greatest of sages, Hillel, taught that the biblical command 'to love thy neighbor as thyself' meant that one should behave so 'that which is *hateful* to yourself, [you] do not do to another!'" [128]

"That makes great sense for two reasons," added Lincoln. "Because love is too soft an emotion to seriously confront something akin to evil, the occasional beast in us needs to hear: No, do not do that! Second, when the wolf in us is anxious to leap out and hurt another, we are more likely to desist from doing so because we ourselves have experienced hurt. Since we *hated* it, we draw back from further acting the wolf."

"Which is why," volunteered Mandela, "as you said, Abraham, slavery and all such evil is that 'which no man ever seeks the good of for himself,' not only because it is not universally good, but because he too would not want to suffer such evil—he would 'hate' it."

"I too appreciate this form of the Golden Rule," added Carter, "what some call I believe 'the Via Negativa.' I would, however, remind us all that the wolf acts out of his own natural instincts. We humans who cause pain and suffering to others do so for reasons far less natural or understandable than the wolves."

"Jimmy," said Lincoln, "you rightly remind us: Even the wolves deserve a good advocate."

"Gentlemen, I hate to put an end to this wonderful discussion about the nature of righteousness. It exceeded my greatest expectations. I wish we had time for you to answer whether ethical behavior can still be right when its motivation is also political, as with your Emancipation Proclamation, Mr. Lincoln?"

Lincoln started to respond....

But I interrupted, "President Lincoln, let us continue with coffee and your wife's almond vanilla cake."

Mandela said, "Rabbi, this has been our pleasure: As we have been sustained by this ethical dialogue so we have also enjoyed its good taste."

Amos and Lincoln added: "Our spirits nourished," and laughing, Carter and Mandela concluded: "Our bodies, too."

RECIPES

MEDITERRANEAN LAMB STEW

Serves 6–8
Serve with Saffron Rice Pilaf

The **Prophet Amos** was a Judean. He so enjoyed the leg of lamb (in chapter one) that he asked me privately if he could have another lamb dish.

A blessing in honor and memory of Amos and his passion for righteousness may be found on page 235.

Ingredients:
    2 ½ lbs. of lamb cut into 1 ½" cubes
    Flour for dredging
    olive oil
    1 med. onion sliced
    2 garlic cloves, minced
    1 red bell pepper
    1 8 oz. can chopped tomato, or 1 large tomato peeled, seeded and
        chopped
    2–3 tbsp. tomato paste
    ¾ c. red wine
    2 tbsp. basil, sliced thinly (julienne)
    2 tsp. fresh or ½ tsp. dried oregano
    1 tsp. salt
    2 ½ slices of large lemon
    1 tbsp. and 1 tsp. honey

Directions:
    Dredge lamb pieces in flour.
    Pour 1 ½ tablespoons olive oil in a large pan and heat oil to very hot. Add the onion, garlic and peppers to the pan and sauté until golden brown.
    Add the tomatoes and tomato paste.
    Add 2 more tablespoons of oil and brown the meat, leaving space between the pieces.

Save the juices from the browned meat and combine with water to achieve 2 cups of stock, or use 2 cups of ready made stock.

In a large pot, add the stock, basil, salt, oregano and the meat.

Add the wine.

Let stew cook, uncovered, for 45 minutes, and add the honey and slices of lemon.

SAFFRON RICE PILAF

Ingredients:

½ small onion
½ small clove of garlic
½ celery stalk
2 tsp. olive oil
1 c. rice
2 c. chicken stock
Large pinch of saffron
1 tbsp. chopped fresh basil
Dried apricots, pistachio nuts or toasted almonds.

Directions:

Chop onion, garlic and celery. Sauté 5 minutes in olive oil until translucent.

Add the rice and stir to coat with oil. Cook for 5 minutes stirring frequently, or until rice is a little opaque.

Stir in the chicken broth and bring to a boil. Stir well, reduce heat as much as possible and cover. Simmer for 20 minutes.

Add the basil.

In honor of **President Carter** who a few pages back said he knew the **Cucumber Salad and the Saffron Rice** would go well with the lamb stew.

Ingredients:

2 Kirby or Pickling cucumbers
½ onion
1 tsp. salt

Juice from 2 lemons

1–2 tbsp. fresh chopped mint

Directions:

Slice the onion and the cucumbers into very thin slices.

Soak the cucumbers and onion in the juice of one lemon for about 1 hour or until soft, then rinse with water and remove moisture (I use a paper towel).

Squeeze juice from remaining lemon; sprinkle juice over salad and add chopped mint. Salt to taste.

RABBI'S BROCCOLI CASSEROLE ALA PECAN

Serves 6

Figuring that there was a restaurant in Plains, Georgia, I found the only one and called. I introduced myself to the nice lady who answered the phone and told her what I was interested in. "Of course, I know Jimmy and Rosalyn," she said. "They brought me here to open the restaurant. And to answer your question, the Carters enjoy plain food, especially vegetables."

"So what do you like to cook for them?" I asked.

"They like vegetable casseroles," she said.

President Carter's other favorite foods are: sirloin steak, any kind of fish and poultry, corn bread, any vegetable except beans, salad with Roquefort dressing, frozen yogurt (from *Fun and Interesting Facts about Presidents*).

President Carter's birthday is October 1 (1924), a nice time to enjoy the casserole in honor of him and Rosalyn and their commitment to righteousness and justice.

For a Baptist grace in honor of President Carter, see page 236.

Ingredients:

½ c. chopped onion

½ c. butter, divided

3 cloves, or 2 ½ tbsp. minced garlic

1 can (10–11 oz.) cream of mushroom soup

1 can (4–5 oz.) mushrooms, drained, or 1 c. sliced, fresh mushrooms

1 c. grated cheddar cheese, reserve ¼ c. for topping

¼ red bell pepper, chopped

1 c. herb-seasoned stuffing mix

3 c. fresh broccoli florets, or 10 oz. frozen broccoli

¼ tsp. nutmeg

¼ c. turkey bacon, chopped in small pieces

¼ c. pecans, finely chopped

¼ c. whole pecans for topping

Directions:

In a large skillet, sauté onion and garlic in ¼ cup butter until tender; add mushrooms, red pepper, nutmeg, bacon and chopped pecans.

When ingredients are cooked, add cheese and mix well.

Scrape ingredients into a lightly buttered 2 quart casserole.

Add remaining butter to skillet, add stuffing mix, and when lightly brown, stir stuffing mix into casserole dish.

Place the broccoli pieces into the casserole with the tops showing

Add the whole pecans, and sprinkle the remaining cheese over the top of the dish.

Bake at 350 F. for about 30–35 minutes or until bubbly.

President **Nelson Mandela**, an Anglican, was born on July 18, 1918.

A blessing in honor of his dedication to righteousness and liberty may be found on page 240.

UMNGQUSHO—CORN MAIZE

Serves 12

This is a favorite, traditional dish of the Xhosa people and a favorite of Nelson Mandela. It is very similar to American hominy or Mexican *posole*. The difference is that the main ingredient, corn kernels, called in South Africa, *stampmielies* or stamp, are crushed. If stamp is not available, one may use hominy and with a rolling pin or mortar and pestle crush or break the kernels, being careful not to grind them into flour. Stamp is sometimes served with fried onions, or as aside dish with any main course that has its own gravy.

Ingredients:

4 c. dry stamp, or *posole* (hominy) (29 oz. can, available in the
Mexican section of market)
2 c. dry cowpeas, similar to black-eyed peas, or any similar bean.
1 tsp. salt

Directions:

Place peas in a large enamel pot or glass bowl. Add cold water to cover peas and let stand overnight. Drain and rinse before cooking.

In a large pot add the hominy and the peas and water to cover the mixture. Bring to a boil for 10 minutes. Reduce heat and simmer on low heat for one to two hours, until the water is mostly absorbed. Add additional water during cooking if needed. Serve hot.

President and Mrs. Abraham Lincoln

Mrs. Lincoln according to more than one source "was a superlative cook: 'Her table was famed for the excellence of its rare Kentucky dishes, and in season was loaded with venison, wild turkeys, prairie chicken, quails and other game, which in those days was abundant.'"[129] However, while the President "enjoyed a good hearty beefsteak now and then," his basic food tastes were simple and food apparently was of little interest to him.

Mary Todd Lincoln as is well known did not live an easy life. She and the President lost two sons, she witnessed her husband's assassination, and she died the lonely widow of a great president.

Mary Todd may have made the vanilla almond cake for Abraham Lincoln when they were courting in Springfield. She continued to make it after she became a wife and a mother, and after she was a first lady. The cake was also baked at the visit of the Marquis de Lafayette to Lexington in 1825, and was such a triumph the recipe was begged for by the Todd ladies, who made it a part of the family repertoire.[130]

President Lincoln, who very much appreciated the wonderful entertaining his wife often did in The White House would no doubt appreciate Americans remembering them both and enjoying this delicious, dense cake on her birthday: December 13th (1818).

MARY TODD LINCOLN'S VANILLA ALMOND CAKE

Ingredients:
1 ½ c. sugar
1 c. butter
1 tsp. Vanilla
2 ¾ c. flour sifted
1 tbsp. baking powder
1 1/3 c. milk
1 c. almonds, – finely chopped
6 egg whites, – stiffly beaten

Directions:
Grease and lightly flour 2 9-inch round cake pans.

Cream together sugar, butter and vanilla. Stir together the cake flour and baking powder (if baking powder has clumps sift with flour).

Add dry ingredients to creamed mixture alternately with milk. Stir in almonds. Gently fold in the egg whites.

Pour into prepared pans.

Bake at 375 degrees F. for 40–50 minutes (longer if at a high altitude). Let cool 10 minutes, remove from pans and cool completely. Frost with white frosting.

White Frosting
1 c. sugar
1/3 c. water
¼ tsp. cream of tartar
Dash of salt

2 egg whites

1 tsp. vanilla

Directions:

In a saucepan combine sugar, water, cream of tartar, and salt. Bring mixture to boiling, stirring till the sugar dissolves.

In mixing bowl slowly pour the mixture in a fine stream into the egg whites, beating constantly with an electric mixer till stiff peaks form, about 7 minutes. Beat in vanilla. [131]

Chapter V

Kindness - The Unusual Rose Garden

I had a rose named after me and I was very flattered.
But I was not pleased to read the description in the catalog:
"No good in a bed, but fine against a wall."
— Eleanor Roosevelt

HOW DO YOU define kindness? Do you consider yourself a kind person?

Knowing kindness is different than being a kind person. In Hebrew the word that comes closest to kindness is *chesed*. The knowledge of *chesed* is but a seed waiting for moisture. When the seed is moistened it flowers into *G'milut ch'sedim*, usually translated as *deeds of loving kindness*.

It is our *deeds* nurtured with love, not our knowledge, which moisten the seed of kindness into flower. Its colors burst forth, bright with, "I am!" What was lifeless becomes a creation—a joy of self so confident—it must kindly act.

It had taken months to get Oprah Winfrey's public relations people to give us permission to meet in her rose garden in Santa Barbara, California. Oprah's garden, like her many, many acts of kindness, seemed the perfect place to meet and explore the nature of kindness. Amongst her roses, chosen to match the gorgeous interior of her home, we would also see beautiful examples of kindness, the character deeds of a few great people.

So on a bright sunny morning Dr. Chuck Wall, who coined the phrase "Today, I will commit one random act of senseless kindness," and I stood at the guard gate to her garden, anxious to see what lay beyond. (Dr. Wall is blind so I had the honor of being his eyes.)[132] The guard briefly looked at our letter giving us permission to visit, and then waved us through. We walked a few hundred yards down a flagstone path and stopped, shocked at what we saw.

To the left there were mounds of garbage, approximately three feet high, thirty feet wide and long.

To the right, we also saw a space thirty feet wide and long, but filled with every imaginable size, shade and type of rose laid out in various patterns of color—all yellow, all red, pink, etc. Between the groups of roses, appropriately placed, were fountains and benches.

To the left the landscape was filled with everything used up, from broken bottles, soiled diapers, mattresses, clothes and decaying food. Looking for something to eat, birds soared overhead.

The overwhelming and decaying smell of everything imaginable that could offend our sense of smell made us feel like throwing up.

To the right, the fragrance of thousands of roses enveloped us, a heady bouquet of perfume, as breathtaking as the glorious colors that were alive before us. What a wonderful workplace it had to be for the gardeners who in black and orange striped overalls meticulously pruned and clipped. Like bees pollinating their flowering clients, the gardeners seemed intent and content in their productive and beautiful labor.

To the left boys, girls and adults with soiled hands, little picks and soured faces, scoured the dump like scavengers; looking for and grabbing anything that attracted their attention, anything that might go into a bag of household waste. And fetch a penny toward a meal.[133]

The need to both hold our noses and enjoy the fragrant panoply of roses was bewildering to our sense of smell and sight. Perhaps we had come to the wrong place. There must be a mistake. We turned back towards the gate to ask. The guard made a call and soon we saw Oprah Winfrey, walking toward us from the rose side of this aesthetic mayhem.

"I have been waiting for you." She inquired sincerely, "Did you get lost? And where is Mr. Rogers?"

"Oprah," I replied, confident that she would explain the mystery we had just observed, "we went to the garden and saw the incredible roses; but there was also a dump with the faces of poverty and suffering strewn all over it."

But before she could answer, a man donned in sneakers and a zip-up cardigan suddenly appeared.

"Hi, glad to be here," he cheerfully said, as if he were simply a neighbor dropping in for a visit.

The three of us introduced each other to Mr. Fred Rogers. Oprah smiled and said, "Welcome to my garden—and my neighborhood. I'm so glad you could all come."

"Garden?" Dr. Wall and I asked at the same time. "What of the dump we just saw?"

"Gentlemen, I won't waste words," she replied, "but let's be seated. You wanted to see my rose garden, a metaphor for beauty and goodness in which we were to discuss the nature of kindness. But until Jesus returns—rabbi, excuse me what you call the messianic age comes—Gertrude Stein to the contrary, 'a rose, is a rose,' is not a rose, outside the context of its opposite."

We must have looked puzzled, especially Mr. Rogers who evidently had not seen what we had.

"Don't misunderstand," she continued, "I too thoroughly enjoy and am proud of my garden. But I refuse to be seduced by its beauty, lest I become unwilling to acknowledge the ugly, the pain and suffering that is so close to everyone's garden, but is not seen."

"Are you saying that the dump we saw was not real, not part of your garden?" I asked.

"In various forms, it exists near every beautiful place. However, until all things are truly beautiful for everyone to enjoy, kindness while it exists remains only a seed waiting to flower. Without our seeing and acknowledging the reality of suffering, what you saw opposite my garden, the seed of kindness does not flower."

Then looking at me, Oprah asked, "Rabbi, isn't it because beauty and suffering compete with each other, like a beautiful individual and a starving child both wanting our attention at the same time, that Jews believe we live in an unredeemed world—one of the reasons why for you the messianic age has not come?"

"Yes, Oprah. What Christians call the second coming, we liberal Jews call the Messianic age. (Orthodox Judaism speaks of *Yemot haMashiach*, literally the days of the Messiah) The price we pay for having been created in a world where goodness and suffering compete as adversaries means that we have the responsibility to join God in *tikkun olum*, the *world's repair*. That is why deeds of loving kindness are so meritorious. Every kindness we humans do is an antidote to the suffering all around us. In fact, the author of an eighth-century Jewish mystical work, Otiot R. Akiva wrote: 'The world could not exist for even one hour without acts of kindness.'" [134]

May I add that without acts of kindness the world actually reverts to its cruel opposite. That's why," continued Dr. Wall who was looking toward Oprah with great admiration, "for every garden somewhere else there are the trash heaps, the dumps of human suffering, crying out to us to replace them with something beautiful and healthy, urging us towards our effort for, what the rabbi called, *tikkun olum*."

Dr. Wall had barely finished, when we suddenly found ourselves seated in the very middle of Oprah's garden. It was as if merely thinking about crushing cruelty, suffering and despair entitled us to a reprieve. However, Oprah must have anticipated our thoughts as she quickly replied, "We are here, as you requested, because my garden truly is a fitting place to witness beautiful examples of 'deeds of kindness.' And also because you saw and were appalled at what was on the other side of my garden."

"We feel extremely fortunate to be in such a beautiful place," said Dr. Wall. "However, Oprah, it is your personal commitment to kindness in the world, that adds significant beauty to this garden."

"I believe in giving back, I... I," she started to say, but Dr. Wall continued.

"As a matter of fact, thank God that there are

The beginning and end of Torah is performing acts of loving kindness. [135]

so many wonderful people like you, 'giving back,'—kindness done with such joy and fervor."

"You are embarrassing me," Oprah said.

"I'm sorry but individuals like you, Bill and Melinda Gates, Bono, Warren Buffet; so many, the famous and the unknown, all deserve society's sincere praise for their individual acts of kindness."

"I can honestly say that every gift I've ever given has brought at least as much happiness to me as it has to the person I've given it to," she replied. "That's the feeling I like to pass on to others."[136]

"Are those not the very words you used the other day," I asked, "when on your show you gave more than 300 audience members $1,000 debit cards to donate to a charitable cause?"

"Yes," she showed obvious delight at recalling that particular show. "I'm kind of famous for giving members of my audience new cars, helping to pay off their debts, fulfilling their wildest dreams but this was my favorite giveaway ever. I said to my audience, 'You're going to open your hearts, you're going to be really creative, and you're going to spend it all at once on one stranger or spend a dollar on every person. Imagine the love and kindness you can spread with $1,000!'"[137]

"That's my point, Oprah. Whether it is seeing to it that hundreds of girls in Soweto, South Africa, get a free education with a contribution of $40 million over 5 years, or giving $10 million for new homes for 50 families that had been displaced from Katrina, you are the personification of personal kindness. In that sense you are by far the prettiest rose in this garden," said Mr. Rogers.

"There's a special verse in the Book of Proverbs that epitomizes people like you," I added. "And Oprah, remember every act of kindness helps preserve the world. And wouldn't you agree the world desperately needs to know of the many acts of kindness—both the 'random' and the premeditated? 'She opens her hands to those in need and offers her help to the poor. Adorned with strength and dignity, she looks to the future with cheerful trust. Her speech is wise, and the law of kindness is on her lips.'"

Oprah looked at us and laughed. "Thank you, but I think I once read those verses are said on the eve of the Jewish Sabbath by a husband to his wife."

"You are correct. How about this, I asked, "Oprah Winfrey has many wonderful friends and is also married to *deeds of loving kindness?"*

Looking a little teary, she started to reply. But before she could, as if Beethoven was complementing Proverbs, Oprah's garden was filled with wonderful music.

"It's the Ode to Joy from the 9th Symphony," said Mr. Rogers, who loved his Beethoven.[138] We looked up to the sky, searching all around for the source of the music, taking in the glorious sound and then we all laughed. It was Oprah's cell phone. She answered and we heard her say, "Send him on."

Looking toward the gate we saw a bicyclist riding toward us. When he got to us we saw he wore a cap inscribed with the words, "We like to bring good messages for kind people."

"Hi everyone, my name is Justin," he declared, as he wheeled his bike over to and stood in front of Mr. Rogers. "I'm sure you don't remember me, but I am one of the millions of people whose lives, at a young age, you made more beautiful with the many examples of kindness you showed us for more than 30 years, on *Mr. Rogers' Neighborhood.*"

Even souls visiting here from the other side blush, and Mr. Rogers was no exception.

"Oh... what a lovely surprise," he said with a very broad smile, and in his rather high voice added, "I am happy to see you."

"In fact," the messenger replied, "we have already seen each other."

"There must be a story," Mr. Rogers chuckled.

"Absolutely, a true one about you; and I've ridden all this way to share it. But I also want to say how much I agree that ethical character attributes like kindness are eternal in time. So Mr. Rogers, in Pittsburgh many still speak in reverent whispers about the time they ran into you while walking across the Smithfield Street Bridge or around town. They say, 'He was so nice! He's just like he was on TV!'"

"Well, thank you," replied Mr. Rogers, "When that happened I would ask for the person's address and within a week they would receive a Mr. Rogers Neighborhood sweatshirt in the mail. As I used to say in my neighborhood and everywhere, 'It's so good to try to be kind to others.'"

"Exactly," said Justin, "that's why after you died, David Newell, who played Mr. McFeely, named after your grandfather, said of you, 'He was so genuinely, genuinely kind, a wonderful person.' And Fred, if I may call you by your first name, my own personal encounter with you personifies that very kindness. So, here's the true story about you and me.

In the summer of '95 I was working as a bike messenger. I walked through an unfamiliar corridor in a familiar building to deliver a package. And on the way in I saw X the Owl's tree sitting on wheels in the hallway; which, of course, I did not recognize as X the Owl's tree until I ran into King Friday's castle around the corner.

Filled with excitement over the proximity of these childhood "Land of Make Believe" icons, I asked the first person to pass by, "Where's Fred?" Without looking up, she nonchalantly pointed to an inconspicuous door with a small unassuming metal tag on it that said "Mr. Rogers Neighborhood."

…Bursting through the door like a little kid bringing home a straight-A report card, I found myself in a very cluttered suite of offices; books, folders, files, papers and things piled high along the walls, on tables, desks and shelves. Two very congenial and grandmotherly women greeted me as they were milling about.

"Where's Fred?" I asked again.

"Oh, he's at home. He's been writing scripts a lot lately and he doesn't come in much when he's writing. Who should I tell him stopped by?" "Just tell him Justin the bike messenger stopped in."

As I said this she began writing it down on a post-it note. "and …oh yes, here's my phone number," I added, not really believing there would be a call.

The next day I came home from a particularly rainy day at work and found this message on my answering machine: "Hello Justin! This is Fred Rogers at Family Communication. Hope you're having a good day, pretty wet for your business though, isn't it? Hope to see you next time you come by… B'bye." I had given notice at the messenger service… in order to move out to the Rocky Mountains to live in a tent, and otherwise find all the neat things life has revealed since then. As luck would have it, a day before my last day I found myself delivering a package yet again in that same building. Barging through the door like I owned the place, I asked the ladies in the front, "Fred here?" They smiled and pointed to a small room in the corner.

Perhaps I should explain that at that time of my life I was a punk rocker of sorts. Appearances can be deceiving, so I made every attempt to appear to be the king of Dante's Seventh Circle of Hell: shoes and socks mismatched, knees and elbows covered with bike related scabs, filthy sweat-soaked T-shirt from bicycling in the ultra humid Pittsburgh summer heat, enormous neon green bike helmet with rag-tag bits of mohawk sticking out, and under the chin hung only half a goatee strictly for the purpose of telling folks I got my razor at a "half off" sale when they ask.

I poked my head into the tiny office.... [An] arm chair was occupied by a professional looking woman attending to some important matter on her clipboard. And on [a] love seat was you, Mr. Rogers, in the flesh and wearing your famous sweater, shoes and make-up, as though you were about to go on camera. "Am I interrupting anything?" I asked, head levitating in the doorway. The lady in the armchair turned looking at me over her reading glasses with a face as sweet as a bulldog with a mouth full of lemons and shouted, "YOU MOST CERTAINLY ARE!!!" And before she could finish, Fred, you stood up with a huge smile on your face. Having to step over her legs to get out, you gently patted the scowling woman on the shoulder and sweetly said, "I'm gonna go talk to him a minute." After a surprisingly firm hand shake, we chatted about life a little and you asked about my plans out west. "OOOOH, that sounds so exciting! Well, Pittsburgh was glad to have ya!" We parted after some kind words and I made my way back to the bike rack.

I must admit that initially I was expecting to have an awkward encounter with a strange famous person that I could laugh about sarcastically for years to come, but being in the presence of you, the real Fred Rogers it became incredibly obvious that your TV persona was no act and that you truly believed that each and every person is special and deserving of love and kindness.

I rode away from this meeting with unmistakable warmth in my heart that brought with it the vivid and serene recollection of a little kid who knew that his mom and her abundant supply of peanut-butter-and-jelly sandwiches spread with love, while watching Mr. Rogers, are what life, kindness and love, past, present and future is all about.[139]

Having finished his story, Justin turned to Mr. Rogers who looked like he was about to cry, and asked, "Is it okay to hug a soul of kindness?"

"Not only is it okay, we souls never stop crying tears of appreciation for beautiful memories."

And with that they embraced, and Justin the beautiful bicycle messenger rode away, leaving us to stare admiringly at Mr. Rogers.

"That was so kind of Justin, so… " his voice fading off, as he seemed to drift into memory's distant neighborhoods.

"You know what made Justin's story and the kindness you Oprah, you Mr. Rogers, and so many others extend to others," said Dr. Wall, "is how kindness affirms us as individuals and as a society. I have written, 'We have become a nation that is quick to condemn and slow to compliment and this MUST be reversed.'" [140]

"Yes, how true," interjected Oprah. "Why is it that we are so fascinated by pulling each other down rather than building each other up? Isn't part of kindness assisting our fellow man in finding happiness rather than in negating them? The best way, I think, is to find the goodness in a person through a compliment, which tends to make that person want to perform at a positive level rather than the negative."

Standing in front of a particularly beautiful rose bush, Oprah was the first to see him. She looked past us and gasped, "President Nixon, is it really you?"

"Yes it's me. I've always loved roses, even though I'm probably more remembered for the thorns," he said with a laugh that had an edge of sorrow. "When I heard about your garden and acts of kindness, I had to come, especially as my girls and I loved seeing and hearing,"—then the 37th President of the United States, obviously amused at what he was about to do, turned toward Fred Rogers and sang—"It's a beautiful day in the neighborhood, a beautiful day in the neighborhood. Would you be mine?"

When President Nixon finished his melodic reminiscence he looked at us and, pointing to Mr. Rogers, said, "And did you know our Mr. Rogers not only composed his own songs for his show, but on the magical trolley ride into the Neighborhood of Make-Believe, where his puppet creations would interact with each other, he personally did much of the puppet work and voices?"

The President sat down, and Mr. Rogers simply nodded appreciatively. Nobody said a word. Each of us was wondering, why had the president come?

"I too have a story about kindness," he said with an air clearly meant to challenge our silence, "I thought you would like to hear."

Again no one said a word, and President Nixon continued, knowing full well that we were too surprised to even say, "Please, Mr. President, do tell us your story."

"On January 15th, 1978 in Washington, DC, there was a funeral for former Vice President Hubert Humphrey. Perhaps, as with mine, you may have seen the funeral service on television. His occurred during Jimmy Carter's presidency and was attended by a great many dignitaries. Everybody else was seated when President Carter and the First Lady came in to take their seats in the first row.

"As President Carter made his way down the aisle he noticed a man he knew very well. There were Secret Service people around the man but nobody wanted to sit with him so he sat in one of the back row of seats.

"After President and Mrs. Carter had taken their seats, he said to her, 'I'll be right back.' President Carter knew it was the first time the man had returned to Washington in years.

"He walked up the aisle, as everyone watched to see where the President was headed. Then, he stopped, extended his hand to the man who had resigned the presidency in embarrassment, humiliation and disgrace, and said,

"'Welcome to Washington, Mr. President—welcome home. Roslyn

and I have a space next to us. We'd be so grateful if you'd do us the honor of sitting with us. I know, Mr. President, what Hubert Humphrey meant in your life.'"

The man's eyes were misty with appreciation and surprise, but he didn't move.

"Carter continued, 'I know of your bond of friendship and it would mean so much to me and to Roslyn if you would honor us by coming and sitting with us.'

"That's the story I wanted to share with you," said President Nixon. "It was the loveliest of gestures. And in the eternity of kindness where I now abide, I continue to bask in that simple act of kindness."[141]

"President Nixon," Mr. Rogers was the first to respond, "I am so glad you shared that event in your very important life with us now, and hope you will share it with others of us on our side."

"I shall be happy to do so," he said, and with that, Richard Nixon, rose, smiled at us and with his hands clasped behind him in that peculiar way he had of walking, disappeared beyond the gate.

"President Nixon experienced that wonderful act in our nation's capital. Ours occurred at the Vatican," said a grey and balding gentleman who had appeared out of nowhere.

"*Shalom*, my name is Rabbi Alexander Schindler. In 1973 I had the honor of becoming the president of the Union of American Hebrew Congregations (UAHC), of Reform Judaism, and about five years later led a delegation of American Jewish leaders to pay our respect to the new Pope, John Paul II, at the Vatican.

"We all knew that Karol Josef Wojtyla had many Jewish friends in Poland and how much he helped the Jews of his home town. We were excited at this opportunity to have an audience with him.

"On the morning of the meeting we were escorted to the large, impressive hall where the Pope meets guests. As we entered the room we were surprised that instead of sitting as is customary, the new Pope stood to greet us. Not quite knowing how to precede we momentarily stood back.

"Then we heard John Paul say in his Polish accented English, 'My brothers, come forward.' In Italian my name is Giuseppe—Josef, in English. 'Come forward,' he continued in a tone that radiated both sincerity and kindness, 'I am your brother Joseph.'

"In the Genesis story, Joseph then embraced his brothers. I do not remember if the Pope embraced us, but we were incredibly touched by his lovely welcome and impressed by how he had used the beautiful verse from Scripture."

"Rabbi Schindler, how kind of you to have come to my garden," said Oprah, "to share that wonderful story."

"Indeed, it is a wonderful example of John Paul's many acts of kindness, and illustrates the wonderful empathic way he welcomed his guests. Yes, it was one of the highlights of my being the President of the UAHC," said Rabbi Schindler.[142]

And before we could respond, he and Mr. Rogers stood up. Mr. Rogers approached Oprah; took her hand and said, "It's easy to say 'It's not my child, not my community, not my world, not my problem.' Then there are those who see the need and respond. I consider those people my heroes."

And before any of us could thank them for enriching our day Mr. Rogers and Rabbi Schindler disappeared.

It was such a gorgeous morning. We remained seated, taking in the smells and sights of Oprah's garden. And I was thinking, perhaps the others were as well, how many wonderful individuals there are who with beautiful acts of kindness make our world a better place with both their random and deliberate acts of kindness

Oprah stood up; looked at her watch. And said, "My new friends, you may not believe this but it has been exactly one hour since we sat down and listened to these examples of loving kindness. Now, let's walk to the house for some refreshments."

"Thanks, Oprah," I said, "because I brought a whole tray of your 'favorite sandwich' for everybody."

"How lovely... . And how did you know what my 'favorite sandwich' is?" she asked.

"Let's just say, the sandwich itself exemplifies another story about your kindness," I replied. (See footnote 144.)

As we headed for the gate Dr. Wall and I looked at each other with utter amazement. The terrible dump had disappeared. "Oprah," Dr. Wall started to ask, "what happened to..." but before he could finish the question, she grinned and replied, "Remember you said, 'the world couldn't exist for even one hour without acts of kindness,' and didn't you suggest, Dr. Wall, that we can replace the dumps of human suffering with 'something beautiful and healthy, urging us towards our effort at *tikkun olum,*' helping repair the world?

"You were right." She continued, "Merely listening to wonderful examples of kindness, the dump opposite my garden has disappeared and the world's clock moved forward one more hour. But do not be misled. If we will look with truth in our hearts we will see that there are, sad to say, many, many other dumps of human misery waiting for our actual deeds of kindness to free them of their stench.

Imagine what one hour of kindness can accomplish in drawing us closer to a world redeemed from suffering."

"That Second coming," I said

"And that messianic age," she added, as we went through the gate from her garden back to the real world.

RECIPES

Mr. Roger's birthday is March 28 (1928) A nice time to remember one of his favorite dishes.

Mr. Rogers was Presbyterian Minister, for a blessing in honor of is kindness, see page 241.

"Here are two recipes for foods that Mister Rogers enjoyed. He was a vegetarian, as seen by "this corn pudding that [his]Grandmother Rogers made every Christmas."[143]

CORN PUDDING

Serves 6

Ingredients:
    1 (1 lb.) can of cream-style corn
    2 eggs
    2 tbsp. flour
    2 tbsp. sugar
    ½ tsp. salt
    ½ c. milk or cream
    2 tbsp. melted butter

Directions:
Beat the eggs. Then add all the other ingredients and mix well. Put it into a buttered casserole dish. Bake at 350 F. for one hour or until well set.

FILIPINO SPINACH EGG ROLLS

"Were a particular favorite of Mister Rogers."
Serves about 16

Ingredients:
    4 lbs. of fresh spinach washed, drained and blanched
    2 tsp. salt

1/8 tsp. nutmeg

12 oz. fresh mushrooms

1 egg white, slightly beaten

1 c. water chestnuts

2 tsp. fresh ginger (or liquid ginger)

1 package large frozen egg roll wrappers, preferably thin ones, de frosted and covered with a damp cloth to prevent drying.

2 tsp. garlic

1 additional egg white for gluing the egg roll firmly with a pastry brush.

Directions:

Sautee the garlic in ½ tsp. vegetable oil until there is no more oil.

Boil the spinach for 2 minutes, drain in colander, and when cool, press firmly so that moisture is removed.

In a food processor grind the mushrooms, chestnuts and ginger.

Combine all the ingredients and mix well.

Working with one egg roll wrapper at a time, brush the four edges with the egg white. At one end of wrapper, spoon about 3–4 table-spoons of the spinach mixture. Fold ½" of the left and right sides of the wrapper over the mixture, also brush these sides with the egg white, roll tightly and seal. (You should not be able to see the mixture on either end of the roll.)

Deep fry in hot vegetable or sunflower oil, making sure not to crowd rolls as they fry. Drain on paper towels.

Enjoy while hot.

Can be served with a raisin sauce or other sweet/sour sauce.

(Recipe adapted from Recipe sent by Mrs. Rogers and Family Communications.).

Dr. **Chuck Wall** describes himself as a Protestant. For a blessing in honor of his contribution to enhancing the concept of kindness, see page 242.

CARROT CAKE

Ingredients:
2 c. all purpose flour

2 tsp. baking soda

1 tsp. salt

2 tsp. ground cinnamon

3 large eggs

1 ¾ c. sugar

¾ c. vegetable oil

¾ c. buttermilk

2 tsp. vanilla

2 c. grated carrot

1 (8 oz.) can crushed pineapple, drained

¼ c. shredded coconut

Frosting

9 oz. cream cheese

½ c. sour cream

1 c. confectioner's sugar

1 tsp. vanilla

Directions:
Sift dry ingredients

Beat eggs together with other wet ingredients and mix into dry ingredients until mixture is smooth.

Add carrot, pineapple and coconut, and mix well.

Pour batter into one 9 x 13" cake pan or two 8 or 9" pans. Bake at 370 F. for 40–45 minutes or until a knife inserted comes out clean. Remove and place on wire rack until cool.

Cream cheese frosting:
Place cream cheese and sour cream in a microwave bowl, cover and heat for a minute or two (Time depends on the individual microwave's wattage and age.) until material is soft to mix.

Stir in sugar and mix until smooth. Spread frosting on cake. extraordinary acts of kindness.

Oprah Winfrey's birthday is January 29 (1954). An appropriate time to celebrate her incredible kindness.

Oprah is a Baptist, for a blessing in her honor, see page 243.

OPRAH'S 'FAVORITE SANDWICH'

With a few changes from original recipe
This sandwich is another example of her kindness. (See [144])
Makes 6 sandwiches

Ingredients:

24 whole black peppercorns
4 bay leaves
6 whole cloves
½ lemon
3 lbs. medium chicken tenders
¾ c. plus 1 tbsp. spicy brown mustard
¾ c. honey
1 ¼ tsp. curry powder
¾ tsp. lemon pepper
1/8 tsp. salt
1 loaf chalah or egg bread, cut into 12 slices* (The sandwich is also
     good with a good whole wheat or grain bread)
½ c. shredded carrots
½ c. slivered almonds
1 bag, about 5 oz., salad greens
Red grapes and assorted berries for garnish

Directions:

In a large saucepan over high heat, add peppercorns, bay leaves, cloves, lemon and 14 cups water; cover and bring to boil.

Add chicken and cook, uncovered and stirring occasionally, 7–10 minutes, or until cooked through; drain. Once cool, cut each tender lengthwise into ½" thick slices.

In a large bowl, combine cooked ingredients with the mustard, honey, curry, pepper and salt, and mix with the chicken.

Cover and refrigerate at least 30 minutes or up to 1 day.

Butter both sides of bread slices. In a heated nonstick skillet over medium-high flame, cook bread in batches 3–5 minutes or until browned, turning once.

Combine carrots and almonds with chicken mixture.

Divide chicken curry and spread on 6 bread slices.

Top with tomatoes, lettuce and remaining bread slices.

Serve with fruit.

*Chalah for sandwiches, see page 243.

(And instead of 4 Tbsp. of sugar use 2, and omit braid).

Chapter VI

"*Courage is rightly esteemed the first of human qualities*
because it is the quality which guarantees all others."
— *Winston Churchill*[145]

This is a work of creative non-fiction. Within this chapter, the author uses creative license to expand upon biographical and autobiographical information. The actual participation of living persons or historical figures as role models in any particular setting or scene is entirely fictional.

DRIVING OUT OF town to visit one of my sons, I was deep in thought about the nature of moral courage. There are so many incredible stories of individuals who personify this noble character trait. But that day my heart was feeling a special empathy for the widow of Captain Roee Klein, an assistant battalion commander in the Israeli army who had just died (August 2006) in the Lebanese town of Bint J'bail.

In the heat of battle, the captain saw a grenade thrown in the direction of his men. Reacting immediately, he jumped on the grenade, blocking it with his body so that it took most of the shock and saved the lives of his comrades. At that terrible moment, he cried out *"Sh'ma... Hear O Israel, the Lord our God, the Lord is One,"* the proclamation a Jew says when s/he knows that death is near.

As I was thinking about Roee Klein's courage, it occurred to me that his first name means "my shepherd," as in the 23rd Psalm, "The Lord is my shepherd, I shall not want."

Then, I noticed that what my car wanted was some gas. I saw a station and pulled in. It seemed strange that other cars were stopping, reading something written on the pumps and driving off.

Puzzled, but curious I pulled in. At the same time a man who looked somewhat familiar stopped in front of the island across from me. We exchanged pleasantries and, as we reached for our respective pumps, like so many others these days, proceeded to grumble about the price of gas. Then he yelled at me excitedly,

"Look at this! Where it usually says 'Choose your fuel,' it reads, **'MORAL COURAGE FUEL.'**"

I looked at the pump, and sure enough that's what it said. "Yea, mine too," I shouted, "and where the price of gas usually appears, instead it reads: 'FREE. See attendant inside.'"

At that moment, I felt a hand on my shoulder. I turned around and, standing next to his bike, was my son. He was grinning, and I was astonished. To say that Micah doesn't usually frequent gas stations would be understatement of monumental proportion.

"Dad, if you are here to get gas, you're wasting your time. Didn't you see everybody else driving away? It's not because they've decided to stop driving cars, as much as that would bring me much joy," he giggled. "This place only serves moral courage fue...."

I cut him off. "Micah, have you been smoking something?"

"Come on, Dad," he said in that special tone reserved for a parent. "If you and he," pointing to the other man who had been listening to us, "don't believe me about the fuel, go and see the attendant. I use to know her."

My new acquaintance and I looked at each other and I said, "Free fuel! Sounds weird."

"Yea, and rather mysterious, like your son....By the way," extending his hand, "My name is Sam."

"I'm Philip, glad to meet you. And may I tell you about my mysterious son?" Not waiting for his answer, I yelled,

"Micah, we'll be right there," as he headed for the office inside the station.

Then I turned to my new friend, "Sam, not that I am objective, but that man is one of the most morally courageous people I know, totally dedicated to the cause of a healthy environment—with as few gas guzzling vehicles as possible."

Two more cars, stopped, looked at us kind of funny and drove away.

"As one of three college students, he co-founded a bicycle delivery service in his town, called Ped-Ex, Peddlers Express, and for over 10 years he rode 30 to 50 miles a day, often starting his deliveries before dawn."

"He must be in incredible shape."

"No kidding. In 1988, he and a girlfriend rode from Washington State to Vermont, and back to the West Coast. And three years later, he rode by himself from Jerusalem to Luxor, Egypt, and back through Cairo to Jerusalem. Imagine Egyptian *Fedayeen* looking down the road from their villages seeing a guy on a bike, coming toward them with a huge backpack. To this day, when I find myself peddling, huffing and puffing, up some little hill, I think of individuals like my son. — bicycling through life, every day, up and down mountains, mile after mile, enduring occasionally the rude driver—the courageous few like Micah, refusing to drive a car, so everything moves or is moved by bike, or a bike trailer.

"And all because he knows that motorized vehicles and fossil fuels are helping to destroy our planet. So now, Sam, you know why I was flabbergasted to see him at a gas station."

"Thanks for telling me," Sam replied, "about your mysterious son." And together we walked toward Micah.

A heavenly, perky brunette, wearing a name tag that said "Dulcenea" greeted us warmly. "Micah has mentioned your social activism," she said looking at me. "And you are Sam Oliner," she said to him, clearly enjoying my surprised expression when she repeated his last name, "Oliner."

"Sam… Dr. Samuel Oliner? Now I know why I recognized you," I said with a delight full of incredulity. "You and your wife Pearl have written major scholarly articles on the nature of altruism, right? And Sam, your book, *Do Unto Others—Extraordinary Acts of Ordinary People—How Altruism Inspires True Acts of Courage,*[146] is an inspiration to everyone interested in character ethics, courage and compassion."

Dr. Oliner said, "I'm honored you know of my work, but Dulcenea," whose name comes from the word sweet, "how… how did you know who I am… that I would be here… in this particular town, looking for gas?

"Rabbi Posner, Dr. Oliner, Micah, in a moment I will introduce you to your other guests and you will understand why we have come to visit you. But for now," she smiled at Micah, " to answer your question Sam, as you may have guessed, being from," she paused, "what you call the 'other side' provides us with energy fields and knowledge of time and place that you have yet to experience. Sam," she continued, "I have also had the honor of meeting the individuals who during World War II saved you when you were twelve years old from the concentration camp. These 'Righteous Gentiles,' as they are called by the Jewish community, asked me to tell you and others how they wish they could have saved many more, like your family."

"I am… needless to say, I, I am… feeling… awe struck, at your presence," said Sam whose face had turned rather pale. "Obviously, we three anxiously wait what else you have to tell us, and why we are here at this place."

"Indeed it is time to answer that question. When we learned that the rabbi was writing a book about how character sustains us, we decided that this gas station would be the perfect place to introduce you to individuals whose energy has personified moral courage. We wish you could meet all the other countless brave souls who over the span of eternity have exhibited such courage. But we chose these three because they also wanted to tell you their story." She then held out her arms as if to embrace us but held back, "before you join us on the other side."

"What you are telling us comes close to terrifying," I replied, "especially as it appears that fate brought us here to a gas station that is obviously something else."

"I understand your feelings. In fact," she looked at us admiringly, "what you are encountering now, the present and future connected, is an aspect of moral courage that we on the other side no longer get to experience. So, we are pleased to be here too, part of our past lives… fond memories...blowing;… blown back with us in time."

"You keep referring to 'we,'" Sam responded, still pale from the shock of what we were experiencing.

"Speaking of we," Micah interrupted, "Dad, I am annoyed to have to be leaving this incredible happening, but I am chairing a meeting about renewable energy, and I'm already late. I hope it finishes quickly so I can return… Dulcenea… Sam, it was an honor to meet you… *shalom*… ." And with that Micah got on his bike and rode off.

"I was waiting for one of you to ask about the 'we,'" Dulcenea continued, "and am glad that you asked, Sam. We thought it would be especially appropriate to include you," now she was looking directly at Dr. Oliner, "because your life and life's work with Pearl have so epitomized the nature of courage and how it is sustained." Then she laughed and said, "Yes,... sustained... and soon you will see how courage is also fueled." And with those mysterious words, she exited through a door that led to the garage. And we heard strange sounds, like fruit dropping from a tree in a wind. And suddenly she stood before us with three individuals.

Imagine our shock when Micah, Sam and I saw who was with her. First came Mahatma Gandhi, wearing his customary white *dhati* and sandals, broad smile, hand extended. Next to him, the very proud and distinguished President Anwar Sadat of Egypt, and a gentleman whom we did not recognize, who was the first to actually greet us.

"Hi-ya." He pronounced "hi" with a particular Midwest twang. "I am Senator Robert Norris, once from... ? He paused to see if we knew and laughed at his question, "from the State of....?" "Iowa," Sam replied.

"No, Cornhusker," he practically jumped up and down as he said the word, "the great State of Nebraska! Yes sir, no corn on the other side," he chuckled, "at least as good as Nebraska's."

"Senator, I could not have recognized you. When you were beginning your career," I said, "first in the U.S. House of Representatives then the Senate, I was some twenty-eight years from yet seeing the light of day. But, I know your name and reputation from President Kennedy's inspiring book, *Profiles in Courage*."[147]

"Yes, sir," replied the Senator, then pausing as if recollecting his political battle scars, "it... was... yes sir... a great honor to be included in Kennedy's book."

President Sadat, speaking for the first time in the very punctuated way he spoke English, "Indeed—my friend—and I—just had—a chat—with JFK, did we not?" He said as he looked at Gandhi.

"Oh yes," answered Gandhi, the way some Indians speak English, combining a gerund with the active tense of a verb. "Speaking, yes Sadat and I were of... how shall I say... of our common destiny? Yes, each of us, assassinated by our own countryman."

"Fellow citizens you mean, Mahatma," interrupted Sadat. "Quite right, Anwar. First me by a fellow Hindu, then you by a brother Muslim, and then JFK by that Oswald fellow."

"All three, fanatics, the precursors perhaps to the terrorism that the world suffers now," added Sadat.

"Speaking of suffering," I said to President Sadat and the others, "Wouldn't you like to sit? And, let me bring some cheese and grapes."

"Grapes?" said Sadat, looking at Gandhi and Dulcenea with an odd smile. "Then you must have some grape juice," he asked.

"I'll see if there is any at the market next door. I'll be right back," I said, wondering if they drank grape juice on the other side.

When I returned my guests were seated, and the Senator was saying, "I remember our President McKinley's assassination. Yes, sir, then T.R. was also shot by an anarchist in Milwaukee. But that scrapper, Roosevelt, he survived. In fact, with blood drying beneath his white vest and dress jacket, the colonel went into the auditorium where he then spoke to his crowd for a period of time before he finally sat down, exhausted, and was taken away to the hospital."

"I did not know that," said Sadat.

"And gentlemen, there were times when I thought I might get a slug in the chest from my, uh at times, dissatisfied constituency," added the Senator; "or a severe punch from one particular, ornery colleague, from the State o-o-f...." His voice trailed off. "No need to mention his name after all these years."

As the senator paused, I said, "Sorry no grape juice, but here's some cheese and grapes."

"Wonderful," said Sadat, who added, "We appreciate your politically polite circumspection, Senator Norris, but now you've got us curious. What exactly took place in your Congress?"

"Yes, please, telling us, it sounds so intriguing," added Gandhi.
The Senator nodded. "As you no doubt remember my country succeeded in staying out of what came to be the Great War in Europe for three years, even though our president, Woodrow Wilson, was determined to have us drawn in to the war. In early 1917 knowing that the public strongly supported him, the President came before an emotionally charged joint session of Congress, asking us for the authorization to arm American merchant ships, something I was very opposed to our doing."

"I was one year old in 1917, but what was wrong with that?" asked Sadat.

"Yes, after all, both our countries were part of the British Empire,"

Gandhi said a bit ruefully. "Why wouldn't you want America to support her allies—colonial Britain and the empire?"

Looking at Gandhi, the senator replied, "Like you, sir, I hated war and feared that big business was the driving force in moving our country 'into a useless, bloody struggle…and that the President's 'Armed Ship Bill' was mainly a device to protect American munitions profits with the blood of American lives."[148]

"I was of forty-eight years," said Gandhi, turning to smile at Sadat and the senator, "when the American President was pursuing, as you said Mr. Norris, a 'useless struggle.' And while, many people have attributed to me the statement, 'In all history there is no war which was not hatched by the governments, the governments alone, independent of the interests of the people,' I wish I could claim it as mine. In truth it was made by my spiritual colleague Leo Tolstoy."

"And indeed sir, it is a fine sentiment. But my problem was that the 'interests of the people' in my home state strongly supported the President in this matter of war. In fact, the Nebraska legislature pledged to the President 'its loyal an undivided support of the entire citizenry… of whatever political party… blood or place of birth… to maintain the rights of America and, the dignity of our nation and the honor of our flag.'"

"What did you do then?" Sam asked.

"I felt I had no choice but to continue opposing the possibility of war. In fact," looking at Gandhi he continued, "it's possible that about this time I read a comment you had made when you were defending the rights of your people, in South Africa: 'What difference does it make to the dead, the orphans and the homeless, whether the mad destruction is wrought under the name of totalitarianism or the holy name of liberty or democracy?'"

"Yes, to answer your question, a 'democracy' in the form of our state legislature had spoken, but I had to follow the 'liberty' that guided my conscience to oppose unnecessary bloodshed. In what turned out to be one of the hardest, most embittering struggles of my political career, I joined a small group of like-minded senators led by the head of the Progressive party, Robert La Follette of Wisconsin, to filibuster the Bill."

"You mean you used the rules of the Senate to block a vote?" I asked.

"Exactly. We, 'a little group of willful men, representing no opinion but their own,' is what the President called us. Unrelentingly, for two days and nights we kept the debate alive, checking every opposition move to end the filibuster, until finally at noon on the second day of the debate the chairman announced adjournment. Our tactics had succeeded."

"Surely, you lost friends in the course of what must have been an exhausting, emotional debate?" asked Gandhi. "I know how difficult it was for me when many of my friends, even relatives, were refusing to give up what they felt was the good life, to join me in our peaceful protest against British rule."

"More than just the loss of friends, sir," replied the Senator. "There were times when, in my judgment, the clash of anger and bitterness has never been exceeded in the history of the United States. On the Senate floor I was called 'a Bolshevist, an enemy of advancement, a traitor and much more,' and in that heat of accusation, as I said earlier, I feared for my person." [149]

"I can imagine your sense of loneliness," volunteered Sadat. "When I told some of my advisers that I was going to address the K'nesset (the Israeli Parliament) some of them never spoke to me again."

"My experience as well," responded the senator. "In such times as those, you learn who your real friends are. But ultimately you face the fact that your best friend has to be your own conscience; and that in the world of politics, victories can be fleeting. President Wilson called a special session of Congress, and eventually had his way—our

Courage is not the absence of fear, but rather the judgment that something else is more important than fear. [150]

merchant ships began to be armed for war."

"My research regarding what moral leaders share in common," volunteered Sam, "includes, 'The position to act in accordance with one's moral ideals or principals... and between the means and ends of one's actions.'[151]

"From what Sam just shared with us," interjected Sadat, "you lost the battle but your 'moral ideals or principals' remained intact."

"Indeed, I have felt from that day to this that the filibuster was justified. We sincerely believed that, by our actions in that struggle, we had averted American participation in the war, at least for a while. I was to say at a latter time:

> I would rather go down to my political grave with a clear conscience then ride in the chariot of victory... a Congressional stool pigeon, the slave, the servant,... whether he be the owner and manager of a legislative menagerie or the ruler of a great nation... I would rather lie in the silent grave, remembered by both friends and enemies as one who remained true to his faith and who never faltered in what he believed to be his duty....'[152]

"Another quality of moral leadership," volunteered Sam "is 'a willingness to risk one's self-interest for the sake of one's moral values.'"[153]

"Yes, there is certainly a risk. But you know my friends, while many a courageous soul has gone down to his political grave for voting his conscience, I was one of the fortunate few. Both in the war matter and again when conscience told me that even though a Republican, I should support Al Smith, a Democrat, for the Presidency (because I believed Smith was truly concerned for the common man, verses Hoover the plutocrat), I faced the hellfire of indignation from my Republican, Nebraska constituency. Even my wife let it be known that she did not agree with me. 'I am not following in all this... I am not going to vote for Smith even if George does,' she told the newspapers."

"Surely all that must have led to the end of your career in politics?" asked Dr. Oliner.

"Yes, sir, you would have thought so," the senator answered. "But in the year 19 and 28 when I faced the music with a series of speeches I called, 'I have come home to tell you the truth,' the voters responded with respect, even at times with thunderous applause. I was elected to three more terms to the Senate. Finally, however my luck ran out. As a strong advocate for Roosevelt's TVA, electrification for the people, I had again supported a Democrat over Hoover. In the election of 1942, the people of Nebraska had enough of my progressive individuality. I lost."

"But not the courage of your convictions," said Gandhi admiringly. "Thank you for telling us about political courage, American style."

"And, thank you!" said the Senator. "By the way we have been awfully formal with each other. May I call you Anwar? And you Gandhi, you are called Mahatma, correct?"

"Of course. Are we not friends?" said Sadat.

"Yes, they are calling me Mahatma for a long time now." The senator then turned to Sadat. "Anwar, when you arrived where our souls now reside, I remember the heavenly buzz upon your arrival. It was October 6, 1981, when they carried you away from the parade stand in Cairo a bloodied corpse. But to us you arrived as a pure soul, with that same air of handsome confidence that you exhibited in Egypt and elsewhere. There was admiration for your courage. We knew after you went to address the Israeli K'nesset, you feared for your life.

"George, you are correct. When I made the decision to talk to the Israelis, I knew I faced a greater risk at home then in Israel."

"But you had to go," said Gandhi more as a statement than a question, "yes?"

"There had been enough bloodshed."

"So, Anwar, like Senator George, you too spoke and acted with the courage of your convictions when you addressed the members of the Israeli Parliament," said Gandhi. "You spoke of the sanctity of life, 'Any life that is lost in war is a human life be it that of an Arab or an Israeli. A wife who becomes a widow is a human being entitled to a happy family life, whether she be an Arab or an Israeli.'[54]

Sadat said, "Yes, it was November 20th, 1977, when I stepped onto the tarmac at Tel Aviv, and to my surprise I was received like a hero. Even my old enemy Golda Meir was there to greet me with a warm smile. Earlier that year I had said to my Parliament, I would go anywhere to negotiate with the Israelis—even to the Israeli parliament to speak for peace. Of course," he continued, "there were many, many people in my country who did not believe me. Some interpreted it as political, to camouflage my intentions of launching a new war.

"I even shared with the Israelis and the entire world, that one of my aides at the presidential office contacted me at a late hour following my return home from the People's Assembly. 'Mr. President, what would be our reaction if the Israelis invite you?' I replied calmly that I would accept it immediately for I want to put before the people of Israel all the facts…"

"The facts?" asked the senator.

"Yes. I meant that there were certain incontrovertible facts that we two nations had to accept about each other—on our part that we would accept Israel as a sovereign nation and she on her part would be willing to return the Sinai desert to us."

"Nor did I hold back with the Israelis. I said, 'No one could have ever conceived that the president of the largest Arab state, which bears the heaviest burden and the main responsibility pertaining to the cause of war and peace in the Middle East, should declare his readiness to go to the land of the adversary while we were still in a state of war.'

"Indeed, I knew it was an enormous risk, but I was serious. *Time* magazine declared that the Middle East had never seen such a moment before. 'President Sadat's courageous initiative for reviving the Middle East peace process,' they wrote, 'took the whole world by surprise.' Nevertheless, you can imagine when the Israelis took up the challenge for peace that I had thrown their way, even though there had been quiet hints that they would welcome me, I too was surprised." Then Sadat looked at Gandhi very seriously, "You know Mohandas," using Gandhi's personal name with real affection, "When I was a young man you made a real impact on my life. My Israeli 'surprise,' had been brewing, like an Egyptian beer, in me for many years."

"Oh," Gandhi replied with his gentle warm smile. "How so?"

"Remember when you toured my country in 1932?" Sadat asked. "You were preaching the power of nonviolence in combating injustice.[155] Mohandas, it was you who may have planted the malt for my decision to go to Israel for peace."

"You are honoring me unduly, and am I taking it with one of my favorite spices, 'a grain of salt,'" he laughed.

Sadat reciprocated with a huge laugh, knowing that Gandhi was teasing him by referring to salt, as Sadat knew very well that one of Mahatma's greatest Indian peace actions was his boycott of salt.[156]

Gentle Gandhi was obviously in a feisty mood. Like an unintimidated chess player boldly moving a pawn to "check mate" he declared, "After all, dear Anwar, I once read when you were young you also admired Hitler."

"Your grain of salt has a fair grain of truth," replied Sadat. "In those anti-colonialist days, I was not alone in seeing Hitler as a potential rival to British control of our nation."[157]

Not to be intimidated, either, Sadat smiled slightly, and pushed his pawn as if it were a queen, "When the war broke out in 1939, with the invasion of Poland by Hitler, after lengthy deliberations with your party leaders, you declared that India could not be party to a war ostensibly being fought for democratic freedom, while that freedom was denied to India herself."

"Anwar, you are correct," Gandhi sighed, "but that decision was simply a cold hearted political one, certainly not because any of us favored the Nazis. And, as you can imagine our decision to put non-violent pressure on the British by refusing our military involvement was strongly criticized by Indian political groups, both pro-British and anti-British. Some felt that opposing Britain in its life-death struggle was immoral, and others felt that I wasn't doing enough."

"You called your movement that the English leave, "Quit India", correct?" asked Sam. "I remember how shocked we refugees, the victims of German terrorism were," he continued, "that you, Gandhi, would even think of advocating pacifism in the face of British power, let alone make it happen."

"Yes, it was a marvel to us in Egypt as well. Thousands of your freedom fighters were killed or injured in police firing, and hundreds of thousands were arrested," continued Sadat, "but you, Gandhi, and your supporters made it clear that you would not support the Allied war effort unless India was granted immediate independence. It must have required incredible discipline."

Just as Gandhi started to answer Sam, a large red and white fuel truck pulled up to the station's underground fuel tank. The driver got out of his cab and appeared to place the fuel hose in the tank.

"There had to be a different way," continued Gandhi, "than the old way of confronting physical force with even greater physical force...."

The rest of Gandhi's answer was drowned out by the roar of expletives coming from the mouth of the fuel tank driver. He appeared to be having difficulty placing the fuel hose in the tank. '...What the f ---' we heard him scream to himself as he headed for his cab. Then, reaching for a cell phone, we could hear him say, with obvious exasperation, "But... I'm telling you I can't get it in. Its blocked with a sign that says, 'Now accepting nothing but moral courage fuel.'"

The driver obviously did not like what was said to him from the other end of the phone, because he jumped into the cab, slammed the door and drove off in a huff and a puff of carbon monoxide.

All this had absolutely no effect on Gandhi. He continued, as if merely a butterfly had disappeared, rather than a furious, bewildered fuel truck driver.

"So I told the British that no matter how many of us would be arrested the movement would not be stopped. Even if they continued committing acts of violence against us, we would still commit ourselves to 'ordered anarchy,' as we called it."

"I hope you don't mind me asking, Mahatma," said the senator. "Were you afraid that your people would ignore your call to non-violence?"

"I am glad you asked," replied Gandhi. "Honestly, there were times when I was fearing the worst, because not all of my fellow Indians agreed with my position. There were parties that were very opposed to our way of dealing with British power. But when I called on the politicians and the people to maintain discipline in *ahimsa* in the cause of ultimate freedom, they responded with noble courage—not all, of course, but many more than I could have imagined. So that even with mass arrests, my own and our entire Congress Working Committee, with violence on an unprecedented scale, *ahimsa* remained."

The senator said, "*Ahimsa*, is not a familiar word to me."

"Understandably so, as the word and our movement of non-violence came together just as you were leaving political office. Literally speaking, it means nonviolence. But to me it has an infinitely higher meaning. It means that you may not offend anybody; you may not harbor uncharitable thought, even in connection with those who you consider to be your enemies. To one who follows this doctrine, there are no enemies."[158]

"Doesn't sound realistic, at least for many Americans," the senator said.

"It is taking an incredible moral courage to live so, but a man who is believing in this doctrine can accomplish a great deal. I once said, in fact, he may find 'the whole world at his feet.' Because, if you can express your love—*ahimsa*—in such a manner, your so-called enemy feels he must return your behavior with love."

"Senator, have you encountered as yet the soul of Martin Luther King?" asked Dr. Oliner. "Dr. King purposely visited India to learn your philosophy and so admired you he had a picture of you, Mahatma, on his office wall. He once said of you, 'Gandhi with only a little love and... a refusal to cooperate with an evil law (accomplished) one of the most significant things in the history of the world—more than 390 million people achieved their freedom, and they achieved it nonviolently.'"[159]

"Though nonviolence was used in a different way in America than in India," added Sadat.

"Yes, 'This doctrine... requires far greater courage than delivering of blows,' but for us in India and for you in America, our concept of *ahimsa* was the spiritual energy behind the pacifism that forced the British in my country and the segregationists in yours to finally give in to our demand for freedom."

"Well, Gandhi, I confess, for a ling time I wasn't doing enough to solve my nation's problems with the Israelis, until I decided to go to Jerusalem. And then everything changed. I declared, 'I have chosen to set aside all precedents and traditions known by warring countries...' And I really believed, as I said, 'If... I wanted to avert from all the Arab people the horrors of shocking and destructive wars I must sincerely... have the same feelings and bear the same responsibility towards all and every man on earth, and certainly towards the Israeli people.'

"In those years, even now, there were few fellow Arab leaders who would accept what I declared at the K'nesset, that '… we all love this land, the land of God, we all, Muslims, Christians and Jews, all worship God….'"

"Yes," said Gandhi, "having such a universal view was particularly courageous and saying it publicly was—revolutionary." "Truthfully, however, I didn't think merely stating that 'we all, Muslims, Christians and Jews, all worship God,' was something revolutionary. I suppose it was more the result of my believing that we and the Israelis had to take full responsibility for working toward a better life for our people, for the sake of all our sons and brothers, for the sake of affording our communities the opportunity to work for the progress and happiness of man, feeling secure and with the right to a dignified life, for the generations to come, for a smile on the face of every child born in our land."

Turning to Sadat, Gandhi recalled, "Anwar, what shocked everyone at the time was that not only did you not consult any of your Arab colleagues or heads of state as to your decision to go, you even declared this fact to the Israelis. That was particularly bold." "Bold? Perhaps, Mahatma," responded Sadat, "but unlike what went on with you and the British, by this time we had fought three wars with the Israelis since they became a state in 1949. In my predecessor's Suez war, 1956, we lost 1,650 soldiers and 4,900 were wounded. In the even shorter war, in 6 days, 21,000 of my soldiers were killed and 45,000 were wounded.

"Yes, it was a risk, but my fellow Arab leaders had not seen their sons die in such numbers. I knew they would all be opposed, except perhaps King Hassan II of Morocco," continued Sadat, "but I wanted no more blood on my hands.

"If in my time, my fellow Nebraskans were cynical as to my motives for opposing war with Germany, I can only imagine what those around you thought of your motives for peaceful dialogue with the Israelis—with whom your country had already fought those three wars."

"True, most of those who contacted me expressed their objection because of the feeling of utter suspicion and absolute lack of confidence between the Arab states and the Palestinian people on the one hand and Israelis on the other."

"Suspicion and fear of change," said Senator Norris, "is the cause of so much misery and denial of basic freedoms, yet you two persevered and succeeded in each of your goals beyond what anyone would have imagined. And, particularly in your case, Mahatma, would you not agree, no one could have thought that you would have been such an advocate of change in your India?"

"Quite so, my American friend," replied Gandhi. "In my early years I was a rather shy and some would say unsuccessful lawyer, passively watching the British occupy and oppress my people. Though what impelled me to act occurred in South Africa where I had been living."

Sadat laughed, "What moved you, as with Rosa Parks many years later, quite literally had to do with movement, simple transportation hinged to discrimination."

"There were other things," affirmed Gandhi. "But yes, Ms. Parks's life was forever changed when she was ordered by the Montgomery, Alabama, bus driver to the back of the bus and she refused to move. My life changed when I was denied a seat on a South African stagecoach.

"A racist driver had made me sit on the outside in the hot sun on a long trip to Pretoria, simply because I was dark skinned. In my heart, like Rosa, I felt 'enough already!' I sued the transportation company and won. And with that act I, much to my own amazement, became a major spokesman for powerless non-whites throughout the British Empire." [160]

"My research regarding what moral leaders share in common," said Sam, "also includes, 'a sustained commitment to moral ideals or principles that include a generalized respect for humanity; or a sustained evidence of moral virtue.'" [161]

"Oh yes, I also remember when your soul arrived to be with us eternally," interjected the senator, "everyone called you the Mahatma or the 'Great Soul' of India. In you was sustained evidence of moral virtue."

"Yes, their calling me Mahatma was the embarrassing price I paid for returning to India after 20 years in South Africa. It took a great deal of pleas and cajoling, but we finally convinced the people that taking up arms against the British was futile. Instead we created a policy of nonviolent protest, or as I called it, 'a weapon for the brave.'"

"Mahatma, you are being too humble," the senator replied. "You arrived to us the 'Great Soul,' not just because your weapon was for the brave, but because you also taught that love would be a better weapon for India's freedom than hate. Confronted by you, a slight man wearing only a plain cloth for clothing, you and millions of followers wore down British power with love and truth. Is that not so?"

"It is not humility, as you are calling it on my part," answered Gandhi, "but the truth of courage and freedom that is innately man's for keeping. The British succumbed to our 20 years of nonviolent protests, marches and strikes, not because of me. But as you, Anwar, suggested earlier, thousands of freedom fighters were killed or injured in police firing, and hundreds of thousands were arrested, until we convinced the Brits that we would not support the war effort unless India was granted immediate independence."

"And two years after that great victory, in 1948, your soul came to us whole, devoid of the body that had been torn by an assassin's bullet," added the senator.

"Did you still love your enemy?" I asked.

"I arrived on the other side disappointed that I left an India struggling to survive its newfound independence, but continuing to believe as I once said, that 'nonviolence exists only when we love those that hate us.

"It is difficult to follow this grand law of love," Gandhi was looking at me, "especially when you see the pistol drawn and aimed at you. But do not all great and good things involve some risk? Love of the hater is the most difficult of all. But by the grace of God even this most difficult thing becomes easy to accomplish if we want to."

Then Gandhi surprised us. "As you know I went to prison on many occasions, but my death was not as difficult as what befell me after my arrest in Bombay in August 1942. In the political and spiritual pursuit of nonviolent action, I was not always the husband or father that I would have liked to have been. During the two years I was imprisoned , my 42-year-old secretary, Mahadev Desai died. And then my wife Kasturba died after an 18 months imprisonment. Her death and the pangs of guilt I felt were far worse than my assassination."

"I have been listening to the three of you," said Sam, "with obvious interest and admiration for the moral courage you demonstrated. So, Mahatma and President Sadat, I hope you won't think my question to you as disrespectful."

They both nodded, ready for the question.

"I wonder if it ever occurred to you both that the creativity and courage of what you did—Mahatma, your replacing hatred against the British with nonviolence and love, and Anwar, your proposal to visit the capital of your enemy—was truly radical?"

"I think," said Gandhi looking at Sadat, "as I have said, we were aware that we were acting in a very different, non-confrontational political way. After all the practice of *ahimsa* calls forth the greatest courage." [162]

"True," nodded Sadat. "Please continue, Sam."

"What you were doing was an incredible example of cognitive dissonance, but… ."

"Cognitive what?" laughed Sadat.

Just as Sam started to answer, a car drove up right in front of the office where we had been sitting. The driver rolled down his window and yelled, "Hey, ain't this a gas station? I need to fill 'er up."

"Come back in the spring," Dulcenea yelled back. "And we'll have grapes."

Amazed by her comment, we merely looked at each other, believing that Dulcenea would explain to us what she had just said. The driver, however, showed no such patience. "F--- you," he screamed as his car squealed off and away.

"Cognitive dissonance is a psychological emotion," Sam continued, "first developed by a psychologist named Leon Festinger, which refers to the discomfort, or dissonance we feel when what we know or believe is challenged with new information or facts. This emotion can play a very important role in the perpetuation of, or the elimination of conflict and has become a very important theory in social psychology." [163]

"It sounds interesting, but what does it have to do with what Anwar and I accomplished?" asked Gandhi.

Sam answered with a question (a very Jewish way of teaching.) "Would you agree, Gandhi, that conflict between individuals and groups is usually perpetuated based on perceptions of each other? In Northern Ireland, for example, the image of Protestants or Catholics as inhuman allowed each side who otherwise believed strongly that 'Thou shalt not murder' to participate in activities that included murder. This process explains how terrorists are capable of such awful behavior. They dehumanize the other in their mind, which eliminates any dissonance between their actions and their beliefs against anti-social behavior like murder or violence."

"Indeed, and we Egyptians believed," acknowledged Sadat, "that Israelis were so haughty that they were not interested in peace."

"And yes, we Indians and the British each had stereotypes of each other that discouraged dialogue, let alone living in harmony."

"Precisely," continued Sam. "These cognitions or emotions can be so dissonant and jarring, that usually each side in a conflict is simply unreceptive to ideas that paint the other in a positive light. Thus an Israeli may not be willing to hear about the thoughts, feelings and family of a Palestinian, because these contradict the Israeli's view of Palestinians as inhuman."

"Of course," I volunteered, "similar examples can be found on all levels of conflict. Individuals on both sides of the abortion debate, for example, are unwilling to look at new information about the other side's stance in an attempt to avoid cognitive dissonance.

"Yes," added Sam, "this emotion can be so unpleasant that individuals would often rather be close-minded than be informed and deal with the repercussions of cognitive dissonance. Anwar, in your speech to the Israelis you used Festinger's concept brilliantly."

"I did?"

"When you said so candidly to the Israelis, 'We used to reject you, we had our reasons and our fears, yes... we refused to meet with you anywhere,' you were acknowledging the dissonance between you and them. Then you declared a new proposal:

Let us be frank with each other today while the entire world, both East and West, follows these unparalleled moments, which could prove to be a radical turning point in the history of this part of the world if not in the history of the world as a whole.

"I never thought of my 'turning point' in this way," admitted Anwar. "But yes, when I said to them, 'There was a huge wall between us... the wall of an implacable and escalating psychological warfare,... a barrier of suspicion, a barrier of rejection; a barrier of fear,' I guess I was acknowledging our situation by using this idea of dissonance."

Turning toward Gandhi, Sam continued, "But Anwar, what made your words so courageous was that like Gandhi's decision to come to challenge the British, you both overcame the wall of suspicion, the dissonance, to create bold, new initiatives—a plea for peace—a plea for a different way of living than the cycle of conflict and hatred."

"All right, my plea for peace and reconciliation with the British, "I am seeing now was an extended form of dissonance, mine based on *ahimsa* and love ,and yours Anwar, based on your courage to advocate peace instead of more violence."

"I even used the C-word *courage* in my appeal to the Israelis: 'Why don't we stand together with the courage of men and the boldness of heroes who dedicate themselves to a sublime aim?

Why don't we stand together with the same courage and daring to erect a huge edifice of peace—an edifice that builds and does not destroy... An edifice that serves as a beacon for generations to come with the human message for construction, development and the dignity of man?

"Yes, yes!" replied Sam, jumping out of his chair with excitement, "and in doing so you and Gandhi forced your adversaries to rethink their actions. While in a political sense you called your behavior nonviolent, in a psychological sense that's exactly what you did—you disarmed them. In fact, gentlemen, 'disarming behaviors,' is another term for cognitive dissonance. Knowing what the British expected, Mahatma, and knowing what the Israelis expected, Anwar, you did the exact opposite—introduced radically new information—creating a new dissonance which forced your adversary to react."[164]

"Sam. I remember to this day President Begin's kind words regarding my courage:

I greet the President of Egypt on the occasion of his visit to our country and his participation in this session of the K'nesset. The duration of the flight from Cairo to Jerusalem is short but, until last night, the distance between them was infinite. President Sadat showed courage in crossing this distance.[165]

"Of course, disarming behaviors do not always succeed in changing another's behavior," I interjected. "But if it is repeatedly and creatively done, or as you two did for the whole world to see, it is hard to ignore. And in your situations it set the path for breaking stereotypes and building trust where none had existed before." [166]

With that, Gandhi and Sadat looked at each other approvingly, and nodded at Sam and me. Before one of them started to say something else, I turned to Dulcenea and asked, "But haven't you forgotten something you promised us?"

"Oh, yes, the courage fuel," answered Dulcenea, who all the while had listened intently to her colleagues discuss moral courage.

"Dulcenea, are you still advocating courage fuel?" Micah asked breathlessly, having just returned to us from his meeting.

"Yes, courage fuel," as she pointed to the pumps where the cars were still parked, "that's the only kind of energy that is really free and makes for a clean and moral environment. Gentlemen, how good is your knowledge of Scripture?" she suddenly asked.

Sadat laughed and said, "You mean the Koran?"

"Or the Bhagavad Gita?" interjected Gandhi, with a wry smile.

She too laughed. "I mean where in the Jewish Torah, or the Christian Pentateuch, is fruit associated with courage?"

"Fruit and courage? The only verse I can even think of that mentions courage," replied Sam, "is when Moses sends the spies to spy out the land of Canaan, with the words, 'Be of good courage!'"

Seeing that was as much information as Sam and I could muster, Senator Norris said with the immediacy of a Baptist preacher, "Numbers 13:20 '…and the time' when Moses urged courage, 'was the time of the first-ripe grapes.'"

"I'm impressed," said Dulcenea to the senator. She then left us and reappeared with a large tray on which were six goblets with a purple liquid.

"'Courage fuel,'" she proclaimed! We all laughed together when we saw what it was.

"Grape juice... ? That's right," said the senator, "what Jews call *'the fruit of the vine,'*"

"*'Borey p'ri ha gafen,'* added Sam, "the blessing we sing, called the *Kiddush,* praising God, the Creator for the fruit of the vine, symbolizing the sweet, good things in life."

"Here have some," said Dulcenea.

We hesitated but Gandhi reminded us, "Do not be afraid, remember, be of good courage!"

We took a goblet and a sip. Sure enough, it was grape juice.

"Are you telling us that grape juice is your courage fuel?" I incredulously asked.

"And yours, too," the senator replied. "As you know it's only a matter of time until there will no longer be any oil left to pollute the world. But the fruits from the earth are unlimited. Who would have known in my day," he continued, "that corn from my old stomping grounds in the Midwest 'would be part of the beginning of a transition to the use of nature's bounty for clean sun-powered fuels, much as Brazil has already accomplished with their sugar cane?'"[167]

"The natural fruits like the grape are the fuel for all things good and ethical on our side, like courage," continued Sadat. "So grape juice is to courage, what corn or sugar is to powering an automobile."

"And, when you join us on the other side," her voice seeming to drift away, "you will see such fruits are the source of our energy...."

Suddenly our visitors from the other side were gone; and in the space they had occupied were six empty goblets floating above where cars were once elevated to be refueled with oil.

Accompanied by laughter, we heard the melody of the Kiddush... *borey p'ri ha gafen...* fade into the space around us.... And in between the notes, that rang out like bells, the words *'ch'zak ve-ematz... '* be of strong courage.'

Then in that place—where what had appeared to be a gas station and had become something else. Sam, Micah, and I, staggered and exhausted by what we had experienced, embraced. There on cement, still stained by grease we felt the courage of their souls, tolling out the words, *'Ch-'zak- ve-e-matz,' Ch-'zak- ve-e-matz,* let courage and energy flow like grape juice, sweet for you and all the earth."

And the last words the four of us heard, as if a proclamation, were, "*l'chayim...* to life... and, 'fill it up'... with moral courage!

Without courage wisdom bears no fruit.[168]

RECIPES:

In honor and memory of **Mahatma Gandhi** who was born October 10, 1869. A blessing for food in the Hindu tradition in honor of Gandhi's moral courage may be found on page 237.

Dr. Rajmohan Gandhi's answer to my question about his grandfather's food tastes beautifully illustrated Gandhi's character:

"Your question cannot elicit an easy answer; for Gandhi believed that controlling the palate rather than pleasing it had to be the aim. After enjoying well-spiced Indian vegetarian food for the first part of his life, from the age of 37 or so, until his death at the age of 78, he lived largely on goat's milk, lentils, boiled vegetables, fruit juices and salads of vegetable or fruit." [169]

INDIAN LENTIL SOUP

Serves 6

Ingredients:
- ½ c. brown lentils
- 4 c. vegetable broth
- 1 medium onion, finely chopped
- ½ tsp. grated ginger
- 2 tbsp. ghee or oil
- 1 large potato, diced into small pieces
- 2 large tomatoes, chopped
- 2 tsps. ground coriander
- 1 tsp. cumin
- ½ tsp. each turmeric, chili flakes, and pepper
- 2 tbsp. shredded coconut
- 3 tsps. tamarind concentrate (if you can't find tamarind, you can substitute lemon or lime juice mixed with a touch of brown sugar)
- 1 1/2 c. shredded cabbage
- ½ c. shredded carrot
- 1 stick cinnamon

Directions:

Soak lentils overnight, rinse in cold water and remove any that float.

Cook lentils for about 20 minutes in fresh water, until tender. Drain well.

Sautee onion and ginger until deep brown.

Add the broth, potatoes and tomatoes, the spices and coconut, and cook another 25 minutes.

Add the lentils and pepper, and bring to a boil. Let pot simmer until lentils and potatoes are soft.

Add the tamarind, carrot and cabbage. Cook until softened.

Serve with coriander or mint as a garnish, if desired.

Note: The dish should be quite tart in favor. Red or yellow lentils, which require less cooking time, may be used instead of brown.

Senator **George W. Norris** was born July 11, 1861, an appropriate occasion to remember him for his moral courage.

A blessing in honor of Senator Norris, who was a Methodist, but who left his library to a Unitarian church, may be found on page 240.

VEAL OR LAMB* FRICASSEE WITH DUMPLINGS

Serves 5 - 6

Linda Hirn of The Nebraska Historical Society found this recipe of veal or lamb* fricassee with dumplings in a cookbook compiled by the senator's wife, Ellie.[170] We have changed it slightly to meet more contemporary tastes.

Ingredients:

2 ½ lbs. thinly sliced veal

1 tbsp. butter

2 ½ tbsp. of flour

½ c. beef gravy

2 c. mushrooms

3 egg yokes, lightly beaten

1 tbsp. cream

Directions:

Very quickly sauté the veal for 30 seconds each side. Remove the veal. Add the butter and sauté the mushrooms. Add the gravy and heat the above ingredients to a light boil. Slowly, while stirring, add the flour, then add the yokes and cream until it is the texture of custard. Remove from heat.

DUMPLINGS (makes 10–12)

Ingredients:
¾ c. milk

2 c. Bisquick

1 14oz. can chicken broth, or more if necessary to cover dumplings.

Directions:

In a large pan bring chicken broth to a boil

Mix milk and Bisquick thoroughly with fork. Drop by spoonful into the hot broth. Cook covered over low heat for 10 minutes.

*Mrs. Norris had noted next to this recipe, "Same with lamb. This recipe is very fine when mushrooms are used to flavor the sauce."

Dr. **Sam Oliner** is especially fond of blintzes.

A Jew; a blessing for his courage and commitment to altruistic behavior can be found on page 240.

BLINTZES

Ingredients:
Batter for about 11 (batter should be thin)

¾ c. white flour

¼ c. wheat flour

1 tsp. salt

1 tbsp. sugar

4 eggs, well beaten

1 ¼ c. milk

1 tsp. vanilla

cooking oil

Directions:

Lightly oil a blintz pan or a 6–8 inch frying pan. Add more oil about every 3rd blintz. or more often as needed.

As you pour the thin batter into the middle of the pan, tip it in a circular fashion so that the batter creates a thin circle covering the bottom of the pan. Cook on one side until pancake is slightly dry. The bottom side should be a light brown. Remove with a metal spatula and place each pancake on a towel, cooked side up.

FILLING

Ingredients:

Filling for about 16–18 pancakes

¾ c., sour cream, or a mix of half sour cream and a fruit yogurt

1 1/4 c. cottage cheese

½ c. cream cheese

6 tbsp. sugar

½ tsp. cinnamon

1 tsp. vanilla

Put the cream, cottage and cream cheese into a microwave-safe bowl and heat in a microwave a minute or so until it is soft. Mix well. Add the dry ingredients and the vanilla. Mix well.

Filling pancake:

Place 1 ½ tablespoons filling in the middle of the pancake. Think of the pancake as comprising four parts, the left quarter, the right quarter, and the middle half. Fold the left and right quarters over the middle, and then, starting from the front roll the pancake to the back end. Lay the side of the blintz with the seam down on a baking pan and refrigerate for at least one hour, and then bake them for 20 minutes in a medium oven, or fry both sides in butter to a crispy brown.

For a dessert, heat your favorite jam and spoon over each blintz.

President Sadat was born December 25, 1918. On November 19, 1977 he flew to Jerusalem for peace talks with Israel, a great occasion to enjoy this salad and a Baba Ganouj to remember him for his moral courage and commitment to peace.

A Muslim; a blessing in his in honor and in memory may be found on page 241.

ORANGE AND OLIVE SALAD WITH CUMIN

Serves 8–10

Ingredients:

8 oranges, preferably navel, peeled, with white pith removed and sliced in half

¾ c. good quality black olives, pitted and cut in half

1 red onion, sliced very thin

¾–1 c. Chickpeas or garbanzo beans

1 ripe avocado, diced into medium size pieces

Juice of one large lemon

2 tsp. ground cumin

3 tbsp. olive oil

3 tbsp.of a sweet white wine

Salt and pepper to taste

Directions:

Toss together oranges, olives, onion, chickpeas.

Combine together lemon juice, cumin, wine, salt and pepper; mix into salad and add avocado.

BABA GANOUJ

A very popular dish in Egypt and elsewhere in the Middle East. The recipe for this side dish that President Sadat no doubt enjoyed comes from my son Hillel, who is an excellent cook. It features artichokes

Ingredients:

2 medium eggplants

4 cloves of garlic

½ c. tahini, available in natural food stores or in the specialty
    section of many supermarkets

4 artichokes

Juice of one lemon

Directions :

Pierce skin of eggplants with a fork in several places; roast eggplants on a cookie sheet at 375 F. degrees until outside is crisp and knife easily penetrates the eggplant. Approximately 40 minutes.

Trim artichokes stem leaving about ¾ of an inch.

Steam artichokes until outer leaves separate easily.

Remove heart of artichoke by removing the outer leaves and the choke (the furry material) in the center.

Remove eggplants, slice open and remove the seeds from the soft flesh.

Place eggplant flesh, artichoke heart, garlic, lemon and tahini in food processor. Process until mixture is smooth.

Dip artichoke leaves in the *baba ganouj.*

Chapter VII

It is possible to avoid the passion of one's times,
but you have to ask yourself if you have been alive.
—Justice Oliver Wendell Holmes

This is a work of creative non-fiction. Within this chapter, the author uses creative license to expand upon biographical and autobiographical information. The actual participation of living persons or historical figures as role models in any particular setting or scene is entirely fictional.

"**I** WONDER IF THEY will recognize us based on these short autobiographical sketches," said an intense looking man with a reddish brown moustache that turned down at the ends.

When I was NYC Police commissioner, 'the midnight trips that... I took with Jacob Riis, [author of *The Way the Other Half Lives*]...gave me personal insight into some of the problems of city life. It is one thing to listen in a perfunctory fashion to tales of overcrowded tenements, and it is quite another actually to see what overcrowding means, some hot summer night.'[171]

When I remarked, with a twinkle in my eye: 'What would my society friends say if they saw me here,' I was referring to my visits and work on behalf of the thousands of Russian Jewish refugees who *were being housed in, to say the least, unsavory surroundings.*[172]

I was incarcerated, once again for merely speaking the truth, and wrote, 'We have waited for more than 340 years for our constitutional and God-given rights.... Perhaps it is easy for those who have never felt the stinging darts of segregation to say, "wait." But when you have seen vicious mobs lynch your mothers and fathers at will and drown your sisters and brothers at whim... the vast majority of your twenty million negro brothers smothering in an airtight cage of poverty in the midst of an affluent society... see tears welling up in your (daughter's) eyes when she is told that Funtown is closed to colored, and see clouds of inferiority beginning to form in her little mental sky... there comes a time when the cup of endurance runs over, and men are no longer willing to be plunged into the abyss of despair...[173]

As I look back on my life, 'I made my greatest strides forward while I was police commissioner, (which)... opened all kinds of windows into the matter of immigrant life for me' and the reality of suffering in the midst of NY opulence.[174]

And I too, as was just described, saw the 'suffering, the heartbreaking, especially the gasping misery of the little children and the worn-out mothers.' And I had the honor, though it was merely one of my 45 poems or sonnets, to successfully muse that theme in my *New Colossus*, "...From her beacon-hand glows world-wide welcome; her mild eyes command... 'Keep, ancient lands, your storied pomp!' cries she with silent lips. 'Give me your tired, your poor, your huddled masses yearning to breathe free, the wretched refuse of your teeming shore. Send these, the homeless, tempest-tost to me, I lift my lamp beside the golden door!'[175]

These three individuals whose reminiscences you just read were seated in the very back row of a Lou Dobb's TV special. And again, the man with the moustache queried his two associates, "With these additional clues do you think they will recognize us?"

"Or what we stood for?" said the other man who sat next to him, who laughed and said, "Your glasses tied to a black ribbon should, give you away."

"And which of our dear presidents," asked the petite, energetic looking woman seated next to the man with the glasses, as if she knew him quite well, "would show up at a TV special with his riding stick except you, Teddy?"[176]

"But you, reverend," she continued, "Excuse the pun, would be a dead give away without those sunglasses and the way you dyed your hair, and besides both of you have recently been on the cover of *Time* magazine."[177]

ANNOUNCER: LOU DOBBS TONIGHT presents a "SNN Special: War on Humanity."

(APPLAUSE)

LOU DOBBS, SNN ANCHOR: Thank you very much. Good evening and welcome to Chicago. We're here today to talk with some of the people who make up this country's middle class, the people who in point of fact are the foundation of this great nation,[178] and who more than anyone know the grave injustices that like a black hole are sucking away our country's greatness.

Then the twenty-sixth President of the United States, 1901–1909, Theodore Roosevelt known by his friends and adversaries as TR, turned to the woman and Martin Luther King, also known as MLK, and said, "That rather bombastic sounding Mr. Dobbs is certainly not referring to us, though candidly," TR laughed, "he does remind me of my old self."

"If there was ever a threesome different in style and appearance than us, I cannot imagine," said MLK.

"And not exactly representatives of 'this country's middle class,'" laughed TR.

"Except for one peculiar similarity," the energetic poetess Emma Lazarus said, "we are distinctly alike in our passion for justice."

As she made that observation to her colleagues, Lou Dobbs, sounding customarily pontifical, was declaring the reason for his SNN Special.

We begin tonight with a complete failure of our leaders to represent the interests of the largest group of constituents in the country, middle class Americans. Republicans and Democrats alike who have been putting their own partisan interests ahead of the concerns of working American families, the common good, justice and the national interest.

"Rabbi Posner, did you know that Lou Dobbs was going to make such a strong accusation about injustice in America when you invited us here?" asked TR.

"I confess I did, Mr. President. I wanted the three of you, who each in your own way were passionate advocates for justice in your day to judge for yourselves what Mr. Dobbs calls 'The War on (America's) Middle Class.'"

"And does he include America's poor in this 'war,' or the suffering of millions outside of America?" MLK asked.

"Not usually, which is another reason why I wanted you to hear and see what's happening not just with the middle class but with millions of Americans who are getting poorer and poorer while the rich of America are getting richer and richer."

Today we want to catalog the hundreds of examples of injustice that are destroying our wonderful nation. But before we continue we want to remind you, following this 'war on America, of SNN's upcoming special on the frightening possibility of a black hole in our very own galaxy.

♦ **In the meantime we hope you will watch the large monitors above you as we show you in bold letters like these, informational bullets of some of the many injustices around us.** [179]

"Yes Mr. President, that is why I put off inviting you to come to this 'side' because I dreaded having to share with you the injustice that is destroying the America you so loved."

"Didn't you trust us to be able to help you?" asked Emma.

I laughed, "I trusted you as exemplars of justice. But I also knew that defining justice would be difficult. Compassion, kindness, forgiveness, righteousness all the other ethical qualities in this book, have a degree of relative objectivity that justice seems to lack."

"That's because justice takes its meaning from the law," said MLK.

"It's interesting you should say that because one of the areas where your and Gandhi's advocacy of 'civil disobedience' was called into question," I responded, "was because you were willing to break the law. As you wrote in your famous 'Letter from Birmingham Jail,'

One may well ask: "How can you advocate breaking some laws and obeying others?" The answer lies in the fact that there are two types of laws: just and unjust…. One has not only a legal but a moral responsibility to obey just laws. Conversely, one has a moral responsibility to disobey unjust laws. [180]

"So, do we agree that it is both the law and something based on some moral authority," asked President Roosevelt, "that informs us as to what is just or unjust?"

"So much so," answered MLK, "that I would agree with St. Augustine's moral view that 'an unjust law is no law at all.'"

"You know, Dr. King, while almost all books about the Civil Rights movement laud your accomplishments and moral philosophy of nonviolence, I happened upon one that faults your view precisely because you favored some laws and were willing to break others:

No matter how many times King drew the fine line between just and unjust laws—no matter how many times he consulted the universe to decide which laws he would obey or disobey—the fact remained that he could not uphold integration laws on odd days, flout segregation laws on even days, and simultaneously proclaim his "highest respect for the law."[181]

"Admittedly, I was vulnerable from a philosophical standpoint for agreeing with St. Augustine. But I was also very aware that I was leading a nonviolent movement and I felt it very appropriate to appeal to moral values like a higher power, conscience, righteousness and justice."

"What we are saying is that while justice may have its roots in an objective law," interjected Emma Lazarus, "like all moral values, justice is also dependent on something ultimately higher."

"Therefore, we have to admit that any understanding of justice and injustice," said Rev. King can not be separated from ethical values associated with what causes pain and suffering to others, as seen in how we live the Golden Rule. "

"As a matter of fact," I said, "as much as Judaism is a religion that assigns a tremendous value to *halacha*, the legal way, as expressed in hundreds of volumes on law and behavior, the Talmud itself recognized that the law can not be independent of ethical values. Therefore it often referred to a concept called '*lifnim m'shurat ha din*,' which some translate as beyond the line of the law,' meaning that one must do more than the law requires.

"Based on various biblical verses including 'you shall do the right and the good' (Deut.6:18) it means that the moral principle must guide and inform the interpretation of the law... and that we must strive to do more than merely conform to the minimal requirements that the law makes.'" [182]

"And that is why I invited you three to share with us your understanding of the 'moral principle' of justice or its opposite. Because in your lives you uniquely personified different aspects of justice, as Ms. Lazarus suggested, with an equal and abiding amount of passion."

"Please call me Emma. And I would submit, having been awakened to injustice and inequality by my reading of Henry George's *Progress and Poverty*, no person who prizes justice or common honesty can dine or sleep or read or work in peace until the monstrous wrong in which we are all accomplices be done away with." [183]

"In fact," she continued, "does not our passion come to us through our mutual conviction, that any definition of justice rests on an individual's awareness that law and morality must include equal opportunities for all God's children?"

"Indeed," declared TR triumphantly, "What I called 'a square deal.'"

"And I cannot imagine that the two of you would disagree," added Emma, "that there can be any justice when the circumstance of a person's passage in life is unequal simply because of his or her background. Further, we who are fortunate in our circumstance and do not act to rid society of injustice bear our own complicity in exploiting the poor and not working to remedy their suffering."

When Emma pronounced the word suffering, we saw the large monitors above Lou Dobbs light up with these words:

♦ **The following table from UNDP (United Nations Development Program) in 2000 shows the inequality of millions of people living without the basic necessities of food, education, water, sanitation.**

Living on less than $1 a day	Total Population under nourished	Primary age children not in school	Children under 5 dying each year	People without access to improved water sources	People without access to adequate sanitation
1,100 million	831 million	104 million	11 million	1,197 million	2,742 million

"I feel a poem coming for our benefit," laughed TR. "And you wouldn't know this, Emma, but as an eclectic reader, I often provided moral and financial succor to a suffering author, now and again. When my son Kermit pointed me to the poetry of Edwin Arlington Robinson, I became such a true fan that later when I learned he was having a hard time making ends meet, I found him a federal job that would not interfere with his writing." [184]

"Mr. President, I had heard that you were a voracious reader, but now I know even more importantly of your kindness to us writers. And," grinning at TR, she asked, "was your comment about a poem a question or a suggestion?"

"The latter," TR replied.

"And I am delighted to respond: from my poem, 'Progress and Poverty':

Oh splendid age when Science lights her lamp
 Fixing it steadfast as a star, man's name
...Launched on a ship whose iron-cuirassed sides
Mock storm and wave, Humanity sails free;
Gaily upon a vast untraveled sea.
O'er pathless wastes, to ports undreamed she rides,
Richer than Cleopatra's barge of gold,
This vessel, manned by demi-gods, with freight
Of priceless marvels. But where yawns the hold
In the deep, reeking hell, what slaves be they,
Who feed the ravenous monsters, pant and sweat,
Nor know of overhead reign night or day? [185]

"What an incredible statement about injustice," said MLK. "As you suggested those were the 'slaves' to circumstance who hardly ever saw the light of day, feeding the coal to the steamships that plied the seas of science and progress. I am so glad you shared it with us."

"I am so glad you liked it."

"Dr. King, and Mr. President, we just heard Emma describe the 'poverty' of her day, despite the 'progress' of science and technology. Now look again at the monitors and see more contemporary examples of how our nation 'is becoming increasingly a divided society—a society of haves and haves not where the rich have gotten richer while working people have gotten poorer." [186]

- **In 2004, the poverty rate for non-Hispanic whites was 8.6 percent, up from 8.2% in 2003; 24.7 percent for black residents, and 21.9 percent for Hispanics, unchanged from 2003 for both Black and Hispanic communities.** [187]

"Given the wide disparity between poverty for blacks and whites," asked Dr. King, "how is poverty in these figures being defined in terms of dollars?"

I replied, "According to the U.S. 2005 Census Bureau, poverty is an individual under age 65 whose income was $10,160 and over 65 was $9,367. And for a household with 2 adults under age 65 with 2 children, poverty meant an income of $15,735.

"Based on that definition of poverty, according to the Census Bureau, the number of fellow Americans living in poverty or below for all races were 37.0 million (12.7 %) in 2004, up from 35.9 million (12.5%) in 2003" [188]

"Now, when we read that there are many below poverty in the wealthiest country in the world," said TR "it is admittedly tragic, but where is the injustice?"

"The injustice," I replied, "is in the incredible disparity between the number of poor who lack decent housing, including 40 million Americans who also lack health care and a government that continues to give tax breaks to millionaires and their corporations."

"That's impossible!" said TR.

"Mr. President, according to Lou Dobbs, 'Fifty years ago, corporate income taxes made up a third of all federal revenues; now corporations account for just an eighth,' and worse still 'many of them have not been paying *any* taxes,' and some 'are actually making more money after taxes, mostly due to tax havens and additional breaks passed by the Bush administration in recent years.'" [189]

Again we saw the monitors light up:

- **The income gap in the United States is greater than many** imagine—the top 29,000 Americans have as much income as the bottom 96 million. And in recent years the tax burden for the richest Americans—especially corporations—has been falling sharply while everyone else's has risen.[190]

"Is it any wonder, as you can see on the monitor that:

♦ The number of millionaires in America reached record highs in 2004, hitting 7.5 million, according to a new survey—a gain of 21%, the largest jump in the number of U.S. millionaires since 1998.[191]

"But don't the heads of corporations deserve a far greater salary than their employees?" asked Emma.

"And deservedly so," echoed TR. "After all, the head of a corporation like Standard Oil of my day bears so much more responsibility than does the oil driller in Texas."

"True," said MLK, "but whose toil is greater? As Emma suggested, the sweating boiler tenders who make a steam ship run, or the fresh white shirted CEO sitting at his desk?"

The President merely sighed.

"Mr. President," said Emma, "may I remind you of what your fellow Progressive, Sen. Robert LaFollette, wrote of you following your last term as President? 'He has preached from The White House many doctrines but among them he has left impressed on the American mind the one great truth of economic justice couched in the pithy and stinging phrase "the Square deal."'"[192]

Again the Prsident merely sighed

"I'm sure we all agree that a CEO, as they are called today, deserves a higher salary," added MLK. "The issue is when does the differential between a CEO and his employees become no longer anything close to a 'square deal,' but an unjust deal for the wealthy whose children, for example, can pay to go to college while the average Americans simply cannot afford the $25,000 per semester and more it costs to go to a university?"

"Just as important, there is the fact that not everyone has the innate intelligence or ability to be a CEO," said Emma. "Have we not all seen the sweating men on a hot summer day, picking up our smelly refuse, running to keep up with the garbage truck (in my day the garbage cart)? Does the hardworking head of a refuse company deserve 100 times more than those hard working garbage men?"

"So will you believe me, Mr. President when I tell you that from the end of the 1980s to 1995 the pay ratio between CEOs and the average worker rose to 431:1—not exactly a 'square deal,' I think you will agree?"

This time the President sighed and said, "I find that most distressing."

"Martin," TR continued, "hearing you talk about this present lack of 'a square deal' for so many of the Americans left behind, reminds me of something you once wrote: 'Deeply etched in the fiber of our religious tradition is the conviction that men are made in the image of God and that they are souls of infinite metaphysical value, the heirs of a legacy of dignity and worth. If we feel this as a profound moral fact, we cannot be content to see men hungry, to see men victimized with starvation and ill health when we have the means to help them. The wealthy... must go all out to bridge the gulf between the rich minority and the poor majority.'"[193]

"Yes, thank you for reminding me of my words, Mr. President Remember when you called the oil magnates of your day, 'robber barons'? A few years ago while thousands of poor people in your state of New York and other cities in the North East were forced to choose between using their money for medicine or heat, the recently retired chairman of Exxon Mobil, Mr. Lee Raymond, appeared before Congress. There he stated that the huge increases in oil prices were the result of supply and demand."[194]

"Am I correct," asked TR, "that Exxon Mobil is the new version of what I knew as Rockefeller's Standard Oil?"

"Certainly, it is Mr. President. It is the same company that in your day the Supreme Court found guilty of 'monopolizing the petroleum industry through a series of anticompetitive actions.'" And in 1911 the Court ruled that Standard Oil be divided up into several competing firms. And now, when Mr. Raymond was telling the American people that gas prices were market driven, Exxon Mobil's financial wealth continued to be larger than the economies of Turkey and Denmark combined. [195]

"Yet in our day, unlike yours, our Congress and our Courts permit giant corporations not only to merge as did Exxon with Mobil in 1999, but because of its vast power, to pretty much do what it wills.

"So Mr. President if you think Standard Oil was a giant, know that in 2002 its successor's GDP was $184,466 million.[196] And last year when poor people in the North East did not have money for fuel to keep warm, Exxon Mobil reported the highest profits in the history of American business."[197]

"And Mr. President, are you ready? During his thirteen-year run as chairman and CEO of Exxon, Mr. Raymond's compensation worked out to be $144,573 a day. On top of that, his retirement package is currently valued at approximately $400 million."[198]

"Friends I am ashamed to say that these salaries are more monstrous than any of the robber barons of my day. Indeed, as Mr. Dobbs writes, they suggest there is a kind of economic war against justice. Imagine, now, how I feel hearing these figures, considering what I once wrote to a friend,[199]

> I utterly and radically disagree with you in what you say about large fortunes. I wish it were in my power to devise some scheme to make it increasingly difficult to heap them up beyond a certain amount. As the difficulties in the way of such a scheme are very great, let us at least prevent their being bequeathed after death or given during life to any one man in excessive amount.[200]

"Mr. President, remember when the steel magnate of your day, Andrew Carnegie, angered his fellow plutocrats by proposing that estates be taxed 100 percent? Over one hundred years ago he said, 'Let the sons of wealth earn their own fortunes.'"[201]

"True, Andrew proved to be a robber baron with a heart," replied the President. "Though in truth if I remember correctly the federal estate tax began prior to the twentieth century as a temporary tax imposed during times of war to provide the government with emergency funds."

"Well, Mr. President," I continued, "such a tax on those who have wealth may have a long history. But in 2001 your old party… "

"You mean," his voice rising, "before I became a Progressive?"

"Yes. A Congress controlled by the same party you abandoned in 1912 passed a 1.3 trillion tax cut, of which 38% benefited the richest 1 percent of America's taxpayers.[202] It included a phased repeal of the very thing, an estate tax, you mentioned to your friend, which by one estimate the present President's cabinet members saved $5 to 19 million apiece."[203]

Now the monitors were practically exploding with surges of flashing lights.

◆ **A study by the General Accounting Office found that almost two-thirds of America's corporations paid no federal income taxes during the late 1990s, when corporate profits were soaring. Nine out of 10 companies paid less than the equivalent of 5 percent of their total income.** [204]

"I am gravely saddened to hear all this. And I know you will all agree that I cannot, nor will I," his soul appearing to redden and rise, "be held responsible for how much my party has changed. I can only say that during my administration I held to the compassionate position that, 'It is better for the government to help a poor man to make a living for his family than to help a rich man make more profit for his company. It is the kind of principle to which politicians delight to pay unctuous homage in words. But we translated the words into deeds; and when they found that this was the case, many rich men… were stirred to hostility….'"[205]

"So I can only imagine how 'stirred to hostility' my Republican descendants would be were I still in power, as I said on more than one occasion, 'The fundamental need in dealing with our people, whether laboring or others, is not charity but justice.'[206]

"But enough of my own concern with American economic justice and the need for a 'square deal,'" the President continued. "Let me hear from you. After all, Martin, you and I were both honored with having received a Nobel Peace Prize, I for brokering a peace agreement between Russia and Japan in 1904, and you for your passionate work on behalf of equal and racial justice. So, do you think there is a greater or lesser amount of equal and racial justice now than there was in our day?"

◆ **Decades after the civil rights movement, racial disparities in income… persist and, by some measurements, are growing.**

"Is that a rhetorical question," Dr. King asked TR, "or do you really want to know what I think?

◆ **White households had incomes that were two-thirds higher than blacks... according to data released by the Census Bureau.** [207]

"Yes, Martin, I want to know what you really think. Have things changed from my early 1900s to your '60s and now?"

◆ **Median income for black households has stayed about 60 percent of the income for white households since 1980. In dollar terms, the gap has grown from $18,123 to $19,683.** [208]

"TR, I guess you didn't see the excellent NBC report called Race in America, that a certain Tom Brokaw presented in July 2006?"

"Martin, as you know, there is so much information available on our side, I guess I missed it."

"Well, let me answer your important question by reviewing a little of what Brokaw reported. He used Jackson Mississippi as an example of some of the racial problems in America and interviewed both blacks and whites. He began by pointing out that, 'Jackson and Mississippi have changed from the bad old days when the state was the epicenter of racism and fierce, often violent opposition to the idea of desegregation.' Then Brokaw interviewed Jackson's mayor, Frank Melton, who said, 'But if you wanna talk about the African American community, I think you just have to be honest. We're in trouble.' He continued interviewing local residents:

Today, the city of Jackson is 70 percent black, with a population that's actually shrinking. There are more people living in poverty than there were 25 years ago. Just across the county line, in the suburbs, it is Anywhere USA, with big box stores, malls, and movie theaters. But not so in the majority black city of Jackson....

'This is the capital city,' interjected the editor of the local newspaper, 'and we have no movie theatre. How many capital cities have you visited without a movie theatre?'

Charlene Priester... a Jackson success story (who) grew up poor said, 'When integration came, the money didn't come, but the door opened and allowed people to move. And so unfortunately you leave behind the people who didn't have the ability. And just like Katrina, when they said evacuate, you know folks couldn't leave.'

To which Brokaw responded by saying, 'So quite simply, integration without economic opportunity was not enough.'

Priester: 'You're right. That's it.'

Brokaw: 'But desegregation [and] the civil rights bill was supposed to change all that?'

To which another resident of Jackson responded, 'It changes what you see. It doesn't change what people think. It doesn't change people's hearts.'"

"Martin thanks for reminding us how in matters of race and economics," said TR, "change is, indeed, subject to 'people's hearts.'"

"TR, to answer your question, I once wrote that Americans are 'infected with racism,' but I also wrote, 'Paradoxically they are also infected with democratic ideals—that is the hope [that] while doing wrong, they have the potential to do right. But they do not have a millennium to make changes. Nor have they the choice of continuing in the old way.'[209]

"So yes, I still believe that the scourge of racism and inequality 'besets the nation' we once called home. But these injustices are a worldwide scourge. And what is frightening, would you not agree my friend, TR, that from where we stand on the other side these evils appear to be worse, not better?"

"Agreed," the President replied sadly. "Even though I had to confront the racism of my day," he added, "the connection between bigotry and huge economic disparities between class and race did not seem as blatant as what we see now. That is not to say we didn't have our own forms of racism. Unfortunately, during the latter part of my term as President certain unwise and demagogic agitators in California showed their disapproval of the Japanese coming into the State, adopted the very foolish procedure of trying to provide by law that the Japanese children should not be allowed to attend the schools with the white children, and offensive and injurious language was used in connection with the proposal."[210]

"Yes," interjected MLK, "and if I remember correctly you dealt with such racism by walking the tightrope of a careful politician."

"Indeed. But I did not fall off. Further, we came to an entirely satisfactory conclusion. The obnoxious school legislation was abandoned, and

I secured an arrangement with Japan under which the Japanese themselves prevented any migration to our country of their laboring people.

"Admittedly, I was using my 'bully pulpit' with the California legislature. I was also very aware that the racism in the far West required soothing words. But I meant them sincerely. 'No part of our success was due to the fact that we succeeded in impressing on the Japanese that we sincerely admired and respected them and desired to treat them with the utmost consideration.'[211]

"I must have greatly irritated the racists of my day by adding that the Japanese are one of the great nations of the world, entitled to stand on a footing of full equality with any nation of Europe or America. I have the heartiest admiration for them. They can teach us much. Their civilization is in some respects higher than our own.'[212]

"And I must say," TR continued, "when we sent 'The Great White Fleet' round the world, it was particularly smooth sailing in the way we were welcomed by the Japanese."

"Too bad your diplomacy, affection for the Japanese, and your standing up to racism did not include what was happening to my people," replied ML King!

Even souls, an inheritance of their previous lives, can show emotion. And TR as we all know was no pacifist. Now his soul's demeanor, once again, seemed to take on a reddish hue. And he said,

"Just what do you mean by that, Dr. King?"

Looking a bit abashed at what he may have unleashed, MLK said, "Mr. President there is no doubt that on many occasions you did right for and by, what was then called the Negro community. In 1908, you threatened the Nashville, Chattanooga & St. Louis Railway with legal action unless it provided Negro passengers with facilities.'[213]

"You also infuriated the South for inviting our brother, the famous African-American educator, Booker T. Washington, for dinner at The White House. And as you no doubt remember, Dixie newspapers like the Memphis *Scimitar* declared your action as simply 'the most damnable outrage ever perpetrated by any citizen of the United States.'[214] And although many southern whites wanted you to appoint only whites to federal government positions, you refused."

"'Yes, I felt that it would be a base and cowardly act not to appoint occasional colored men.'"[215]

The word, "occasional" stood out like a sore thumb, but MLK graciously ignored it, knowing that in the early 1900s there were limits on what even a fairly progressive president on issues of race could accomplish.

"And you even spoke out against the ghastly injustice of Jim Crow lynching, as a part of the broader oppression that kept blacks poor and powerless despite the paper guarantees of the 13th, 14th and 15th Amendments to the Bill of Rights," continued MLK.

"As a matter of fact I said, 'All thoughtful men must feel the gravest alarm over the growth of lynching in this country, and especially the inhuman aspect of putting to death by torture—usually by burning alive so often taken by mob violence when colored men are the victims—on which occasions the mob seems to lay most weight, not on the crime but on the color of the criminal.[216]

"But remember earlier, Mr. President, when we spoke of the complexity and relativity of defining justice? Yes, compared to President Woodrow Wilson's willingness to allow Jim Crow to hang thousands of my brothers by looking the other way, you were Mr. Justice. But occasionally even you in the name of justice, perverted it."

Again the President had that reddish hue about him.

"And to what, my dear man, do you refer?" he asked in a voice that indicated he was clearly irritated. .

"The incident regarding soldiers in Brownsville, Texas," MLK replied.

"Yes, I remember reading about that," I interrupted, hoping to break the rising tension between the two of them. "In 1906, some black soldiers from a nearby military installation (Fort Brown) allegedly killed a white bartender and wounded a policeman in a wild midnight raid on the town."

"Yes," said TR, "that is the case."

"But Mr. President, none of the alleged participants was ever positively identified; nor did any one of them ever admit responsibility," continued MLK. "They were never brought before a court of law, military or civil, and to this day their guilt remains unproved. Yet you ordered almost the entire three companies in question, about 160 black soldiers, 'discharged without honor and forever barred from re-enlistment.'" [217]

TR sighed and replied, "I admit to being a bit embarrassed about the whole affair, particularly since several of the soldiers were near retirement and six had won the Medal of Honor for their heroism in previous wars."

"Evidently, as you said, you rationalized your decision on the basis of the constant need for 'military discipline,' but you also released the information regarding your order a few days after the November elections of that year, possibly to avoid losing the vote of Northern Black voters.[218]

"And," MLK continued, "While eventually, Mr. President, you rode out the storm of protests from both northern blacks and whites, this one event stained your otherwise good reputation with the black community." [219]

"Martin, while I never deviated from the rightness of my decision during my life time, I admit now I wish I had ordered a fuller investigation of the matter."

"Thank you, Mr. President," replied MLK, "in the heat of the Civil Rights battle, I know I made mistakes I wish I could take back."

"Friends, I need to say," Said Emma, "While all these numbers and this discussion are helpful in understanding how injustice like some giant vortex is swallowing up anything just and right in its path, the numbers do not adequately portray the suffering, the depravation, that is the awful face of suffering. How to describe what it must feel for an individual on his/her way to a lean-to; a home that is only a place to sleep, that lacks clean water, where one's children play next to raw sewage to see the opulently clothed, drive by in their fancy cars?"

"Emma, thank you for having the soul of a poet, reminding us so passionately," said MLK, "that an absence of justice means that millions of our fellow human beings, whose blood is the same as ours, who want the same thing for their children as do we, endure suffering and deprivation, hour after hour, day after day until they leave this world."

"Maybe it is better for those in Europe and much of North America," said TR, "but the souls we meet from much of the world tell us how bad it is—the inequality, violence, religious hatred—it's all threatening any sense that justice can exist."

"Seeing what the world we once occupied is like now, a place of increasing poverty for the vast majority, increasing wealth for a small minority and remnants of race and class that keep towns like Jackson largely segregated," MLK asked "is there something called justice?" His voice soaring with an old and earthly passion, "Does it even exist?"

"Or perhaps justice still exists," proclaimed, TR, "but it is slowly disappearing into some kind of black hole?

RECIPES

in honor and memory of Emma Lazarus, Dr. Martin Luther king and President Teddy Roosevelt, are at end of Part II of this chapter, page 199.

Chapter VII Part 2

Someone From the Audience answered, 'It's only Science Fiction — Justice with a Terrible Twist'

*"And he waited for Justice, but instead
there was an expanding hole of violence."*
— Isaiah 5:7 [220]

THE THREE OF them had not realized how passionate their discussion had become. Their voices, however, grew louder with every mention of justice, so much so that someone in Mr. Dobbs's audience finally turned around and told them, "Will you three quiet down!"

Then someone said, "Hey you look like a recent picture of President Teddy Roosevelt that was… " he paused.

"… On a recent cover of Time magazine,"[221] another shouted.

"And even with those funky sunglasses, you sir, look like Martin Luther King… "

People were turning around to look, "They do, they do," someone screamed. Another said, "Are you some kind of ghosts?"

And with that all hell broke loose. Ushers were running everywhere. One of them ran up to Mr. Dobbs, who looked totally stunned. Collecting himself, he motioned to the three to come forward. On the stage, they introduced themselves and tried to explain to an unbelieving audience.

"We are souls from the other side, sent to learn about justice in the world we once inhabited. We thought we could remain anonymous, learn what we need to and report to…." TR didn't finish the sentence.

"And then return," MLK continued, "to tell you what has happened to another part of the univ…."

Totally stunned by all this, the audience in the vast hall had gone totally quiet.

"NO," screamed Emma, interrupting MLK, "Not yet, Martin! We don't have permission to tell… ."

Realizing the situation around him could easily break out into total panic, Lou Dobbs decided to intervene and break the tension in the hall by announcing, "As we said earlier, we are now going to our Science Editor, Tim Spivac, to this developing and frightening news bulletin."

It worked. Again the audience went totally quiet, and no one seemed to notice the three surprise mystery visitors quietly take seats at the back of the stage.

Thank you Lou: As many of you listening know, "black holes are among the oddest objects believed to populate the universe. Long sought, they have recently been found lurking in the centers of galaxies, tipping the scales at a million to a billion times the mass of the sun.[222]

Now the SNN monitors not only lit up with collaborating information, but even these inanimate lights seemed to radiate a glowing indignation regarding the injustices that were being portrayed

♦ The world's 358 billionaires are "tipping" the scales with assets exceeding the combined annual incomes of countries with 45 percent of the world's people.[223]

But astronomers have debated for years, Tim Spivac continued to explain, whether "primordial" black holes could still exist, roughly 14 billion years after the big bang. Surprisingly, the answer depends on the number of spatial dimensions in the universe.

In Albert Einstein's theory of general relativity… the universe is understood as having three dimensions of space (plus one of time)… That could change, though, if the universe has more than three spatial dimensions… [224]

Again the SNN monitors were proclaiming in **bold** letters these bullets of injustice.

♦ Of the world's "dimensions" of life sustaining resources, a mere 12 percent of the world's population uses 85 percent of the water.

Physicists Lisa Randall of Harvard and Raman Sundrum of Johns Hopkins University have turned [what they call the] "braneworld" concept into a specific model that they and others are examining as a possible alternative to Einstein's general relativity.[225]

♦ Ethical "relativity" asks where is the justice that of the 6.2 billion people in today's world, nearly 3 billion people live on less than $2 a day and 1.2 billion live on less than $1 per day?

In the Randall-Sundrum braneworld model, the fourth dimension of space changes how gravity operates on small scales, which changes the rate at which small black holes form and evaporate.[226]

♦ Socially and economically our world's "black holes" form in the great disparities of wealth with a minority of the world's population (17%) consuming most of the world's resources (80%).

The upshot is that… primordial black holes… may have been able to survive to today.[227]

♦ The other "upshot" today is that billions of people are surviving with barely the very basic necessities of life, food, water, housing, sanitation, health to sustain them.

…(and) if (these black holes) make up 1 percent of the dark matter in the universe, thousands of tiny black holes may lie within our solar system!… So your neighbors could have a pet black hole, and you might not realize it.[228]

Lou Dobbs, interrupted these dark matters to announce:

On February 2, 2007 ABC News reported:

"At the Dome Restaurant in Bangkok, Thailand, after 10 courses… each diner was presented with a bill for… about $30,000…. One of the event's organizers told the AP '-Yes, it is expensive, but when you look at the whole experience, it's the experience of a lifetime.'"

The lights of the monitors almost seemed as if they were on fire.

♦ Every day, 34,000 children under five die of preventable diseases resulting from hunger or 6 million in a year—their "experience of a lifetime."

And Dr. Tim, continued his analysis: And incredibly we now realize much to our amazement, that in fact one of our neighbors, astronomically speaking, is an evolving black hole.

◆ An analysis of long-term trends shows the distance between the richest and poorest countries as "an evolving black hole" that went from:

5:1 in 1820

11:1 in 1913

44:1 in 1973

72:1 in 1992

"With me," said Dr. Tim, "to explain this possibly frightening event in our galaxy is Dr. William Knowles of NASBH—the National Astronomical Black Holes Society."

◆ Is it not more frightening that a massive black hole of poverty exists in our very world? So that 800 million go to bed hungry every day, and 30,000 to 60,000 die each day from hunger alone... while the world's 500 or so billionaires have assets of 1.9 trillion dollars, a sum greater than the income of the poorest 170 countries in the world?

"Thank you, Tim. Though all of us from the Society wish we did not have to report this incredible astronomical event: We have just learned that ESA's gamma-ray astronomical observatory, known as Integra, has spotted a rare kind of gamma-ray outburst. This vast explosion of energy has allowed astronomers to pinpoint a possible black hole in our very own galaxy." [229]

◆ But in our very own world the true "possible black hole" is an unacceptable "outburst" of inequality. In 2006 the average CEO of a company with at least $1 billion in annual revenue made $10,982,200 or 262 times what the average worker made.

"The outburst was discovered on 17 September 2006 by staff at the Integral Science Data Centre (ISDC), Versoix, Switzerland. Inside the ISDC, astronomers constantly monitor the data coming down from Integral because they know the sky at gamma-ray wavelengths can be a swiftly changing place."

◆ The "changing place" for the average employee and CEO is an "outburst" of continuing inequality, as the average worker who earned $41,861 in 2005 made about $400 less last year than what the average large company CEO made in one day. Nevertheless between 2000 and 2005, median CEO pay rose 84% to $605 million on an inflation-adjusted basis. [230]

It was during one of the first of these observations that astronomers saw the outburst take place. An unexpected event of this kind is known as a "target of opportunity"

♦ "Target of opportunity," for whom? For the "median worker (who saw his) pay during the same period fall an estimated 0.3 percent to $33,852?

Again, Mr. Dobbs: The meal at the Dome restaurant in Bangkok, according to Britain's Guardian newspaper...included about $200,000 of some of the finest wines in the world, including rare Rothschild estate wines.

♦ The cost of providing basic health care and nutrition for all in the world would be less than is spent in Europe and the US on pet food.

It should be noted that we have only bulleted universal justice and injustice issues—hunger, etc. There are thousands of individual examples of injustice, especially in countries that lack honest and fair judicial systems. But in the U.S. as well there are thousands of heart-wrenching examples of injustice.

In these systems, the gravity of the black hole is ripping the sun-like star to pieces. As the doomed star orbits the black hole, it lays down its gas in a disc, know as an accretion disc, surrounding the black hole. Occasionally, this accretion disc becomes unstable and collapses onto the black hole, causing the kind of outburst that Integral witnessed.

♦ Those who watched ABC's 60 Minutes of 11 February 2007 "witnessed" an "unstable," psychotic individual; Timothy Souders die in a Michigan Jail. One of thousands of very emotionally ill individuals who are confined to prison following the Reagan administration's decision to close hospitals for the emotionally ill, Souders had been held in restraints for three consecutive days. He "collapsed" and died in "the black hole" of his cell a victim of dehydration.

President Roosevelt and the others had been quiet during the astronomer's announcement and the above bullets of injustice. But watching them, it was obvious that they were becoming increasingly agitated and were quietly disagreeing about something.

"We must tell them now. They have a right to know," I overheard MLK say to the others.

"No," said Emma. "We don't have permission to reveal this to them. We did not learn of these black holes, no one told us about them until we got to the other side."

TR's soul once again took on that reddish hue as it had earlier, "And Emma you are correct about us," his voice rising, "but maybe if they know... ,"

MLK interrupted him. "... Perhaps there will be fewer black holes and it won't happen to earth and its sun, as it just happened to... . "

"But... ,"

She was too late. MLK, then rose, came to the front of the stage to where Mr. Dobbs had been speaking and said very slowly, "You here in Mr. Dobbs's audience and those listening everywhere, those bullets of statistics and information you have seen on the monitors regarding injustice are ascending into space as we speak, like the gasses that are contributing to global warming."

TR joined MLK and added, "Perhaps you recently heard on your Public Broadcasting Station what is being referred to as 'the World Wide Mind,' which involves individuals having the ability to feel what others feel, a kind of world wide empathy.[231] "The SNN report you just heard is correct about developing black holes in the universe, but the 'gamma ray outbursts' they referred to are the 'accretion' discs which become 'unstable and collapse onto the black hole, causing the kind of outburst that Integral witnessed.'

"And the reason why the accretion discs collapse is because they are similar to 'the Randall-Sundrum braneworld model, the fourth dimension of space [which] changes how gravity operates,' causing black holes to form and evaporate."

"What you may have heard us disagreeing about, and what Emma didn't want us to reveal to you because you will not want to accept this, is that these black holes occur because injustice, the result of a lack of compassion and empathy for others, equals the 4th dimension that you just heard the SNN science editor refer to.

"What we are able to see, from our perspective on the other side, is that the energy of selfishness, greed, an absence of feelings for anyone except oneself or his/her corporate interests eventually accumulates into 'unstable' matter. Eventually this matter 'collapses into a black hole' so intense that it consumes all other forms of pro-social behavior or ethical character attributes that are necessary to sustain life."

"All right, you've told them," sighed Emma, who continued, "And what that astronomical observatory known as Integra spotted was a 4th dimension back hole—what they referred to as an 'outburst.'"

"Indeed," said MLK. "'Outbursts' of humanity's injustice."

"But how does it happen?" screamed someone from Mr. Dodds's audience.

Emma continued, "Imagine millions of pieces of matter in space in the shape of a giant clock. This 4th dimension is different from other life dimensions because over eons of time like a huge clock or pinwheel, it turns ever more quickly until it moves faster and faster resembling a funnel. Fed by humanity's injustices it eventually becomes a black hole sucking up every other thing nearby it into its abyss."

"That seems to be what happened to the planet closest to the nearby solar system that Integral witnessed," said TR. "On our side of life we are in contact with souls who have told us, that the once habitable planets of their solar system became so concentrated with greed and injustice that all of the planet's energy turned in on itself, like a huge drain... and apparently the only thing left of that solar system... is... silence."

Someone from Lou's audience shouted. "Does that mean such an "outburst" could envelop and consume our own solar system?"

"We're not exactly sure," answered Emma. "But evidently just as with the solar warming that is endangering the planet Earth, the world can only take so much pollution before it has to react. So in the 4th dimension the universe can only take so much injustice before it has to react."

"Think of all the bullets of injustice that you saw today on Mr. Dobbs's monitors," said MLK. "One after another like rockets going off, they leave us at the speed of light and eventually begin to form a vortex. Of course, we're referring to an astronomical phenomenon that takes place over millions of years. But slowly its light grows dimmer and dimmer until in time, accelerating faster and faster, it obliterates all other forms of matter until it becomes a black hole and… and… ."

It was obvious to everyone who saw him that MLK was having a difficult time laying out this tragic scenario. TR picked up where MLK had left off.

"…And because we are talking about such vast distances, we don't see the black hole disappear until its light is gone. But if you were out in space looking back at what is happening in our 4th dimension, you would see that huge pinwheel of injustice slowly forming a vortex at this very moment. And if it continues, it will accelerate until… from out there our universe of being will disappear in our own black hole… ."

Then Lou Dobbs sighed, and said in a tone very far removed from his usual pomposity, "Injustice consuming justice until we are no more."

Once again, the audience grew terribly silent.

TR said "Let's hope not,"

"Perhaps our earthly descendants," said Emma, "will learn and behave so that social, equal and economic justice will apply equally to everyone, which is why we are commanded, '*tsedek tsedek,* justice, justice shall you pursue.'[232] 'Justice' is repeated twice, so that we will 'pursue' its mandate for everyone."

"Otherwise, the planet Earth and its inhabitants are in grave peril," the three of them said in unison.

And with the word "Earth," President Teddy Roosevelt, Rev., Martin Luther King and the poet Emma Lazarus disappeared to the other side—where justice is inclusive and eternal.

RECIPES

Martin Luther King, Jr. and **President Roosevelt** both enjoyed Southern Fried Chicken.

But first a story about ML King, told to me by Rev. Fred Shuttlesworth.

In 1957 Rev. Fred Shuttlesworth, with Reverends Martin Luther King, Jr., Ralph Abernathy and Joseph Lowery founded the Southern Christian Leadership Conference (SCLC). Its purpose was to fight segregation and other forms of racism, with a commitment to non-violence.

A fearless civil rights activist, Rev. Shuttlesworth survived two attempts on his life in 1957, the bombing of his house and being beaten up by KKK members. His wife was also stabbed.

Rev. Shuttlesworth was also known for not being shy in asking King to take a more active role in leading the fight against segregation. He warned that history would not look kindly on those who gave "flowery speeches" but did not act on them. Nevertheless, he was a close friend of MLK, and I was honored and delighted to get from him the following story about his close associate.

In March 2006, at 84, Rev Shuttlesworth retired as the minister of his church in Cincinnati, where he continues to live.

Seven months later, Rev. Shuttlesworth and I talked by phone. After a couple of minutes reminiscing about the Freedom Rides, he said to me, "You know, rabbi, I do have a story about Martin for you," and he introduced the story by saying, "Martin and Ralph [Rev. Abernathy] were terrific eaters and they both liked their chicken and steak."

"Rabbi, here's the story:

In '62 we, the SCLC Board, were having a board meeting at the AG Gaston Motel in Birmingham to discuss the upcoming demonstration in Washington, when Martin got a call from President Kennedy. They were having an animated discussion, evidently about the demonstration, and I remember Martin looking at his arm and saying, "Mr. President, segregation is like a boil and you see if you don't excise it and let it get some light and air it will only get worse. That's why a nonviolent demonstration is necessary."[233]

At that point Martin looked up and saw Ralph heading for the kitchen in our suite. "Excuse me, Mr. President," Martin said, as he put the phone down, and whispered to Abernathy, "Ralph bring me back some chicken and a piece of bread too," Then he said to me, "Fred, isn't that some great bread?"

I pointed to the phone and whispered: "Martin, the President, you were talking to the President."

"Of course, of course," he said just before he picked up the phone. Then I heard him say, "Sorry for the interruption. Mr. President, it takes nonviolent action to bring about creative tension to make people aware of what is wrong in the community.

"Oh yes, Martin liked eating," Fred said with a laugh, "almost as much as he enjoyed talking to the President of the United States."[234]

Chicken aside, Dr. King's phone call may have helped turn the President around. In MLK's autobiography, we learn, "The President at first publicly worried about the wisdom of such a project... [but] the spirit behind the ensuing march caused him to [have]...a handsome new interest... in seeing the march take place."[235]

In July 2003, Paschal's, the diner in Atlanta "where Martin Luther King was a regular, served its final meals."[236] While the then owner, James Paschal, was unwilling to share the chicken recipe that MLK enjoyed at his restaurant, his office manager said to me the recipe included, "flour, salt and pepper, and lots of love."

[237]Our recipe includes the probable missing ingredient Mr. Pacahal did not want to reveal: buttermilk. And, we have added some garlic.

Dr. King was born January 15, 1929

For a Baptist grace in honor and memory of ML King, and his incredible commitment to equal justice, see page 238.

Fried Chicken in honor and memory of President Teddy Roosevelt and Dr. Martin Luther King.[238]

GARLIC FRIED CHICKEN

Serves 4–6

Ingredients:
1–2 ½ lb. chicken (fryer)
1 egg, well beaten
1 pinch baking powder
2 tbsp. or to taste garlic, pureed
2 tbsp. olive oil
1 c. buttermilk
Salt and pepper to taste
Seasoned flour

Directions:
Mix egg, baking powder, garlic, olive oil and buttermilk in a container large enough to hold chicken in a single layer, or in a plastic bag with a tight closure.

Cut chicken into serving pieces, salt and pepper it, and soak it several hours (preferably overnight) in the egg mixture.

Heat shortening or oil on low heat until oil is very hot.

Put seasoned flour into a plastic bag, add chicken pieces and shake to coat, or on a shallow plate and roll the chicken pieces in the seasoned flour.

Heat oil in a large, deep frying pan and fry the chicken pieces on low heat for 10–15 minutes, turn pieces over and fry another 10–15 minutes until brown.

Regarding his taste in food, President **Teddy Roosevelt** wrote, "Our menus are a legacy from my Georgian mother. She taught us to have rice twice a day and hominy every morning for breakfast, and we group simple meats around it." [239]

President Roosevelt was born October 10, 1858.

For an Episcopal grace in honor and memory of Theodore Roosevelt's passion for economic justice, see page 241.

CRANBERRY NUT RICE

Serves 6.

Ingredients:

1 ½ c. long grain brown Jasmine or Basmati rice

1/3 c. chopped parsley

½ tsp. salt

2 tbsp. olive oil

¼ c. dried cranberries

½ c. pine nuts

1 tsp. garlic powder

Directions:

Cook rice until tender. Add salt and garlic powder and mix well. Add olive oil, nuts and cranberries and mix well.

Alice Roosevelt Longworth recalled that all the Roosevelt children took after their father in his penchant for sweets. Cookies, such as vanilla wafers and sand tarts "were a Roosevelt weakness." [240]

In honor and memory of President Roosevelt, who as a New Yorker may have tasted mandebrot or biscotti, but assuredly not mine:

RABBI'S CHOCOLATE MANDELBROT

Makes about 4 dozen.

Ingredients:

3 ¾ c. all purpose flour

1 ¼ c. wheat flour

2 ½ tsp. baking powder. Sift all dry ingredients together to remove lumps

½ c. plus 2 tbsp. Hershey's cocoa

1 ¼ c. sugar

1 ½ tbsp. Cinnamon

¼ tsp. salt.

¼ c. strong coffee, or whisky,

½ c. plus one tbsp. vegetable oil,

4 large eggs

2 ½ tbsp. vanilla

1 round Mexican chocolate (Ibarra or Abuela brand)

1/3 c. chocolate chips

1/3 c. almond slivers or currents (optional)

Directions:

Mix dry ingredients well.

Slowly add wet ingredients to dry and mix well until dough is tight but moist. If too dry, add a little more liquid.

Pre-heat oven to 350 F. and slightly oil two 12x18" baking pans.

On a floured surface roll out dough into one long strip about 3" x 30." Cut the strip in half and roll out each half pastry to about 5" wide.

Place the strips on the baking pans and sprinkle the half of the strips closest to you with the almond and chocolate mixture, pressing it into the dough. Then fold the other half over the part with the mixture and firmly press down the edge for a good seal.

Bake on top rack of oven at 350 F. for 30 minutes or until brown, remove from oven. While the pastry is still hot use a cleaver to cut pastry into ¾ inch wide slices. Slightly separate them, and return to the oven to bake for another 25 minutes.

Emma Lazarus was born July 22nd, 1849.

A Jewish blessing for food may be found on page 239.

Rellenos or *reynadas,* meat or vegetable stuffed vegetables, are especially popular in the Jewish Sephardic tradition from which Emma Lazarus came. They can be served as a main course, with a lemon based sauce, or as a side dish.

Reynadas de pipirushksas
STUFFED PEPPERS WITH LEMON SAUCE

Ingredients for the filling:

¼ c. olive oil

2–3 onions, chopped

3 garlic cloves, minced

¼ c. finely chopped red pepper

2 tbsp. chopped, fresh parsley

1 tsp. salt

1 tsp. allspice and black pepper

1 ½ tsp. cinnamon

½ c. pine nuts or chopped walnuts, toasted

½ c. currants or raisins, chopped

1 lb. ground lamb or meat of your choice

¾ c. white rice

2 Tbls. soy sauce

Directions for the filling:

In a large pan sauté the onions in the olive oil. Add the garlic, red pepper, parsley, the other spices, the nuts and currants or raisins. Sauté for 2–4 more minutes. Add the meat and the soy sauce, mixing the ingredients until the meat is done and blended all together, about 6 minutes.

Add the rice and water, and cook for about 5 minutes.

Vegetables:

About 4 pounds of favorite large vegetable to stuff: tomatoes, egg plant, red and green bell peppers or zucchini. (A mix of the vegetables makes a beautiful plate at the end).

Following is the directions for *reynadas de pipirushksas*, stuffed peppers, but the concept is the same for the other vegetables.

Directions:

Preheat the oven to 350 F.

Cut off the top of the peppers and remove the seeds. Boil the pepper shells for 5 minutes and drain, or if you prefer a more crisp pepper do not boil. them.

Stuff the filling into the peppers, being careful not to fill all the way to the top, as the rice will continue to expand.

LEMON SAUCE

Ingredients
1 c. of your favorite stock
2–3 eggs or egg yolks
Juice of 2 small lemons, 4–5 Tbsp.
3-4 Tbls sugar
1/4 tsp. nutmeg
1/8 tsp. paprika

Directions:
Bring the stock to a simmer in a saucepan or in a microwave-safe dish in the microwave.

Beat the eggs or yolks with the lemon juice, the sugar and the nutmeg until frothy. Slowly whisk in a little of the hot stock, and then stir the eggs into the rest of the stock. Heat the mixture in the microwave or in a saucepan until slightly thickened. Spoon the hot mixture over the stuffed peppers. Sprinkle with the paprika.

VIII

Empathy
The Indian Hospital Room

If you want something really important to be done,
you must not merely satisfy the reason; you must move the heart also.
— Mahatma Gandhi

EVERYONE WAS RUNNING, as if the hospital were on fire. No one except Mother Teresa seemed to know where they were running to or from. A stranger approached me and asked, "Is there an emergency, a code blue? Did someone die?"

"Ask her," I said, pointing to a frail looking, grey haired woman whose face radiated great strength and contentment.

"You mean the woman with the white and blue sari?" he asked. "Isn't that Mother Teresa?"

I nodded. The stranger approached her. They exchanged greetings, and I heard her say, "Yes, there is death everywhere in Calcutta but here," she smiled and pointed to Room 204. "See there, a mother is giving birth to her first child. We are worried because she has been in labor for such a long time."

"Do you know her name?" the man asked.

"No, she is another stranger," Mother Teresa answered. "This is the hospital of strangers. We are all strangers here looking for those who need our love."

"But how can that be? This is a hospital. Surely the doctors, the nurses, the cafeteria staff, and the others who work here must know one another?"

"In the beginning," Mother Teresa explained, "when we start our required tasks, we are strangers, even to each other. Then from a certain room we hear someone scream or a doctor telling a patient's wife, 'I'm sorry we did what we could.' Or we see a child's leg bleeding so profusely from a dog bite that it might require being amputated.

"Then we remember the last time we felt our own pain, saw our own blood or that of a loved one. We identify with those who are suffering around us, and we are no longer strangers, either to them or ourselves."

There was more commotion, running and loud voices. Turning toward Room 202, we heard horrible screams. Someone said, "She must be in terrible pain."

What I have just described, I was not alone in observing. Grey hair and slight of build, the Nobel Prize recipient Elie Wiesel, himself no stranger to strangers, had agreed to meet me, Mother Teresa and one other very empathic soul from the other side to discuss the nature of empathy.

This would not be the first time Mother Teresa and Elie Wiesel had met, but it was my first encounter with these two incredible individuals. I was almost giddy with excitement at seeing them together, a feeling one Eileen Egan felt as well when she described the two of them, in 1971, at a symposium in Boston: "Wiesel's presence as a witness to man's death-dealing powers, in the same room with Mother Teresa's witness to life's inviolable sacredness and the duty to nurture it, formed the most poignantly dramatic conjunction of the symposium."[241]

One a devout Christian, the other a humanitarian, storyteller and Jew who is never afraid to question God's goodness; both of them exhibit a profound and similar quality—the ability to feel the suffering of others.

Room 202 had been quiet for a while. Then the screams began again. There was a pause. Suddenly we heard voices and a woman's laughter, and someone proclaimed "It's a girl!"

In the meantime as we were waiting for the other empathic soul to arrive, I asked, "Elie, Mother Teresa, how does suffering so touch you that it evokes a compassionate response toward others?

Mother Teresa's answered:

When I pick up a person from the street, hungry, I give him a plate of rice, a piece of bread, I have (am) satisfied, I have removed that hunger. But a person that is shut out, that feels unwanted, unloved, terrified, the person… that has been thrown out from society—that poverty is so hurtable [sic.] and I find it very difficult. To be able to do this, our lives have to be woven with Christ to be able to understand, to be able to share. Because there is so much suffering—and I feel that the passion of Christ is being relived all over again—and we are to share that passion, to share the suffering of people.[242]

Wiesel and I, borne out of our historical sensitivity toward those who had persecuted our people in "Christ's name," listened intently to how Mother felt her Lord not in the destruction of others, but as one who reached out to their suffering.

"Dear Mother Teresa," Wiesel's whole body leaned toward her as if he wanted to touch her soul, "listening to you speak such beautiful words reminds me how much I have changed, but also remain the same. I know you have visited Buchenwald. So, I trust you will understand.

"Once in 1954, it seems so long ago now, I listened to a devout Roman Catholic, a Nobel laureate for literature, Francois Mauriac, speak similarly as did you. My emotional wounds from Auschwitz were still burning in me; and I lashed out at Mauriac, my anger exposed as when ash falls from a red hot piece of coal. 'You speak of Christ. Christians love to speak of him. The passion of Christ, the agony of Christ, the death of Christ. In your religion, that is all you speak of. Well, I want you to know that ten years ago, not very far from here, I knew Jewish children every one of whom suffered a thousand times more, six million times more than Christ on the cross. And we don't speak about them. Can you understand that, sir? We don't speak of them.'[243]

"And you know what," Wiesel continued, "Mauriac's face went pale. At first he said nothing. And then he began to weep, looking at me, engulfed in grief.[244] And Mother, though it took years for the burning coals to cool, eventually I came to understand what Mauriac's Christ meant for him and what Christ means to you."

As much as these two souls, one from the other side, one from here could, they were touching and being touched by each other's identification with the other's experience.

Wiesel continued, "Mother, even though thanks to Mauriac's understanding and encouragement, I began to 'speak' and write my feelings of the Holocaust, never shall I forget those flames which consumed my faith forever—those moments which murdered my God and my soul and turned my dreams to dust.[246]

"True, unlike some I never accepted the idea that 'God is dead.' Instead, because of the Holocaust I have challenged my readers and myself to live in a world with God, standing against evil, not allowing God or humanity to ignore suffering, or remain indifferent to the stranger."

It was not difficult to see how touched Mother was by Wiesel's words. She simply said, "Elie, you and I born of the same century of grief have both seen such suffering—you a Jew, I a Christian. What we saw and absorbed cannot be separated from our destiny."

The next morning the three of us returned to the hospital to continue our discussion. Mother Teresa asked me how I had slept the night in an Indian hard bed.

"Thanks for asking. Truthfully, I did not sleep well, but not because of the bed. I couldn't stop thinking that something must have prevented Etty, one of my favorite people in the whole world, from coming yesterday. But I am positive she will join us today. Mother," I continued, "have you heard of Etty Hillesum?"

"I think so. Didn't she have something to do with Anne Frank?"

"There are similarities. Etty like Anne Frank lived in Amsterdam, and both started writing their diaries around the same time—July 1942—separated from each other only by a few miles. They both died at Auschwitz, and both exposed their beautiful souls so that the millions who read them had a different view of what matters in life.

"But Etty was not hidden, like Ann Frank. In fact," Elie added, "she refused to hide. She was

It seems clear that there are qualitative as well as quantitative differences... in the way people react emotionally when confronted with others in distress... [However] there is clear evidence that... to the degree we take the perspective of the other, we are likely to experience a second, more other-oriented emotion; this emotion has been labeled empathy.[245]

also twenty-nine when she wrote her diaries and letters, which have been published as *An Interrupted Life*. Her work reveals the passion, compassion, intellect and spirituality of a mature woman, suffering with dignity in the exposed hellhole of life under the Nazis.

"As one who has written more than 40 novels, plays and essays many having to do with the Holocaust," Elie continued, "I have to agree with one of the literary reviews of her writing as I remember it, that hers is 'one of the greatest testimonies to personal potential and spiritual resource that will emerge from the 20th century.'"

No sooner had Wiesel spoken those words, when a pretty young woman, wearing a blue turban, with a cigarette in the corner of her mouth, suddenly appeared.

"I am the late Etty Hillesum, and I am sorry to be so late," she said with a wry smile. "Yesterday there was a great number of strangers who arrived on our side, and I am in charge of helping them acclimatize to their new environment." Then her smile broadened, as if amused with her own recall of what she was about to say. "I once asked those in charge of souls and administration why me? 'Etty,' they answered, 'who better than you? When you came to us, everyone concerned with welcoming the new arrivals remembered that you once wrote, "strangely I heard a stranger say: 'I am with you.'"'" [247]

Fascinated by the way she had introduced herself, Elie and Mother Teresa finally managed to say, "Welcome, Etty."

"No," I interjected, "at least for me, 'welcome' is insufficient to express the joy I feel in finally meeting, even with a cigarette, the woman I have loved ever since she broke into my heart."

"It's not lit, is it?" she asked with a giggle. "You know in my day smoking was quite fashionable, particularly for a woman nonconformist, bordering on rebellion like me."

"Do souls really smoke?" Elie asked quite incredulously.

"Not where I've just come from. In fact," her smile turned upward just enough to look slightly mischievous, "as much as I was intrigued by the invitation to come and meet, the rabbi, Elie and you, Mother Teresa, I couldn't wait to find a cigarette. But now that I have one, other than rather enjoying the way I remember myself in Europe, it has lost its appeal.

"'Broke into my heart,' you said a second ago, my dear Rabbi; I so wish I could have found a way before now to tell you how grateful I am for your love and so many others. When I thrust my manuscript into the hands of my friend Maria, just before my parents, brother and I were pushed onto that horrible transport, I could only fantasize a dream that my diary would survive, let alone finally be published."

Etty's countenance then took on a rapturous glow that radiated such beauty and sincerity that I blurted out, in the way that one says words to others but aim them to one whom you especially love, "Now you see why I love her so."

And with barely the hint of a blush, she continued, "As Elie knows only too well, every victim of the Holocaust survived as long as possible, always with the hope that our stories will survive."

"Oh Etty, remember you wrote that very thought?" I asked, rhetorically.

> And I shall wield this slender fountain pen as if it were a hammer and my words will have to be so many hammer-strokes with which to beat out the story of our fate and of a piece of history as it is and never was before... Still, a few people must survive if only to be the chroniclers of this age. I would very much like to become one of their number.[248]

"Yes, I remember those words as if they were hammered out of me yesterday." Then, with a great deal more emotion than we might imagine of real souls, she continued, trying not to weep, "To know that my words have been translated around the world, studied and appreciated... I can't begin to describe... what I feel. So yes, while the cigarette to make a bad pun was a draw, I really came to say *dank u*, thank you, thank you, for remembering me."

"And Etty, when we enjoy some *Erwtensoep*—pea-soup in your honor, because of a recipe sent to me from a lovely young lady from Holland whom I recently met, you will be sustained once again. She said to me, just what a difference you have made: 'I think she would have been very pleased that her diary is sold in so many countries and that she and her philosophy live on and help other people to cope with difficult situations.'[249]

"And my Dutch friend's comment is especially meaningful to me because she had not read the diary until I told her how happy it would make me, if she read it."

"Etty, last night Mother and I at the rabbi's prompting shared a few thoughts about God. And now the beautiful words you just spoke as a fellow chronicler," Elie said, "prompt me to ask you half a century after you wrote them, do you agree with me that we Jews "are God's memory and the heart of mankind... and to be a Jew means to remember'? I ask because, you were such a universal soul, some even questioned your Jewishness."

"Elie, thanks for asking. Perhaps I was seen that way because, yes, I admit sometimes I didn't act or pray like a Jew. I didn't know how. I just prayed. And one time, probably there were others, when I still had my own room in Amsterdam, I even fell on my knees in gratitude to God. I remember," Etty looked over towards Mother, "thinking 'This is very Catholic.' But, Elie most of the time as I wrote, 'I never pray for myself, always for others.' That's Jewish isn't it?" she looked inquiring at Elie and me.

"Of course," I said.

"Praying to God for something for yourself has always struck me," she continued, "as being too childish for words. Instead one should pray that another should have enough strength to shoulder his burden. If you do that, you lend him some of your own strength.[250]

"Admittedly my prayers were very personal, in my own space, and perhaps that is why some Jews find them, well... different. But then, Elie when things grew much worse, I felt myself all the more 'glad to be a Jewess,' and all the more aware of my prayers.

> Ours is a common destiny, and that is something we must not forget. A very hard day. [in Nazi occupied Amsterdam] But I keep finding myself in prayer. And that is something I shall always be able to do, even in the smallest space: Pray. And that part of our common destiny which I must shoulder myself, I strap tightly and firmly to my back, it becomes part of me, as I walk through the Amsterdam streets even now.[251]

"So yes, Elie, I totally agree with you about us being 'God's memory,' though it would never have occurred to me to write as did you that we Jews are 'the heart of mankind.'"

"Etty, you know what I find so commendable is that you chronicled your thoughts and feelings while in the very midst of hell, right up to the end. I admire you for that, because as you may know I not only did not write in the camps, but also after I survived I vowed that I would not write anything about it for 10 years."

"You are too gracious," she responded, "Each of us as with death and dying deals with the Holocaust and suffering in our own unique way."

"Etty, I wonder if that is why," said Mother, "your prayer is so universal. But you could never even dream, let alone write as did Elie that God must be in 'every thought, in every tear, in every joy, and in evil. And it's up to us to redeem that evil.'"

"Yes Mother I would like to think that had I survived on earth, my universal prayers would have spread their wings, would have flown as a messenger for a redemptive God to humanity, as have yours and Elie's. But you two have been so dedicated to humanity it's hard to believe that I... "

But Mother did not let her finish. "Etty, I once said, 'Prayer does not demand that we interrupt our work, but that we continue working as if it were a prayer.'[252]" Then she looked at Elie and with a deep sigh said, "Somehow, God allowed you and me to continue to work our prayers."

"Now may I ask a question, Mother. Why did you suggest to the rabbi that we meet here in this Indian hospital to discuss empathy? I could have gotten my cigarette anywhere back here on Earth," she laughed.

"The rabbi asked me that, too," replied Mother. "Perhaps I too just wanted to see again where I grew up, became a real person... "

"Some would say where you became a saint," interjected Elie.

Acknowledging his remark with a slight smile, she continued, "but more than that I was sure the rabbi invited me," she looked at me, "because he knows that the source of empathy is found not just in memory itself, but in our ability to not repress our suffering. And Etty, other than that terrible place where you died and Elie survived, there is hardly a more real place for remembering pain and suffering than what goes on here in this hospital in the middle of Calcutta where so much anguish exists, and where so much of it is ignored."

"Mother, your answer is not only true, but beautiful, because it says so much about you and this place," said Elie. "In the early '50s, I visited India, eager to learn something about life from this great and old culture, its mystic appeal. But to be honest, I returned from India even more Jewish than before.[253] I was disheartened by the caste system and the appalling misery of the poor on the streets, especially in Calcutta. But you, Teresa, you came, remained and did exactly what you taught the Sisters of your Order, 'I ask you one thing: Do not tire of giving, but do not give your leftovers. Give until it hurts, until you feel the pain.'"[254]

"Yes, those are the words and the behavior of a saint," concluded Elie.

"Oh my, let's not talk of me," Teresa said somewhat dismissively, but it was clear by her look that she appreciated his accolade.

"Fine, but I need to say one more thing related to what I shared with you and the rabbi last night. Eventually I came to appreciate what Mauriac's Christ meant for him and what Christ means to you, because I came to understand that Christians and Jews empathize differently."

"What do you mean?" Mother Teresa asked.

"Elie," I said, "since my doctoral dissertation is on what I call empathy ethics, do you mind if I attempt an answer?"

"Please do,"

"Mother, your empathy with the suffering of Jesus moves, even inspires, you to identify with the suffering of others, in love. The various empathy-based ethical commandments of Exodus, Leviticus and Deuteronomy were forged out of our own suffering as Hebrew slaves in Egypt, and pounded out in the anvil of our history as Jews in Medieval Europe.

"So, for example, even though we were present in Spain some three to four hundred years before Christianity arrived, we were treated as strangers to be severely discriminated against by the Visigoth Christian Spanish rulers, some three hundred years later.

Judaism insists, therefore, that we not be allowed to forget. The verb z'chor, remember, appears 169 times... in the Tanach—Bible. Through our memories come the emotional energy that we channel into our 'trait empathy' and our empathic imagination, moving us to feel the suffering of others and the desire to help them. In Judaism this energy of memory is what also fuels many of the ethical injunctions, chief among them are these most important empathy based commandments: [255]

'You shall remember that you were slaves in Egypt... therefore I enjoin this commandment (regarding the compassionate treatment of slaves and the needy) upon you this day. (Deuteronomy 15:15)

(And) 'When a stranger resides with you in your land, you shall not wrong him. The stranger who resides with you shall be to you as one of your citizens; you shall love him as yourself, for you were strangers in the land of Egypt. I am the Lord your God.' (Lev. 19:34)

"Thus, the catalyst for our empathy to treat the stranger lovingly is in our hearts—our feelings—based on the memory of our own suffering in Egypt:

You shall not oppress a stranger, for you know the heart—the feelings—of the stranger, having yourselves been strangers in the land of Egypt. (Ex.23:9)

"So, Mother, both the Christian and Jewish forms of empathy elicit the religious attributes of love and righteous behavior, but are inspired by our unique individual history and understanding of God."

"Elie, do you agree?"

"Not only do I agree, the connection between empathy, the stranger and the needy is also at the very heart of our Passover celebration—the *seder*."

"Yes, and Elie, you express that relationship beautifully in the commentary you wrote for the Passover Haggadah: 'The larger piece of the *matzah* represents *lachma anya*, the bread of the poor. It is meant to remind us of the hungry. At that moment, we should identify with those who are afraid to eat their bread, and always leave something for later.'"[256]

"However, the role of the stranger in Jewish life," continued Elie, "is not only based on, as you call them, rabbi, 'empathy ethics'; the ethical treatment of the hungry or stranger has a practical implication for community. As I have written elsewhere, 'To live without strangers could result in an impoverished system; to live only amongst ourselves, constantly in-breeding, never facing an outsider to make us question again and again our certainties and rules, would inevitably lead to atrophy.

The experience of encountering a stranger—like that of suffering—is important and creative.'"[257]

"I am very appreciative to you both," interjected Etty, "because while I died as a Jew, there was so much I did not know about my religion, including these links between suffering, righteousness, empathy and love."

"Speaking of love," Elie glanced at me and then Etty, "I have never heard a married rabbi talk so openly about his love of another woman. It almost sounds inappropriately passionate?"

"Elie, I am grateful for your comment. I once began a High Holiday sermon, 'You my congregation need to know,' with my wife seated in the sanctuary, 'I love another woman,' I paused to extend the drama, "her name is Etty Hillesum.'"

Having shared that event, I looked at Etty and replied, "I meant I love your soul, Etty, especially the empathy you and Elie feel for the stranger—even the supposed enemy. But yes, Elie, I admit there is a special passion I feel for Etty, as if she and I are soul mates, so that although I could never hold her in my arms, I feel her spirit as one with mine."

"I remain incredibly touched by your kindness and love," Etty said quietly.

I wanted to get up and kiss her right then, but imagining that souls express love non-physically, I contained myself and said, "Let me give you an example of your empathy and why your soul, as with all character, remains a part of every soul.

"Etty, remember the incident when you wrote, '… a large group of us were crowded into Gestapo hall'… with 'the disgruntled young Gestapo officer'?

"In Amsterdam, or in the camp?" she asked, referring to Westerbork where she and her family were imprisoned before she boarded the transport to Auschwitz.

"In Amsterdam. You wrote, 'How rash to assert that man shapes his own destiny. All he can do is determine his inner responses. You cannot know another's inner life from his circumstances. To know that you must know his dreams, his relationships, his moods, his disappointments, his sickness and his death.'"[258]

"I remember one officer who was especially obnoxious, but the specifics have faded."

"You said of him:

He kept looking for pretexts to shout... 'Take your hands out of your pockets... and so on....' When it was my turn to stand in front of his desk, he bawled at me, '... get the hell out of here,' his face saying 'I'll deal with you later.' And that was presumably meant to scare me to death....[259]

"And were you not scared?" Mother asked.

"In fact, Etty you answered, as if Mother were there asking,

I am not easily frightened. Not because I am brave but because I know that I am dealing with human beings and that I must try as hard as I can to understand everything that anyone ever does. And that was the real import of this morning: Not that [he] yelled at me, but I felt no indignation, rather a real compassion, and would have liked to ask, 'Did you have a very unhappy childhood, has your girlfriend let you down?[260]

"You behaved as if you were 'dealing with human beings'?" Mother asked.

"Perhaps your ability to believe that saved you emotionally," added Elie.

"Yes," she replied, "perhaps, but... I also wrote: 'Something else about this morning: The perception very strongly borne in, that despite all the suffering and injustice I cannot hate others.'"[261]

"Even toward the end, before you boarded the transport?" inquired Elie.

"In resisting hatred, Mother, you and I share a love—your love for your Jesus—me for my neighbor."

Last night during yet another hard struggle not to be overwhelmed with pity for my parents, which would paralyze me completely if I succumbed, I told myself it must be wrong to be so overcome with grief and concern for one's own family that one has little thought and love left over for one's neighbour.[262]

"Oh, yes, I remember as if it were yesterday when in 1928 I left my home, mother, sister and brother. We lived for each other and we made every effort to make one another happy, and it was only my love of God that allowed me to tear myself away from them. In fact," Mother continued, "I once wrote, 'If you are glad at the thought that God may be calling you to serve him and your neighbor, this may be the best proof of your vocation. A deep joy is like the compass which points out the proper direction for your life. One should follow this, even when one is venturing upon a difficult path.'"[263]

"And so it was, when I departed Skopje for Calcutta it was not only a tearful farewell, I would never see my family again."

"I think" said Etie, "like Mother's 'direction' for her 'life,' to answer your question, Elie, even though it became harder and harder not to hate, I managed to keep hatred out of reach by embracing my neighbors.

"I saw more and more that love for all our neighbours, for everyone made in God's image, must take pride of place over love for one's nearest and dearest."[264]

"But Elie, as you also suggest in your writing, what was increasingly difficult for me, as more trains seemed to leave everyday was to remain without anger at the injustice of it all. I wrote:

I see a father, ready to depart, blessing his wife and child and being blessed in turn by an old rabbi with a snow-white beard and the profile of a fiery prophet. I can see... ah, I can't begin to describe it all... Suddenly there are a lot of green-uniformed men swarming over the asphalt... Knapsacks and guns over their shoulders. I study their faces. I try to look at them without prejudice. [265]

"I also used to get angry sometimes, when I saw waste, when the things that were wasted were things that could have saved people from dying," interjected Mother. "But the suffering I witnessed and tried to alleviate all of my life," continued Mother, "was the result of indifference, the opposite of love, not hatred. So I could only answer such apathy with love and be strengthened by the love that was given back to me.

"I understand the suffering," interjected Elie, "could you give us an example of the love?"

"Once, there was a man we picked up from the gutter, half-eaten by worms:

> And after we had brought him to the home, he only said, 'I have lived like an animal in the street, but am going to die as an angel, loved and cared for.' Then after we had removed all the worms from this body, all he said—with a big smile—was: 'Sister, I am going home to God.' And he died. It was so wonderful to see the greatness of that man, who could speak like that without blaming anybody, without comparing anything.[266]

"Mother, I once read in a 1989 *Time* interview that you picked up around 54,000 people. That was a lot of love," I said.

"But Elie and Etty, the both of you had to construct your own love, like a tower of compassion and peace out of your own personal circumstance, and I can't imagine being able to do that in a place of such monstrous evil."

"Mother, it seems to me," responded Etty, "that ultimately, we have just one moral duty: to reclaim large areas of peace in ourselves, more and more peace and reflect it toward others. And the more peace there is in us, the more peace there will be in our troubled world.'"[267]

"Yes Etty, I agree about such inner peace as a moral duty. But I think you would agree that as those trains were arriving closer and closer to your being taken away, you also felt the duty as you said earlier to bear witness?"

"Elie, my friend, you are correct. Peace became not the peace of healing but a peace of acceptance borne out of the knowledge that I was, I hoped by my deeds and by my words, bearing witness."

> My God, are the doors really being shut now? Yes they are. Shut on the herded, densely packed, mass of people inside. Through small openings at the top we can see heads and hands, hands that will wave to us later when the train leaves. ... One more piece of our camp has been amputated. Next week yet another piece will follow. This is what has been happening now for over a year, week in, week out.... A hundred thousand Dutch members of our race are toiling away under an unknown sky or lie rotting in some unknown soil.[268]

"The last words I was able to write reflect that final acceptance."

It is only a short while, perhaps before we find out, each one of us in his own time, for we are all marked down to share that fate, of that I have not a moment's doubt. But I must go now and lie down and sleep for a little while. I am a bit tired and dizzy. As for the future, I am firmly resolved to return to you after my wanderings. In the meantime, my love once again, you dear people.[269]

"Your 'wanderings,' Etty and Elie, are your fountain pens as eternal chroniclers, forever spelling out 'love once again' to all who will listen, and who love life," responded Mother.

They both nodded, and Elie said, "Thank you very much."

"Thank you, thank you," Mother declared, "that in such a place of evil, somehow you did not give up on life."

Hardly had those words left Teresa's lips, when there was a sudden commotion in the hospital hall. The family of the mother who the day before had given birth swept by us to congratulate their loved one in Room 204 for both the pain and the life she bore.

We were watching them, enjoying their chatter and laughter, when Mother suddenly turned and asked, "Would you agree everything that we have been discussing these last few days, suffering, justice, God, peace, injustice, love, and empathy—compassion are in that room?"

Mother paused, as if she were contemplating what she was going to say next, then continued, "There a mother survived her pain to give life, and with such a being comes the opportunity for empathy to move one more individual to acts of caring and love."

Nodding to Mother Teresa, I said, "It is so interesting that you said that because the Hebrew and Arabic words for compassion, *Rachamim* in Hebrew, *rachma* in Arabic, come from the root R-Ch-M. And from that same root comes the Hebrew word *ReCheM*—womb. However the concept of empathy is a fairly modern concept, so that *rachamim* really comes closer to how we define empathy as compassion's partner in action.

So Mother Teresa, illustrative of what you just said, in childbirth a mother feels the conflicting emotions of love for the emerging infant and the physical pain of childbirth. In the struggle to give birth she pushes, as if pushing on the pain itself. And from her womb comes her and God's creation, for which she feels an intense identification with her new born infant. That wonderful emotion, maternal empathy epitomizes *rachamim*."

"Rabbi, I never connected the birth process with empathy," said Mother, "but it... ."

"Excuse me, it not only makes sense," interjected Elie, "but wonderfully explains the nature of *rachamim*, which those who speak Yiddish know as *rachmones*. However, Mother, I'm intrigued that you seem to hold up empathy as the source for other ethical attributes like kindness, righteousness, justice, forgiveness and peace. I understand it as a catalyst for compassion, but... ."

I couldn't contain myself. "Elie, Mother, Etty," I said, jumping up with unbounded enthusiasm, "the three of you personify those qualities precisely because like a mother giving birth you feel the suffering of others. You identify with suffering so much it's as if it is your pain, and your suffering becomes one with theirs. As Mother said, through her Savior, and the two of you said, regarding the stranger, you feel their pain with such urgency that you choose to act on their behalf."

Then, with the words "on their behalf," Elie said, "Oh my God," and looking up we saw Presidents Lincoln and Roosevelt, Dr. Schweitzer and Viktor Frankl, Amos and Joseph, Gandhi and Sadat, Mr. Rogers, Emma Lazarus and Dr. King coming toward us, with Dulcenea.

"'Oh, my God,' somebody said," President Lincoln laughed and replied, "No, just us souls from the other side; Dulcenea insisted we all return to add our support to character and what you, rabbi, call empathy ethics."

As you can imagine, Elie was flabbergasted at seeing these special souls. I was surprised and delighted to be with them again, and Etty and Mother Teresa seemed casual, almost blasé at their arrival. In truth, Mother Teresa must have acquired a knowledge of Hebrew on the other side because we heard her say, "*Mah Pitom*," a very succinct Hebrew idiom, meaning something like, "What's (the) sudden surprise? I expected them."

"It's wonderful to welcome you all again, but President Lincoln what do you mean, 'support', and where is Senator Norris?" I asked.

"The senator couldn't get away from energy stuff," answered Amos. "He sends his regrets as he especially wanted to support the idea that moral courage should be included with the other character attributes and their connection to empathy."

"Is that what you mean, Dulcenea, by coming to 'support' me," I asked.

"Yes, that too, but as Etty suggested to you yesterday, we souls enjoy returning to our old homes to interact with you."

"When we are here we especially feel the eternity of time and our connection to you, the past and present and our continuing future," said Sadat. "Yet, I admit, coming back also reminds me of how much I miss my dear wife and family. But I feel healed by her courage, and all the others who so valiantly work to pursue the quest for lasting peace."

"Beautifully said, Anwar," Teddy Roosevelt added. "Coming back reminds me of hunting out West, only there is no game. Rather it's like gathering all our souls with yours as we share memories about ethical values and ideals."

"It keeps us," beamed Schweitzer, "young in spirit, as if we are all moving back and forth between the past and the present on a great bridge."

"A bridge not of steel and cement, but of values that span time itself," said MLK.

"And these values, justice, kindness, courage, etc., all the ones we have been talking about," said Mr. Rogers, "carry us along on the bridge from where our souls reside, to here and back again."

"And on that passageway, the ability to identify with and feel each other's circumstance continually," added Lincoln, "nurtures and sustains our eternal empathy, keeping our souls alive for each other, where we reside, and, yes with you on Earth as well."

"Without the ability to identify with our neighbors and others," added Etty, "without feeling their life situation as our own, compassion would not flower."

"The lights of justice and liberty would never shine," said Emma Lazarus with such passion it was as if we could see her holding up a torch.

"Nor would the tree of kindness you ascribed to me bear fruit for any other," said Mr. Rogers.

"Or the righteousness, and ability to forgive, that you so kindly attributed to me," said Lincoln, "would never see the light of day, rather there would be only night after night of continuing hopelessness.

"Without empathy," Sadat and Gandhi asked in unison," would we have had the courage to change hearts of fear to hearts for peaceful hopes?"

"As a matter of fact, by which I mean the fact of our spirit, without empathy to enable us to feel individually touched, or the embrace of our neighbors, there would be less 'meaning' in our decision to care for and love each other," said Viktor Frankl.

"Not only would there be less meaning and purpose to our existence," added Joseph, "how could we ever forgive each other without the ability to feel the other's trespass and connect them to our own mistakes, or sins? And yes, rabbi, I must say," Joseph continued, "I felt really honored that you included the story of how John Paul welcomed his 'brothers' by quoting what I once said to my brothers."

"In fact," added Amos, "by that I also mean our spirit; I meant to tell you, Joseph, that the Pope and I were discussing Scripture at that very moment when Rabbi... uh... a senior moment... "

"Schindler," I helped.

"... Yes, when, Schindler told you about that Vatican greeting. And John Paul was delighted, once again, as if it had just happened."

"Friends, it seems that empathy is a little like me," giggled Dulcenea, "a sweet messenger that motivates pro-social behavior. A catalyst for pushing the ethical in us, causing us to remember and acknowledge our own feelings; and when we lack empathy, not feeling for another or others, we are physically alive but spiritually dead.... "

"And, I don't mean to frighten you," interjected Martin Luther King, "but our future, what religion calls salvation, ceases when love is expressed conditionally without empathy. A false love, a form of selfish narcissism, such love confuses us and others. More importantly, such a conditional love, lacking in empathy, dies with our bodies—no future, no salvation, no soul."

"Which reminds me of a story, with which to almost end this chapter and book about ethical character, soul and food.," (When I said, "almost", I laughed because we clergy so often say we are going to conclude, but keep going on.)

So here's the story: "Sh'muel (Samuel) and his dear friend Yitschak (Isaac) were enjoying each other's company, as they often did, tipsy, in the local tavern. With each *l'chayim* toast to life came the required shot of whiskey—a Polish version—which could be dangerous for Jews on two counts, if you know what I mean.

"'Sh'muele, do you love me?' asked Yitschak.

"'*Nu*, Yitschak, what kind of question is that? Am I not your best friend? Of course, I love you.'

"'Well, Yitschak' continued Sh'muel, 'If you love me, do you know what causes me *tsurus*, suffering troubles, I mean what really hurts me in my *kishkas*, like deep in my heart?'

"'How should I know what causes your *tsurus*, suffering?' his puzzled friend answered sincerely.

"'If you don't know my *tsurus*, after all these years,' replied Yitschak, also sincerely, Do *not say you love* me.'"[270]

For a minute or two, no one among us spoke—as silence laden with meaning hung in the place we had occupied.

Finally, someone asked, "Does anybody know where Mother Teresa is? She didn't share any words about empathy, or compassion?"

Suddenly, flying out of Room 202, Mother appeared as a rolling answer to the question. And she was headed right toward us, pushing a wheelchair with a very happy mother and sleeping baby. Moving the chair, its occupants and herself as if they were all one spirit, she looked unbelievably delighted. "They are going home," she declared authoritatively.

Then she paused, and in perfect Hebrew said to us, quoting Rabbi Shimon ben Gamliel, "*Lo ha midrash ikar, ela ha ma-a'se:* It is not study that is the root [of our being] but the doing [of good deeds]!"[271]

"That's where I've been—adding one more brick to my ethical, eternal foundation." And with both a smile that radiated sweetness and a prophetic voice that challenged, she asked, "and where have you been?"

Then, without waiting for a reply she declared, "Come now, let us all go and eat...."

RECIPES

Etty Hillesum was born January 15, 1914, and died November 40, 1943, at Auschwitz. Her birthday would be a wonderful time to remember her on a frigid day in the camp serving out empathy's warmth with only memory's ladle—not a drop of soup in sight.

A Jewish blessing in honor of her noble empathy and compassion, can be found on page 237.

ERWTENSOEP—A DUTCH PEA-SOUP [272]

Also called Snert

This soup serves 6–8 and freezes well. It is not a starter, but a substantial meal, and should be thick enough, suggests some, that on a cold day it would be thick enough to slice. "My father always used to say that his spoon must be able to stand upright and won't fall to the side. Well, my father can exaggerate a little!" [273] Traditionally Erwtensoep is served with a rye or a pumpernickel bread. *(see page 59)*

Ingredients:
    3 ½ c. dried split green peas, soaked overnight in 3 liters of water.
    1 ox tail, or 1 lb. beef ribs .
    3–4 kosher frankfurters or knockwurst cut in slices
    ½ lb. bacon (cut in slices) or beef bacon or smoked pork, or turkey
        sausage
    2 medium leeks, washed carefully and chopped, including the green
        part
    1 medium diced celery root or bulb, or 3 c. chopped celery.
    1 carrot, peeled and sliced
    1 grated potato
    1 bouillon cube, to taste, optional
    Chopped celery and fresh parsley leaves microwaved in a little water
    Salt and pepper to taste

Directions:

Wash the peas and soak them overnight in water. Next day carefully pour out the water and replace with 3 litres fresh water.

Bring the peas, ox tail or ribs, and bacon to a boil and then simmer on a low heat for 1–1 ½ hours, stirring occasionally.

Add the leeks, potato, carrot and celery, and cook for another hour or until the soup becomes thick. If ribs are used, remove the meat from the bones and return the meat to the pan.

Add the frankfurters, knockwurst or sausage, cook for another half hour and season to taste, including bouillon cube(s). Add the liquid from the chopped celery leaves and parsley before serving. The soup is even better the next day.

Elie Wiesel was born September 30, 1928, and the date is a nice occasion to honor him for his devotion to empathy and human understanding.

A Jewish blessing in his honor can be found on page 243.

RABBI'S CHICKEN SOUP AND KREPLACH

Ingredients for broth for 7–8

1 chicken, whole or cut in quarters
3 ½ quarts water
2 large carrots, sliced
2 stalks celery, sliced
2 sprigs parsley
1 onion, quartered
1 bay leaf
1 tbsp. salt to taste
¼ tsp. pepper
1 or 2 chicken bouillon cubes (optional)

Bring water and chicken to boil. Add seasonings and vegetables. Simmer about 3 ½ hours until chicken falls off the bone.

Remove chicken, strain soup and use chicken and vegetables as desired. Refrigerate the broth until cold. Then skim off the fat.

Ingredients for Kreplach dough:
Makes about 18
　1 large egg
　½ tsp. salt
　1 c. flour sifted
Beat eggs slightly and add salt, slowly add flour. Add more flour if necessary to make a stiff dough. Knead for about 5 minutes until dough is soft and elastic.

Flour surface and roll out dough to about a 13x13 square. It should be fairly thin. Cover dough with a moist cloth to prevent drying.

Filling:
　½ lb. beef, sautéed and chopped fine (or use the set aside chicken, chopped)
　1 large onion, chopped and sautéed in 1 tbsp. butter
　Mix meat or chicken with:
　¼ c. finely chopped red pepper
　1 tsp. salt and pepper to taste
　1 egg mixed with 1/3 c. French dressing
　¼ c. finely chopped raisins
Place about one teaspoon on a square of dough; moisten the edges of the dough with a finger dipped in water. Fold dough over filling to form a triangle. Press down to make a firm seal with a fork. Kreplach can be dropped into hot soup and cooked for about 20 minutes or can be fried and served as a side dish.

Mother Teresa was born August 26, 1910, and died September 5, 1997. Either date would be a meaningful occasion to honor the memory of Mother Teresa's empathy and compassion for the poorest of the poor.

A blessing in honor of Mother Teresa can be found on page 242.

In January of 2006, I asked Sister Leticia of Missionaries of Charity, the Bronx in New York, what Mother Teresa most enjoyed eating. "Grapes—Mother loved grapes!"

So here is a **Curried Chicken Salad with Grapes** in honor and memory of this amazing person.

CURRIED CHICKEN SALAD WITH GRAPES

6 Servings

Ingredients:
3 c. cooked chicken breasts, cubed
2–3 tsp. curry powder (start out with 2) to taste
½ tsp. powdered ginger
¼ tsp. cumin
1 ¼ c. plain yogurt
¾ c. sour cream
2 tbsp. orange juice
½ c. sliced celery
2 tbsp. green onion, sliced
1 tbsp. cider vinegar
1 tsp. sesame oil
½ tsp. brown sugar
¼ c. shredded coconut
¾–1 c. pecans, coarsely chopped
2 c. grapes, halved

Directions:
In large bowl combine dry ingredients, then celery, coconut and brown sugar. Mix well. Add liquids, pecans and grapes.

Best served chilled.

Epilogue

I T WAS MY birthday, and after the surprise reunion I was anxious to get home. I tearfully said *"shalom"* to Amos and my other inspiring role models. I had barely driven a few miles when I noticed two large billboards on the side of the road.

The first asked:

Anybody reading this that has never experienced suffering?

I had to drive a little further to read what the next billboard said. It was like having to turn the last page of a book to see how it ends:

Yes, I could have created you all without any suffering. But had I done so, I believe you would be even less willing to help me eradicate evil—yours and humanity's.

And yes, I hear your laughing cynicism, "An end to evil, here? Not likely."

So if you really want to help me—be my partner in putting an end to suffering, hatred, apathy—injustice and war... I'm telling you again, try "loving your neighbor as you love yourself"! But if you cannot do that one, if you don't have enough love for yourself to flow out to others? Then try this:

"WHAT IS HATEFUL TO YOU,"
BECAUSE IT CAUSED YOU REAL SUFFERING,
REMEMBER HOW IT MADE YOU FEEL?
SO, DO NOT CAUSE SUFFERING
TO ANY OTHER PERSON"!![274]

And "for God's sake," and your mother's, don't forget to eat good, healthy food!!

— GOD

Advertisingforgood@Hilleland.com

Chapter IX

G RACE OR BLESSINGS of thanks for the values and food that sustain us, from different religious traditions, in honor or memory of our role models. To recite such blessings on their birthdays, as we enjoy good food, enhances both memory and deed.

Following these blessings is Rabbi Posner's Chalah (egg bread) in honor of all our readers and in honor and, or, memory of all our role models.

AMOS THE PROPHET, A JUDEAN—RIGHTEOUSNESS

There is a total absence of blessing and certainly no grace in the Book of Amos. To the contrary, for Amos the Israelites and the other nations around them face destruction for their unrighteous, evil behavior. Thus, when the Prophet speaks of bread, the staff of life, he declares that the Israelites "lack bread" because they "have not returned" from doing evil. [275]

In honor and memory of this great prophet of righteousness,"*Baruch ataw Adonoi,* Blessed are You God," for commanding us to enjoy our bread with the desire to live righteous lives, so that we will not "lack" our daily bread."

ANTONIA, MOTHER, A CATHOLIC—COMPASSION

Mother Antonia was born in 1926.

This grace or blessing is recited in some Roman Catholic monasteries, convents and other communities that are served by outstanding individuals like Mother Antonia.

"The eyes of all hope in thee, O Lord, and thou wilt give them food in due time. Thou openest thy hand, and fillest every living thing with thy blessing." [276]

Dear God, as we are sustained with Thy food, so are we with gratitude sustained with the overflowing compassion of individuals such as Mother Antonia. With faith and courage they open their hands and hearts, spiritually "rescuing prisoners from confinement, those who sit in darkness out of the prison-house." [277]

CARTER, JIMMY, A BAPTIST—RIGHTEOUSNESS

President Carter was born on October 1, 1924.

In the Baptist tradition, as is seen in this blessing, there is a strong emphasis on gratitude.

"We thank you for this food and all the good things of life. Thank you for the people gathered here and all the people who prepared this meal." As we are grateful for all the "good things of life," we are grateful to President and Mrs. Carter for their devotion toward alleviating suffering by emphasizing the necessity of righteous behavior.

CLINTON, BILL, A BAPTIST—FORGIVENESS

President Clinton was born on August 9, 1946.

"We thank you for this food and all the good things of life that sustain us," including our friends and family who nourish us during difficult times with their love and forgiveness.[278]

CLINTON, HILLARY, A METHODIST—FORGIVENESS

Senator Clinton was born October 10, 1947.

"Be present at our table, Lord, be here and everywhere adored. Thy creatures bless, and grant that we may feast in paradise with Thee," but until we find our place on high, grant us the courage to love and forgive.[279]

FRANKL, VIKTOR, JEWISH— COMPASSION, MEANING AND COURAGE

Viktor Frankl was born on March 26, 2005, and died on September 2, 1997.

In the Jewish tradition we praise God both before a meal—the *motsi*—and after with the *birchat ha mason*—blessing for sustenance in which we are reminded of how values like compassion sustain us.

"*Baruch ataw A-do-nai*, we praise you, Eternal One, our God, sovereign of the universe, whose goodness sustains the whole world. With grace, love and compassion, you provide food for all your creatures, for your love is everlasting."[280]

Dear God, when your "love everlasting" is difficult to find in the behavior of your children, may we be sustained by the courage and meaning in life that exists in every heart, as seen in the teaching, strength and courage of inspiring individuals such as Viktor Frankl.

GANDHI, MAHATMA, HINDU—MORAL COURAGE

Gandhi was born on October 10, 1869.

Physical health and strength cannot be separated from spiritual and moral values as seen in the Hindu Vedic Code. In Gandhi's life as well, these virtues of health and spirit all combined to make him the great individual he was.

So, "May there be voice in my mouth, breath in my nostrils, sight in my eyes, hearing in my ears... May I have power in my thighs, swiftness in my legs, and steadiness in my feet. May all my limbs be uninjured and my soul remain unconquered."[281] Also, "May Brahman protect us all. May he nourish us all. May we work together with great energy. May our being together be vigorous and fruitful. May we not hate each other. Peace, Peace, Peace."[282]

HILLESUM, ETTY, JEWISH— EMPATHY AND PERSPECTIVE

Etty was born on January 15, 1914.

As the Nazi net of terror and violence closed around her, Etty's perspective and gratitude for life helped sustained her

She wrote,"As life becomes harder and more threatening it also becomes richer, because the fewer expectations we have, the more the good things of life become unexpected gifts which we accept with gratitude."[283]

"*Baruch ataw A-do-nai*, we praise you, Eternal One, our God, sovereign of the universe who brings forth bread," sustaining us with courage and perspective with the "unexpected gifts which we accept with gratitude."

JOSEPH THE SON OF JACOB AND RACHEL, A HEBREW—FORGIVENESS

As the Joseph story preceeded the revelation at Sinai, Joseph identity is more of a Hebrew than a Jew. The word Hebrew comes from the three letter root, *ayin, vet, resh*, which means pass through or over to the other side.[284] And the name Joseph comes from the root, *yod, samech, fe*, meaning add on, continue, move on.

"*Baruch ataw A-do-nai*, we praise you, Eternal One, our God, sovereign of the universe who brings forth bread, sustaining us with the spiritual strength to pass through and overcome our anger that we may forgive and move on with renewed health."

KIELBURGER, CRAIG, A CATHOLIC—COMPASSION

Craig's birthday is December 17, 1982.

"Bless us O Lord and these Thy gifts, which we are about to receive from Thy bounty through Christ our Lord." And may our compassion be a favorite gift to give and receive that all God's children, with the help of organizations like Free the

KING, REV. MARTIN LUTHER, A BAPTIST— EQUAL JUSTICE

Rev. King's birthday is January 15, 1929.

Unfortunately, I could not find a specific Baptist blessing recited by MLK for food. However, like his friend and colleague Rev. Fred Shuttlesworth, he no doubt varied the theme of his blessing depending on the occasion, maintaining some of the traditional phrases as quoted to me by Mrs. Shuttlesworth: "We give thanks for all things that have come our way. May the food we are about to partake sustain our bodies," and our recollection of Martin Luther King's passion for justice continue so that everywhere righteousness and justice may flow down like a mighty stream.[285]

LAZARUS, EMMA, A SEPHARDIC JEW— SOCIAL JUSTICE

Emma's birthday is July 22, 1849.

Many of the Jews who were expelled from Spain in 1492 continued to speak their old Spanish, which is called Ladino. I came across this lovely Ladino version of the Jewish Blessing after the meal:

"Ya comimos y bevimos, y al Dio santo Barukh hu u-Barukh Shemo bendishimos; que mos dio y mos dara pan para comer y panyos para vestir, y anos para bivir. Siempre mejor, nunca peor, nunca mos manke la meza del Criador: We have eaten and drunk; Let us thank the holy God, ever to be praised, who gives us bread to eat, and clothes to wear, and years to live. May things always get better, never worse, and may the Creator's goodness toward us never cease."[286]

Also, Esther Schor, the author of a beautifully recent biography of Emma Lazarus shared with me, "My favorite, and the favorite of the Emma Lazarus Federation, is: 'Until we are all free, none of us is free.'"[287]

Ribon shel ha olum, Master/Mistress of the universe, how grateful we are not only for the food we are about to enjoy, but grateful as well for passionate poets of freedom and justice, like Emma Lazarus. As we are sustained with this food may we also be sustained with Emma's eloquent words and her passion for justice.

LINCOLN, PRESIDENT ABRAHAM, DEIST (PROBABLY CLOSEST TO BEING A UNITARIAN)—RIGHTEOUSNESS

President Lincoln's Birthday is February 12, 1809.

Praised art Thou O Lord, Creator of such holy and magnanimous souls as Abraham Lincoln, without whose righteousness these United

States would be no more. As we are sustained with the food before us, may we Americans continue to be forever sustained by President Lincoln's vision for a just, righteous and compassionate nation.

MANDELA, PRESIDENT NELSON, AN ANGLICAN—RIGHTEOUSNESS

President Mandela's birthday is July 18, 1918.

President Mandela's great commitment to righteousness for the people of South Africa and the world cannot be separated from his love of life and the knowledge that with our freedom is the wisdom to never take life for granted.

"Thank you to God for everything; for life, for good health, for food, for safety in travel, for joy, for laughter, for friendship, for fish caught, for a job, for the stars, for the sun, for birds, for grace, for God." [288]

NORRIS, SENATOR ROBERT, A PROTESTANT WHO ALSO APPRECIATED THE UNITARIAN CHURCH—MORAL COURAGE

Senator Norris's birthday is July 11, 1861.

"Sustain us with the food we eat and give us the grace, O God, to dare to do the deed which we well know cries to be done. Let us not hesitate because of ease, or the words of men's mouths, or our own lives." [289]

OLINER, DR. SAM, JEWISH—MORAL COURAGE

Sam Oliner dedicated his book, *Do Unto Others—How Altruism Inspires True Acts of Courage*, "to the many heroes and moral exemplars who have exhibited courage, caring, and social responsibility for others in need." [290]

"*Baruch ataw A-do-nai*, we praise you, Eternal One, our God, sovereign of the universe who brings forth bread," giving so many the virtue of moral courage that we and our world may be sustained by caring and altruistic individuals who sustain life and not death, for good and not evil.

ROGERS, FRED,
A PRESBYTERIAN MINISTER—KINDNESS.

Mr. Roger's birthday is March 20, 1928.

His wife, concert pianist Joanne Rogers, wrote: "Yes, we had a family blessing we used to recite, though I can't say it is particularly Presbyterian, though it definitely is Christian. Here it is: 'Come, Lord Jesus, be Thou our guest, our morning joy, our evening rest; and, with Thy daily bread, impart Thy love and peace to every heart. Amen.'"[291] And as we remember Mr. Rogers, may we labor that our neighborhoods will be places of peace and kindness.

ROOSEVELT, PRESIDENT THEODORE,
AN EPISCOPALIAN—ECONOMIC JUSTICE.

President Roosevelt's birthday is October 10, 1858.

As we enjoy one of President Roosevelt's favorite dishes, in honor and memory of his devotion to Justice, we may say:

Blessed are you, O Lord God, King of the universe, for with good food and a passion for justice our lives are sustained. May the holy and life-giving spirit move every heart in all lands that barriers which divide us may crumble, suspicions disappear, and hatreds cease. So that we may live in justice and peace; making our hearts glad through Jesus Christ our lord. Amen.[292]

SADAT, PRESIDENT ANWAR,
MUSLIM—MORAL COURAGE

President Sadat's Birthday is December 25, 1918.

Muslims, as in the Jewish tradition, pronounce blessings before and after the meal.

Before: "In the name of Allah the most merciful, the most kind who expands the provisions for us."

After: "Praise to the Almighty who provided us with the solid food and the liquid food and created us in peace. Our Lord feed those who feed us."[293]

SCHWEITZER, ALBERT,
THE SON OF A LUTHERAN PASTOR—COMPASSION

Dr. Schweitzer was born January 14, 1875 and died September 4, 1965 while still working at his hospital in Lambarene.

The Evangelical Lutheran Church of America's Prayer Ministry sent me 15 blessings. This one seems to most reflect Albert Schweitzer's compassion and concern for others:

"Bless, O Lord, this food for thy use, and make us ever mindful of the wants and needs of others." Amen

TERESA, MOTHER, CATHOLIC—EMPATHY

Mother Teresa's birthday is August 27, 1910.

Grateful for the "gifts" of Mother Teresa's overflowing "bounty" of empathy and compassion for the poorest of the poor, individuals may say, "Bless us O Lord and these Thy gifts which in Thy bounty we are about to receive through Jesus Christ our Lord. Amen." [294]

TUTU, DESMOND,
ANGLICAN ARCHBISHOP—FORGIVENESS

Archbishop Tutu's birthday is October 7, 1931.

Archbishop Tutu possesses a wonderful and abiding faith in humanity's ability to be sustained by forgiveness and our character virtues. He reminds us that we are sustained both by our food and gratitude for our values:

"We thank you for the commitment among all people to seek justice and peace, homes and jobs, education and health, reconciliation and reconstruction." [295]

WALL, CHUCK,
A PROTESTANT—KINDNESS

Dr. Wall's birthday is January 12, 1941.

"Thank you for the food we eat. Thank you for the friends we greet. Thank you for the birds that sing. Thank you God for everything," [296] including those who like Dr. Wall sing out for kindness.

WIESEL, ELIE, JEWISH—EMPATHY

Elie Wiesel's Birthday is September 30, 1928.

In Judaism, compassion is one of the important virtues necessary for humanity's ultimate redemption and the coming of a messianic age. And so, in the *Birchat ha Mazon,* the blessing after eating, God is referred to as *Ha-Ra-cha-man,* the Compassionate One. The blessing reads, "May the Compassionate One permit us to witness the time of redemption."[297]

May the food before us and the compassion—empathy—of special people like Elie Wiesel inspire and sustain us for our own compassionate acts that we may be partners with God to "witness the time of humanity's redemption."

WINFREY, OPRAH, BAPTIST—KINDNESS

Oprah Winfrey was born January 29, 1954.

"We thank you for this food and all the good things of life. Thank you for the people gathered here and all the people who prepared this meal."

And we thank incredible individuals like Oprah Winfrey who freely choose to sustain so many with her virtuous kindness, that instead of suffering and want they are more likely able to enjoy "...the good things of life."

RABBI POSNER'S SWEET CHALAH

Ingredients:

  2 ¼ c. white flour

  1 ¼ c. whole wheat flour

  ½ c. plus 1 or 2 tbsp. water

  2 eggs

  2 ½ tbsp. oil (or 4 tbsp. if chalah is all white flour)

  4 tbsp. sugar*

  1 tsp. vanilla

  1 tsp. cinnamon or nutmeg, or ½ tsp. of each

  1/3 c. raisins, heated in water two minutes in microwave (can use this water instead of plain water mentioned above.)

  1 tbsp. orange zest (optional)

2 ¼ tsp. yeast (1 packet)

1/8 c. of sesame seed or poppy seed

1 egg yoke and a little honey, for gloss

Directions:

Mix flours and add yeast.

Heat water or milk to warm but not boiling. Add eggs, oil, sugar, vanilla, spices, and zest; mix with flour. Dough should be moist, but not stick to side of bowl. If too moist, add a little flour.

Remove raisins from hot water, pat them dry in a folded paper towel, and add to mixture.

Prepare the dough in a bread mixer on the dough cycle, or knead and prepare dough by hand. Punch the dough down and cut dough in half. Then divide each half into two amounts, one about 60% of the mass and the other about 40%. Divide each of those into three strips and braid, so you have six braids. Place the larger three braided amounts on a greased pan, cut a line in the middle and place the other smaller three braids inside and on top. Do the same with the other half, so you have two medium chalahs. (Or, you may divide the whole into two amounts, with the six braids for a larger chalah.)

As with all breads there are many ways to let challah rise.

Before you braid the chalahs, turn the oven on to 200 F. Turn it off just before you put the breads into the oven to rise. Or, instead of preheating the oven, you can put a baking pan on the floor or lowest rack of the oven and pour boiling water into it and put chalahs on racks above water in oven to rise.

(If you live in a warm climate, or in the summer you can also let dough rise outside in the sun with the dough in a plastic bag, or in a car with the windows closed, for about 45 minutes, until it has almost doubled in size.)

Preheat the oven to 350F or 180C.

Beat an egg yoke with a fork dipped in a little honey. Use a pastry brush to paint bread with yolk mixture and add seeds.

Bake for 25–30 minutes or until brown.

Cool on wire racks.

Notes

(Endnotes)

1   Jane Grigson, *Food with the Famous*, p.110

2   Ibid.

3   Psalm 104, verses 14,15, author's translation

4   *Food with the Famous*, ibid, pp. 44 and 48

5   A Chassidic tale based on Midrash

6   William Lee Miller (2002), *Lincoln's Virtues*, p.4

7   Op. Cit., p. 87

8   Carl Sandburg (1964) *Abraham Lincoln*, The War Years, Vol. 3, p. 822

9   Ibid., p. 823

10   "*Perkey Avot,* Sayings of the Fathers," From the *Mishna*, Author's translation

11   Poppy Cannon, Patricia Brooks, *The Presidents' Cookbook*, p.239

12   Ibid., p.249

13   *The San Francisco Chronicle*, "The American Prison Angel of Tijuana," 4/21/02

14   Mary Jordan and Kevin Sullivan, *The Prison Angel*

15   Ibid.

16   The Dalai Lama

17   Ibid., Inside book jacket, *The Prison Angel*

18   Ibid., *The Prison Angel*

19   Ibid., p.182

20   Ibid., pp. 77–78

21   Maguelonne Toussant-Samat, *History of Food* (2003) pp.45–46

22   Union of American Hebrew Congregations (UAHC) RAC Consultation on Conscience, March 2001

23   Op. Cit., History of Food, p 231

24   Craig Kielburger, *Free The Children* (1998) p.7

25   Personal correspondence, Craig Kielburger, April 2006

26   Op. Cit., Viktor Frankl p.46

27   George Marshal and David Poling, *Schweitzer—A Biography* pp. 138 - 139

28   Albert Schweitzer, *Memoirs of Childhood and Youth*, p. 9

29   Op. Cit., *History of Food*, p. 177

30   Personal interview with Mother Antonia, Tijuana, Mexico, 5/16/06

31   Op. Cit., Personal Correspondence, Craig Kielburger,

32   Op, Cit., Viktor Frankl p. 35

33   Ibid. pp. 43–44

34   Ibid. p. 79

35   Katz, editor, *Encyclopedia of Food and Culture*, p. 90

36   Op. cit., Viktor Frankl, p. 90

37   Ibid. p. 92–3

38   Op. cit., Personal Correspondence, Craig Kielburger

39   Op. cit., Personal interview with Mother Antonia

40   Op. cit., Mary Jordan and Kevin Sullivan, p. 67

41   Op. cit., Albert Schweitzer, p. 15

42   Op. cit., Personal interview with Mother Antonia

43   Op. cit., Viktor Frankl, p. 172

44   Ibid., p. 176

45   Dr. Franz Vesely, Viktor Frankl Institut, Viktor Frankl's son in law, wrote, "Viktor did NOT describe suffering as meaningful in itself. What he said was that it is a humane and meaningful achievement if one shoulders an unavoidable(!) suffering in a courageous manner. Bearing a predicament with dignity and courage was the point, not the predicament itself." Personal Correspondence, 6/23/07

46   Samuel P. Oliner, *Do Unto Others—Extraordinary Acts of ordinary People*, (2004) p. 43

47   Bill Clinton, *My Life* (2004) p.800

48   Ibid., *History of Food* p.313

49   Re. Cholent and French—Yiddish, from a lecture by Dr. Arnold Band, UCLA, 1960–61

50   Op. Cit., The Encyclopedia

51   Desmond Tutu, *No Future Without Forgiveness* (1999), p. 269

52   Paul Boese, from Quoteland.com

53   Hillary Rodham Clinton, *Living History* (2003), p. 401

54   Ibid., p. 480

55   Ibid., p. 401

56   Op. Cit., Desmond Tutu, p. 10

57   Ibid., p. 287

58   Bill Clinton's speech, September 11.1998 at the Annual White House Prayer Service: www.historyplace.com/speeches/clinton-sin

59   Ibid.

60   Op. Cit., Hillary Rodham Clinton, p. 476

61   Ibid., p. 480

62   Ibid., p. 476

63   Ibid., p. 469

64   Ibid., p. 442–443

65   Ibid., p. 401–402

66   Op. Cit., Desmond Tutu, p 85.

67   Ibid., p. 270–71

68   Ibid., p. 286

69   Ibid.

70   Ibid., p. 102

71   What has come to be known as Ken Starr's Whitewater investigation began as an investigation into an Arkansas real estate venture dating to the late 1970s and its connection with a now-defunct Arkansas savings and loan institution. It lasted 6 years, was 445 pages in length, mentioned "sex" more than five hundred times, cost an estimated 64 million in tax money, and led to the impeachment of Clinton in 1998–99. In his final report issued on March 20 2002, Mr. Ray, Starr's successor, declared that insufficient evidence existed to prosecute the president or his wife.

72   Op Cit., Bill Clinton, p. 671

73   Torah, Book of Exodus 44

74   Op. Cit., The Encyclopedia

75   Op Cit., Desmond Tutu, p. 154

76   Ibid., 152–53

77   William Lee Miller, *Lincoln's Virtues—An Ethical Biography* (2002) pp. 412, 416

78   Ibid.

79   James R. Gilmore, *Personal Recollections of Abraham Lincoln and the Civil War*, p. 155

80   Yom Kippur—Day of Atonement—Prayer Book

81   From Sephardic Flavors, Joyce Goldstein, Chronicle Books, San Francisco

82   *The Autobiography of Martin Luther King, Jr.*, Edited by Clabome Carson, p.342 (It should be noted that this work is not an autobiography in the strict sense of the term autobiography)

83   Op Cit., *Encyclopedic Dictionary of Judaism*, Ed. du Cerf

84   Op Cit., William Lee Miller, *Lincoln's Virtues—An Ethical Biography* (2002) p.313

85   Jimmy Carter *Our Endangered Values—America's Moral Crisis* (2005) pp. 6

86   Ibid., p. 66

87   Apartheid, meaning '"apartness,"' was the legalization of an oppressive system that kept Africans in an inferior position for centuries, though the term was introduced by the Nationalist party in 1948

88   Op. Cit., William Lee Miller, Letter to Ann Rutledge, August 16, 1837, p. 77

89   Op. Cit., Jimmy Carter, *Source of Strength* (1997) p. 199

90   Op. Cit .,William Lee Miller, Op. Cit., pp. 311–315

91   Op.Cit, p. 363

92   Op. Cit., *Sources of Strength*, Ibid., p. 150

93   Op. Cit., *Our Endangered Values*, p. 79

94   Carl Sandburg, *Abraham Lincoln—The War Years* (1965) pp.38

95   Ibid., p. 39

96   Ibid., p. 40

97   Nelson Mandela, *Long Walk to Freedom*, (1994) pp.625–26

98   Ibid., p. 627

99   Ibid.

100 Op. Cit., *Sources of Strength*, p. 124

101 Ibid., p. 125

[102] Op. Cit., Nelson Mandela, p. 582

[103] The Prophet Amos, 6:21–24

[104] Op. Cit., *Sources of Strength* pp. 124–126

[105] Op. Cit., William Lee Miller, p. 87

[106] Ibid., p. 84

[107] Ibid., p. 42

[108] Dr. Elizabeth Hirschman, *The Last Lost Tribe in America*

[109] The Melungeon DNA Surname Project, Dr. Elizabeth Hirschman and Dr. Donald Panther Yates. Also, see online, "The Melungeons, The Last Lost Tribe in America."

[110] This author is grateful to the American Jewish Archives of the Hebrew Union College—JIR, Cincinnati, Ohio, for sending me a copy of Rabbi Wise's eulogy. As the editor of the *Israelite* (Cincinnati's Jewish newspaper), Rabbi Wise published his eulogy to Lincoln in the Friday morning edition of the *Israelite* April 25th, 1865. The eulogy first appeared in the Cincinnati *Commercial* (newspaper) April 20th (1865).

[111] Ibid. The word after "sacred" in the manuscript sent to me is very blurred

[112] Andrew Ferguson, *Land of Lincoln, Adventures in Abe's America*. p. 76

[113] Amos, 5:24

[114] Op. Cit., *Sources of Strength* p.126

[115] *The Mishna*. "Sayings of the Fathers," 2:21, author's translation.

[116] Op. Cit., *Our Endangered Values*, p. 147

[117] Ibid, p.171

[118] Op. Cit., *Our Endangered Values*, p.147

[119] Op. Cit., Carl Sandburg, 301-302

[120] Ibid., p. 291

[121] In *Our Endangered Values*, President Carter refers to "the War between the States."

[122] Ibid., p. 72

[123] Op. Cit., William Lee Miller, p.281

[124] Ibid.

[125] Ibid., p. 280

[126] Ibid.

[127] Ibid., p. 281

[128]   The Talmud, Shabbat 31a

[129]   Poppy Cannon and Patricia Brooks, *The Presidents Cook Book*, p. 238

[130]   Janis Cooke Newman, *"Mary: A Novel,"* MacAdam/Cage

[131]   Alastra.com/misc/famous recipes

[132]   Dr. Chuck Wall is a published author and lecturer in supervision, leadership, communications, and human relations issues, including *"Random Acts of Kindness"*. He has co-authored a book on organizational renewal, written several scholarly articles, produced a multi-media look into the 21st Century for a White House conference, hosted his own television and radio programs, and with the Stroud Puppets, has published a 5-act video program entitled *"Kindness for Kids."* He is the author of *"The Kindness Collection,"* and with Kimberly Walton, *"Selling Lemonade for Free.* Dr. Wall continues to be deeply involved in the "Random Acts of Kindness" project, which has received international attention.

[133]   "What we saw is like the life that is lived in the Payatas garbage dump, just outside Manila in the Philippines, where 30,000 other people live. They are too poor to afford housing, so they live in the dump, scavenging for things to sell...." Craig and Marc Kielburger *Born and raised in a trash dump.* (10/19/ 2006)

[134]   Eugene B. Borowitz and Frances Weinman Schwartz, *The Jewish Moral Virtues,* p. 42

[135]   The Talmud

[136]   CBS 11tv.com, (Dallas/Fort Worth) "Oprah Winfrey Gives Audience 'gift of giving back'" (10/30/06)

[137]   Ibid.

[138]   Copyright 2003 The Associated Press. All active hyperlinks have been inserted by AOL. Friday, January 27, 2006

[139]   A true story about Mr. Rogers, written by Justin Short, personal correspondence, 8/19/06

[140]   Dr. Chuck Wall, Personal Correspondence, 12/20/06

[141]   The story about Carter and Nixon appears in a sermon, "The most Surprising Payday In History," by Rev. Thomas k. Tewell on 1/27/2002 at 5th Ave Presbyterian Church, NY www fapc.org/semons. However, Rev. Tewell was unable to confirm the source of his account.
    Ret. Colonel Jack Brennan, who was President Nixon's Marine Corps Aide, states that the story is not true. ""I was at the funeral and the reception preceding, which was in Sen. Baker's office, Pres. Carter was very cordial. I do not remember the invitation to sit with him and it did not happen. It would have been awkward for Pres. Carter to invite Nixon as Pres. and Mrs. Ford were also present at the reception and the service." Personal correspondence 11/12/06
    Whether the story is apocryphal or not, we may all ask ourselves how would we have treated President Nixon, if we were President Carter?

[142]   Based on a written account by Rabbi Alexander Schindler, which I remember

reading, but have been unable to find the source. However, Garry Wills, author of *Papal Sin*, writes "…Pope John had greeted a delegation of American Jews by saying, '*Son io Guiseppe, il fratello vostro*—I am Joseph your brother'—echoing the words of the biblical Joseph (Gen. 45:4)," p.23

[143] From Mrs. Rogers with permission of Family Communications, William Isler, President, (5/18/2005)

[144] "On a Thursday in July," writes Margot Dougherty an editor at *Los Angeles Magazine*, "Margaux Sky the owner of the Art Café & Bakery, in San Luis Obispo, California "put together what she thought was her last batch of sandwiches. She packed up the sandwiches, along with salads and homemade double chocolate fudge cake. Her sister, Mary Bennett, who'd ordered the food, picked it up.

That night, Margaux got a call from Mary's husband, Tim. "Your sandwiches were a hit," he said. "They were a big hit."

Tim Bennett is the president of Harpo Productions, and his guest that afternoon was his boss, Oprah. When the platter was passed around the table, Oprah chose the curried chicken. "I don't think she was completely through the first bite before she said, 'This is unbelievable—the best sandwich I've ever tasted,'" Tim recalls. He told her to enjoy it, because Margaux was closing her café the next day. She had been working nonstop, barely making ends meet, for two and a half years and was just too tired to continue.

Oprah thought about the sandwich and about Margaux on the hour-long drive back to her home in Santa Barbara. When she got there, she emailed Tim: "Anybody this good shouldn't go out of business." The timing was uncanny. At 9 a.m. the next day, Margaux was to sign the Art Café over to a new owner. At 8 a.m. she got the call from Tim to say that Oprah was sending her a big check to hire help so she could keep going.

Two weeks later, Oprah and Margaux met for the first time at the café. …Now "…with Oprah's gift," not only was the business saved but the "business is booming."

[145] Chris Wallace, Character—*Profiles in Presidential Courage*. 2004

[146] Samuel P. Oliner. *Do Unto Others—How Altruism Inspires True Acts of Courage* (2003)

[147] John F. Kennedy *Profiles in Courage* (1963)

[148] Ibid., Story about George W. Norris and direct quotations, pp. 161–177

[149] Years later he was still seen as too progressive for even Nebraska's politicians. Just after noontime on March 12, 1959, a festive crowd jammed the U.S. Capitol's Senate Reception Room to honor five of the Senate's "most outstanding" former members….. As their top choice, (a committee of scholars) named Nebraska's Progressive Republican *George Norris*. Unfortunately for Norris, the two Nebraska senators then serving—*Carl Curtis* and *Roman Hruska*—did not share the scholars' enthusiasm for their progressive predecessor (and) removed him from further consideration.

[150] Quotation about courage by Ambrose Redman

[151] Op. Cit., Samuel P. Oliner, p. 140

[152]   Op. Cit., John F. Kennedy pp.161–162

[153]   Op. Cit., Samuel P. Oliner p. 140

[154]   Story about Anwar Sadat and direct quotations come from President Anwar Sadat's Address to the Israeli Knesset, November 20, 1977.

[155]   AnwarSadat@Everything2.com

[156]   The British monopoly on the salt trade in India dictated that the sale or production of salt by anyone but the British government was a criminal offense punishable by law. Protesting the salt tax as an injustice to the people of India was an ingenious choice because every peasant and every aristocrat understood the necessity of salt in everyday life. It was also a good choice because it did not alienate Congress moderates while simultaneously being an issue of enough importance to mobilize a mass following.

[157]   Anwar Sadat Biography, www.ibiblio.org

[158]   Wikipedia.org/ahimsa

[159]   *Op Cit., The autobiography of Martin Luther King, Jr.,* Edited by Clayborne Carson (2001) p. 129

[160]   Comprehensive Site by Gandhian Institutes, mkgandhi.org

[161]   Op. Cit., Samuel P. Oliner, p140

[162]   *All Men Are Brothers: Life and Thoughts of Mahatma Gandhi as Told in His Own Words* compiled and edited by Krishna Kripalani, Chapter IV Ahimsa or the Way of Nonviolence

[163]   Leon Festinger, *A Theory of Cognitive Dissonance* (1957) pp.19-20

[164]   *"An Introduction to Cognitive Dissonance Theory and an Overview of Current Perspectives on the Theory,"* Chapter 1, p.22

[165]   Address of President Menachem Begin to the Knesset. 11/22/77

[166]   Sadat's speech to the Israeli Knesset initiated a new momentum for peace that eventually culminated in the 1978 Camp David Accords, when on March 26, 1979, President Anwar Sadat of Egypt and Premier Menachem Begin of Israel put their seal on a comprehensive peace treaty. It was also signed by American President Jimmy Carter, the man largely responsible for keeping the negotiation process alive when all had seemed lost. Of the treaty Carter said, "I think this was a kind of answer to those who are cynical about basic human attitudes and attributes. I think the inclination toward peace and love transcended those toward war and hatred."

[167]   Personal correspondence, regarding the information on "clean sun-powered fuels." I am grateful to Dr. Donald Aitken, currently principal of his own consulting company, Donald Aitken Associates. Dr. Aitken has also served as the executive director of the Western Regional Solar Energy Center for the U.S. Department of Energy, and senior staff scientist for renewable energy policy and economics with the Union of Concerned Scientists. He has over 100 publications in these

various fields.

168   Quote by Baltasar Gracian

169   Rajmohan Gandhi, Personal correspondence (9/2/06) "…I think you could match him either with (a) a fruit salad or (b) a vegetable salad or (c) a lentil soup. Best wishes with your imaginatively conceived project."

170   Based on Ellie Norris's *Congressional Club Cook Book* compiled and published by The Congressional Club, Washington D.C., 1927.

171   Theodore Roosevelt, *An Autobiography* (1985) p. 204

172   Esther Schor *Emma Lazarus* (2006) p. 148

173   *The Autobiography of Martin Luther King, Jr.* Edited by Clayborne Carson, Letter from Birmingham Jail, p. 193

174   Eric Rauchway, *Murdering McKinley—The Making of Theodore Roosevelt's America*, pp. 141–2

175   *Emma Lazarus—selected poems* John Hollander, editor (2005) p.58

176   National Park Service Ranger Joshua Reyes, personal correspondence 2/23/07, "According to the Harvard Library index of Theodore Roosevelt papers, TR and Emma Lazarus never exchanged any kind of correspondence. However, it is possible they may have encountered each other because both families were part of similar social circles. Emma grew up around Union Square which put her in the vicinity of Theodore Roosevelt, who grew up on East 20th Street. Like Theodore Roosevelt Sr., Emma's father (Moses Lazarus) was a member of the Union League Club. Therefore, it is safe to say they most likely knew of each other. However, if such a meeting occurred it would have been before either was immortalized in the American conscious."

177   *Time Magazine*," "The Secret Agony of Martin Luther King, Jr.," January 9, 2006 and "Teddy—How Roosevelt Invented Modern America," July 3, 2006

178   Based on, but not exactly the same as: CNN America Votes 2006 Special: War on the Middle Class." Live from Kansas City, Missouri, Lou Dobbs, aired 10/18/06

179   The "bullets of injustice" come from "Social/Economic Injustice," www.World Centric.org

180   Op. Cit., *The Autobiography of Martin Luther King, Jr.*, p.193

181   Lionel Lokos, *House Divided—The Life and Legacy of Martin Luther King*, p. 88

182   I am grateful to Dr. Barry Kogan, Professor of Ethics at the Hebrew Union College – JIR, for clarifying for me the complexities of 'lifnin m'shurat ha din.' Personal correspondence, November 14, 2007

183   One of Emma Lazarus's favorite quotations, personal correspondence, Esther Schor, author of Emma Lazarus, 6/9/07

184   Nathan Miller, *Theodore Roosevelt—A Life* (1992) p. 426

[185]   Op. cit., Esther Schorr, p. 116–17

[186]   Lou Dobbs, *War on the Middle Class*, (2006) p. 10

[187]   See *www.census.* Gov/prog/Press-Release (2005) Race and Hispanic Origin in the United States, U.S. Census Bureau

[188]   Ibid., Poverty, Overview.

[189]   Ibid., pp. 3, 31

[190]   David Cay Johnston, *Perfectly Legal: The Covert Campaign To Rig Our Tax System to Benefit The Super Rich—And Cheat Everybody Else* (Pulitzer Prize Reporter for the *New York Times*)

[191]   Survey by the Spectrum Group, a Chicago-based research firm

[192]   Op. Cit., Theodore Roosevelt, p. 406

[193]   Op. Cit., Martin Luther King, Jr., p. 261

[194]   Op. Cit., Lou Dobbs, p. 26

[195]   Ibid., p. 30

[196]   Ibid., p. 255

[197]   Ibid., p. 54

[198]   Ibid., p. 26

[199]   Letter of April 26, 1906. *The Works of Theodore Roosevelt*, Memorial Edition, XX, p. 484

[200]   *Theodore Roosevelt Cyclopedia*, Edited by A B Hart and HR Ferleger, 1941, p. 190

[201]   Jack Huberman, *An A–Z Guide to the Bush Attack on Truth, Justice, Equality, and the American Way*, (2006), p. 65

[202]   According to Senator Hillary Clinton of New York, the Tax Reconciliation bill "... will mostly benefit the wealthiest Americans. Indeed, under this bill, the average millionaire will receive an additional $42,000 tax cut while middle income Americans will see an average of $20." And Senator Harry Reid of Nevada said,"The tax reconciliation bill giveaway on capital gains and dividends will do much more for Exxon Mobil board members than it will do for Exxon Mobil customers."

[203]   Ibid., p. 68

[204]   Op. Cit., David Cay Johnston

[205]   Op. Cit., Theodore Roosevelt, p. 417

[206]   Ibid., p. 505

[207]   *Chicago Sun-Times, Nov 14, 2006 by Stephen Ohlemacher*

208 The median income for white households was $50,622 last year. It was $30,939 for black households. According to the American Community Survey, based on the Census bureau's 2006 annual survey of 3 million households nationwide.

209 Op. Cit., Martin Luther King, p. 351

210 Op. Cit., Theodore Roosevelt, p.393

211 Ibid., p.395

212 Ibid., pp. 394–96

213 William Henry Harbough, *Power and Responsibility—The Life and Times of Theodore Roosevelt* (1961) p. 307

214 H. W. Brands, *T.R. The Last Romantic.* p. 423.

215 Ibid., p. 498

216 Ibid., pp. 496–97

217 Op. Cit., William Henry Harbough., p. 304

218 Ibid., pp.305–06

219 "Booker T. Washington… was able to place the affair in perspective… possibly because of his friendship with Roosevelt. (He) wrote in June, 1908,… the intelligent portion of the race does not believe it is fair or wise to condemn such good friends as President Roosevelt and Secretary Taft because they might have done what they considered right. (Further)… it is not part of common sense to cherish ill will against one who has helped us in so many ways as the President has." Ibid., p. 307

220 Author's translation. The word *mispach* is usually translated as violence. The root is *s-p-ch* and means an outpouring, i.e., something expanding. I have taken liberty with the verse from Isaiah to add the word hole. The Jewish Publication Commentary, Soncino books of the Bible, rightly points out "the assonance of the Hebrew strikingly emphasized the contrasts, instead of *mishpat* (justice) there is *mispach* (violence) p. 23

221 *Time Magazine*, "Teddy – How Roosevelt Invented Modern America," 7/3/06

222 Charles Keeton and Arlie Petters, "Twin Black Holes."

223 The "Bullets of Injustice" come from "Social/Economic Injustice," www.World Centric.org

224 The material on black holes and "the braneworld concept" for the science fiction aspect of this chapter is based on a 6/9/06 article, "Little Black Holes," San Francisco Chronicle by Keary Davidson, Chronicle Science Writer. However, "Tiny" in the context of the braneworld concept represents something around a billionth of a billionth of the mass of the sun—a couple billion tons, or the mass of a small asteroid. A black hole of this mass would actually be the size of an atomic nucleus. Physicists have speculated that, when the universe was very young and hot, copious numbers of miniature black holes may have been produced. To our

knowledge, however, tiny black holes cannot form today.

225   Ibid.

226   Ibid.

227   Ibid.

228   Ibid.

229   The material about Esa's Observatory and black holes, and the "World Wide Mind" for my science fiction is based on PBS *Nova's* wonderful production, "Monster of The Milky Way," 10/31/06 and an article titled "Tiny black Holes" by Charles Keeton and Arlie Peters (Charles Keeton is an assistant professor in the Department of Physics and Astronomy at Rutgers University. Arlie Petters is a professor of mathematics and physics at Duke University.)

230   Based on 260 days of pay (52 weeks x 5 days a week).

231   PBS 22nd century, 10/31/06

232   Deuteronomy 16:20

233   In Dr. King's Letter From Birmingham Jail, he used the very same analogy for engaging in nonviolent direct action "…Like a boil that can never be cured so long as it is covered up but must be opened with all its ugliness to the natural medicines of air and light, injustice must be exposed… to the light of human conscience and the air of national opinion before it can be cured."

234   Phone conversation and personal correspondence with Rev. Shuttlesworth and his wife, Sephira Bailey Shuttlesworth, 10/17/06

235   *Op Cit., the Autobiography of Martin Luther King, Jr.* (2001) p. 221

236   "Martin Luther King Diner Shuts Down," CommonDreams.org News Center, by Andrew Buncombe, Aug. 3, 2003.

237   Personal discussion with Cheryl Evans, August 27, 2007

238   As for President Roosevelt's other food tastes, "President Roosevelt loved to eat southern fried foods because he grew up on a southern diet due to the fact his mother was born and raised in Georgia."

   Poppy Cannon and Patricia Brooks, The Presidents' Cookbook (1968), pp 358, 364. "Our menus are a legacy from my Georgian mother," he (TR) explained.

   Unfortunately very little is known about the fried chicken recipe used by the Roosevelt's. I spoke with Charles Markis, Chief of Visitor Services, who oversaw a project involving Roosevelt recipes. According to Ranger Markis, he came across several fried chicken recipes in various journals, but was never able to find documentation to the so-called Roosevelt fried chicken recipe. "Currently our search is ongoing." Ranger Joshua Reyes National Park Service at Sagamore Hill 3/1/07

   President Roosevelt "also had a fondness for game and terrapin, but he could be just as happy with Irish stew, pork and beans or bread and milk. Quantity was more important to him than quality." *Theodore Roosevelt—A Life*, Nathan Miller,

p. 425–6

239   "She taught us to have rice twice a day and hominy every morning for breakfast, and we group simple meats around it." (*T.R. The Last Romantic*, p.496)

240   "He loved coffee, in fact, he devoured many cups of coffee a day. President Roosevelt also loved desserts, such as fresh peaches and cream with the cream over flowing his bowl."

      Personal Correspondence, Sagamore Hill National Historic Site, National Park Service. Mark J. Koziol Museum Technician

241   David Aikam, *Great Souls—Six Who Changed the Century* (1998) p. 235

242   Ibid., pp. 238–39

243   Elie Wiesel, *A Jew Today*, p. 18

244   Op. Cit., David Aikam, p. 342

245   "Suffering and Memory: A Study of Empathy Ethics In Judaism," Author's unpublished doctoral dissertation, p. 34

246   Elie Wiesel, *Night*, p. 32

247   Etty Hillesum, *An Interrupted Life—The Diaries of Etty Hillesum 1941-43* (1984), p. 22

248   Ibid., p. 181

249   Personal correspondence, Marjanne (from Holland) 12/20/06

250   Op. Cit., Etty Hillesum, p.192

251   Ibid., p. 181

252   *Mother Teresa in My Own Words—1910-1997,* (1996) p. 7

253   Op. Cit., David Aikam, p. 339

254   Op. Cit., Mother Teresa, p. 17

255   Op. Cit., "Suffering and Memory: A Study of Empathy Ethics in Judaism," author's unpublished doctoral dissertation, p. 34

256   *A Passover Haggadah,* as commented upon by Elie Wiesel, p. 161

257   Elie Wiesel, "*The Stranger in the Bible*," (UAHC-JIR 1980) p. 47

258   Op. Cit., Etty Hillesum, p.88

259   Ibid., p. 89

260   Ibid.

261   Ibid.

262   Ibid., p. 251

263   Op. Cit., David Aikam, pp. 202–03

264   Op. Cit., Etty Hillesum, p. 251

265   Ibid., pp. 267, 268

266   Op. Cit., David Aikam, pp.223–24

267   Op. Cit., Etty Hillesum, p. 229

268   Ibid., p. 272

269   Ibid., p. 273

270   Based on a story by Martin Buber in *Tales of the Chasidim*

271   Mishna Perkey Avot, 1:17, author's translation.

272   Hello Rabbi Philip, I finished the book yesterday. I am very impressed in the way Etty coped with all the horrible things that happened in her life, and she must have been a very special person for the people surrounding her! I think she would have been very pleased that her diary is sold in so many countries and that she and her philosophy lives on and help other people to cope with difficult situations.... About the soup I think that Etty and her friends would have liked the soup and it is very much possible that they have eaten it, because it is a soup recipe that is very old and very Dutch, my grandmother also made it in winter and my mother always makes it in wintertime.... Personal correspondence Marjanne, 12/20/06 from Holland.

273   Ibid.

274   Babylonian Talmud, Shabbat 31a, The author has translated *rea,* usually *neighbor,* to the more inclusive "person."

275   Amos 4:6

276   Thomas J. Craughwell, *Every Eye Beholds You: A World Treasury of Prayer* (1995) "A Blessing before Meals," p. 284

277   Isaiah 42:7

278   Rev. Louis Twyman, Louisville, Ky

279   Based on a grace by John Wesley

280   *Siddur Lev Chadash* Union of Liberal and Progressive Synagogues (Services and Prayers...) (1995) p. 554

281   Thomas J. Craughwell, Op., Cit., "Health of mind and body," (Atharva-Veda XIX, 60) p. 171

282   Professor Bhafnagar, Louisville, KY

283   *Op. Cit., An Interrupted Life, p. 165*

284   The 12th century sage, Nachmanides, comments on the word "Hebrew" (Genesis 40:15) "Abraham having come from the other side (*ever*) of the Jordan, and his descendants were known likewise...(hence Hebrew)."

285   In discussion by phone with Rev. and Mrs. Fred Shuttlesworth, 6/6/07

286   Op Cit., *Siddur Lev Chadash* ,p. 551

287   Personal correspondence, Esther Schor, 6/9/07

288   From Desmond Tutu, *An African Prayer Book*, p. 54–55

289   Op Cit., Thomas J. Craughwell, "A Prayer for Courage," *An African Prayer* by W.E. B. Du Bois, p. 176–77

290   Op. Cit., Samuel P. Oliner, *Do Unto Others*, Dedication page, v.

291   Email from Elaine Lynch, Mrs. Rogers' administrative assistant, 6/7/07

292   Based on the Episcopal Book of Common Prayer, pp. 835 and 823

293   Dr. Shareef, Louisville, KY

294   The blessing used by the Sisters of Charity Leticia, New York

295   Op cit., Desmond Tutu, *An African Prayer Book*, p. 54–55

296   Joan Bosert, Chicago IL.

297   Op Cit., *Siddur Lev Chadash*, p. 558